Industrial Organization, Antitrust, and Public Policy

MIDDLEBURY COLLEGE CONFERENCE SERIES ON ECONOMIC ISSUES

An Incomes Policy for the United States
Michael P. Claudon and Richard R. Cornwall, Editors

Welfare Reform in America
Paul M. Sommers, Editor

Industrial Organization, Antitrust, and Public Policy
John V. Craven, Editor

Middlebury College Conference Series volumes are made possible by the generosity of the Christian A. Johnson Endeavor Foundation. These volumes are edited at Middlebury College and represent articles drawn from conferences held there. Due to costs of publication, the Series volumes are not intended to be full records of the conferences as they were presented. In some cases the contributed papers have been revised for publication.

Industrial Organization, Antitrust, and Public Policy

John V. Craven, Editor

Kluwer-Nijhoff Publishing
Boston / The Hague / London

Distributors for North America:
Kluwer-Nijhoff Publishing
Kluwer Boston, Inc.
190 Old Derby Street
Hingham, Massachusetts 02043, U.S.A.

Distributors outside North America:
Kluwer Academic Publishers Group
Distribution Centre
P.O. Box 322
3300AH Dordrecht, The Netherlands

Library of Congress Cataloging in Publication Data
Main entry under title:
Industrial organization, antitrust, and public policy.

(Middlebury College conference series on economic issues)
Selection of the papers presented at the 3rd annual Middlebury College Conference on Economic Issues, held in Apr. 1981.
Bibliography: p.
Contents: The relevance of industrial organization / Alfred E. Kahn — The anti-antitrust movement / Willard F. Mueller —Antitrust enforcement / Oliver E. Williamson — [etc.]

1. Trusts, Industrial — United States — Congresses. 2. Industrial organization (Economic theory) — Congresses. I. Craven, John V., 1921– . II. Middlebury College Conference on Economic Issues (3rd : 1981) III. Series.
HD2783.I5 338.8'0973 82-6622
ISBN 0-89838-103-7 AACR2

Printed in the United States of America

Contents

Volume Editor's Introduction

This book contains a selection of the papers presented at the third annual Middlebury College Conference on Economic Issues, held in April, 1981. The theme of the conference was "Industrial Organization and Public Policy." It is perhaps testimony to the complexity of our industrial structure that thirty years have passed without legislative action on antitrust even as the field of industrial organization has been heavily mined by scholars. Evidence that Congress prefers a hands-off policy seems now stronger than ever. This book seeks to present analyses and assessments that would aid the reader in judging the correctness of such public policy.

Alfred Kahn, in Part I, questions whether scholars whose concerns lie in the field of industrial organization can contribute significant insights to the major problems of the day — inflation, declining productivity, rising costs of resources, and income allocation. Although the paper following is not a direct response to Professor Kahn's skepticism, Willard Mueller presents in it a lively attack on those who discount the importance of an activist antitrust policy. Given the rather sharply contrasting views of Professors Mueller and Kahn, Oliver Williamson's contribution is an opportune perspective of where antitrust enforcement has been in the past two decades, and where it is going in the 1980s. Part I concludes with David Audretsch's assessment of the effectiveness of the enforcement of our merger law, followed by Robert Smith's proposal that we tie antitrust action more closely and more logically to macro stabilization policies.

The selections in Part II emphasize the industrial organization trinity: market structure, behavior, and performance. Coauthors Ralph Bradburd and A. Mead Over, Jr. deal with the special problems of critical concentration ratios. Edwin Mansfield provides analysis that relates technological change to market structure. Concluding Part II, Peter Meyer, with the assistance of Katherine M. Garber and Barbara A. Pino, shows the results of an investigation into concentration in local retail markets, a relatively neglected but important geographic delimitation.

Part III is embodied in a single paper — William Shepherd's pursuit of the key to the antitrust dilemma: how to distinguish profits arising from scale economies from those derived through market power.

What activities would an optimal antitrust policy cover? The selections in Part IV provide a partial answer to that question. Steven Schwartz suggests in "Micro Determinants of Conglomerate Mergers" that the puzzle of what to do about conglomerates is partially solved by enforcement of existing antitrust laws, if that enforcement is vigorous. In reaching that conclusion he provides a number of useful tests of the determinants of mergers. Katherine McElroy, John Siegfried and George Sweeney conclude Part IV with an inquiry into the distributive effects of antitrust policy.

In less than a decade from now, the one-hundredth anniversary of the Sherman Act will be noted, perhaps celebrated. It is the editor's fond hope that this collection will contribute to a keener appreciation of the strengths and weaknesses of our antitrust laws and to a clearer perception of important issues in the field of industrial organization.

I THE RELEVANCE OF ANTITRUST

1 THE RELEVANCE OF INDUSTRIAL ORGANIZATION

Alfred E. Kahn

It is now on the order of 45 years since Professor Edward S. Mason, working out of the Chamberlinian tradition, began to develop the rationale and organizing principles for the field we refer to as industrial organization. The organizing principle was the trinity — market structure, behavior, and performance; the basic premise, that the first of these, structure, is the conditioning, causal variable, the influence of which can be traced in the behavior of the active parties, and in the economic results they produce. The taxonomy of structure ran, in highly neoclassical fashion, along the competition-to-monopoly axis — that is, market structure was to be defined principally in terms of location on the competition-to-monopoly spectrum; and the most important focus of antitrust policy, it followed, was on market structure, not on behavior, let alone the intent that might be inferred from that behavior.[1]

At the cost of some oversimplification and at the risk of revealing my inability to keep up with the professional literature during the last ten

I acknowledge, with gratitude, the very helpful — and often very critical — reactions to an earlier draft of this paper by Jeff Boldani, Douglas Greer, Joel B. Dirlam, Paul Joskow, Scott Lindsay, and Irwin Stelzer.

years, I suggest that three major trends have developed during that decade, within and to this branch of our discipline, that have a bearing on its continued validity, usefulness — and, yes, relevance.

First, we have witnessed a veritable renaissance of microeconomics — an increasing and now close-to-universal recognition that microeconomic phenomena, institutions, and policies are at the core of the major economic problems of our age. Since I, a confirmed microeconomist, have lived professionally through 35 years in which, thanks largely to Keynes, micro has taken a back seat to macro, my feeling that the resurrection of the former has come not a moment too soon should come as no surprise.

Second, while industrial-organization economics has retained the trinity of structure, behavior, and performance, it has (in theory, if not in practice) discarded the simple characterization of the first of these along the competition-monopoly axis, as well as the notion that structure is to be regarded exclusively as the exogenous determinant of behavior. Furthermore, there has been an increased concentration on behavior — on advertising, product-quality variations, research and development (R&D), and particularly on such forms of strategic behavior as predatory and limit-pricing, and of the ways in which they may affect structure in general and the condition of entry in particular.

Incidentally, as one who has historically emphasized the behavioral over the structural approach to antitrust when it was quite unpopular with most economists, I take a good deal of satisfaction, as well as instruction, from Oliver Williamson's persuasive argument (see chapter 3) that the analysis of strategic behavior is going to be the central preoccupation of antitrust economics in the 1980s. Joel Dirlam and I bid you welcome.[2]

But third, despite these advances — and here I speak with trepidation — I have the impression that what I have characterized as the organizing principles and premises of our particular branch of economics, along with its very heavy traditional emphasis on antitrust policy, have come to be — or to be perceived to be — of sharply diminished relevance to our most pressing national economic concerns.

I suspect most economists would not have great difficulty agreeing on something similar to the following list of those problems and issues:

- Inflation — or, more descriptively, the dilemma of stagflation;
- Energy — or, more broadly, the apparently rising real costs of some critical natural resources, including a desirable physical environment;
- The proper relationship of government to the private economy — in particular, regulatory policy;

- Declining productivity growth, and the apparently declining competitive position of our industry in relation to the rest of the world;
- Major allocation issues — the distribution of our gross national product between consumption and investment, between the provision of public and private goods — along with such related income distributional issues as the definition of the social minimum (or President Reagan's "safety net"), the ballooning of government transfer programs and entitlements, the reconciliation of income redistribution with private incentives.[3]

What I am going to suggest, as a challenge that I only two-thirds believe myself, is, first, that the structure of markets and industries is not a very important explanation of most of these problems; and, second, that even where it is important (as I will argue is the case with inflation) the antitrust laws and other such remedies aimed at restructuring industries in some preferred direction along the competition-monopoly axis have become increasingly beside the point.

Inflation

Since monetarists continue to claim that inflation is nothing but a monetary phenomenon, I insist that I not be misunderstood as denying the relevance to this problem of the way in which our markets are organized and behave. I intend the contrary.

At times, the argument of the monetarist is wholly tautological: since inflation is the difference between the increase in aggregate spending in monetary terms and the increase in real output, the argument goes, inflation is caused by excessive spending and can be cured by reducing it.[4] The identities — total spending equals total sales in real terms times prices; and the same for their respective increments — obviously do not, however, demonstrate which is cause, which effect.

Moreover, while it is undoubtedly true, as a matter not only of definition but also of historical process, that inflation could not take place were not the policies that determine total spending accommodating; that most of the inflations in history, including even those of the last fifteen years, have indeed been largely caused, or at least set off by excessive increases in aggregate spending, financed largely by increases in the money supply; and that inflation could unquestionably be brought under control by a sufficiently restrictive monetary policy, those propositions simply do not answer the highly pertinent question of the costs of any such policy in terms of the distribution of its restrictive effects between prices and real output.

The terms of that trade-off — the location and slope of the Phillips Curve — are a micro, not a macroeconomic phenomenon, and it is precisely the apparently unfavorable character of those terms that is at the heart of the United States' (and the United Kingdom's) stagflationary dilemmas today.

A more specific formulation of the same argument, on both sides, revolves around the question of whether it makes sense to attribute any causal role in inflation to such microeconomic phenomena as what happened in world oil and grain markets in 1973–1974 and in oil again in 1978–1980. With the proper monetary policy, one side of the argument goes, increases in the relative prices of some commodities would be balanced by decreases in the prices of others. This argument is undoubtedly correct — tautologically. The question remains what would have been the cost to the economy, in terms of the effect on real output, of macroeconomic policies sufficiently tight to get declines in all prices other than oil and food sufficient to achieve stability in the average.

No doubt reflecting my incorrigibly institutionalist inclinations, I find it illuminating to think of inflation as a consequence of competing, and, in the aggregate, of incompatible, income claims — claims we exert not merely in spending out of our incomes, but also in the wages and profit margins we set, in the social and protective regulations we lobby for, in our demands for credit, for tax shelters and subsidies (consider only the inflationary consequences of the deductibility of mortgage interest for income-tax purposes), and for government expenditure programs — with inflation being the consequence of those claims exceeding, in the aggregate, the ability of the economy to satisfy them. This rather broad political or sociological explanation has the virtue of answering the question: granted that a sufficiently restrictive monetary policy would forestall inflation, why is it that some societies at some times have been able to practice the necessary restraint — and stop inflation dead in its tracks — and others at other times have not? Monetary and fiscal policies are not disembodied, exogenous visitations on the polity from some distant planet, affecting only the aggregate; each component of them has micro and distributional as well as macroeconomic consequences. They are part and parcel of the political-economic process in which people and groups of people struggle for income shares.

This continuous struggle for income shares, and the terms of the trade-off between real and price effects of macroeconomic restraint to which it gives rise — that is to say, the nature and intensity of our stagflationary dilemma — are importantly conditioned by the structure of markets and industries. I make no effort to spell this generalization out in detail, partly because its main components are, I think, obvious, and partly because I have already done so at length in what must be one of the least influential articles in the history of economic literature.[5]

Clearly, monopoly power, exerted in product and labor markets, is one important vehicle for the exertion of these excessive income claims in the face of aggregate demand that is either only sufficient for full employment or intentionally restricted in order to combat inflation. It is market power that permits the negotiation of wage increases far in excess of productivity, even when unemployment is growing, and the routine passing on of those cost increases with or without an increased *ex ante* profit margin even when product-market demand is weak or declining. It is market power, in important measure, that explains the ratchets — the temporal ratchet (prices and wages going up when demand expands more readily than going down when it contracts), interindustry ratchets (the asymmetrical behavior of wages and prices in markets experiencing increasing and declining demand) — and the perverse pricing behavior that threatens to divert the downward thrust of a restrictive monetary policy from prices to output.

Of course, in attempting to explain how market power could produce a secular upward drift in prices, we find ourselves confronting the neoclassical notion that, while profit-maximizing monopoly produces statically higher prices than competition, there is no reason for expecting it to increase that difference over time.

Once again, I attempt no thorough reconciliation, partly because I know of no wholly satisfactory one. Instead, I confine myself to a number of brief observations. First, since labor unions are obviously not maximizers of profits or even, quite possibly, of the total wage bill, the neoclassical logic does not seem to apply to the behavior of their wages over time. I do not know how to embrace their tendency to follow the Consumer Price Index (CPI), or the preceding highly visible union settlement, within a static maximizing framework that, in turn, seems to exclude the possibility of a wage/price and wage/wage spiral.

Second, there seems to be some relationship between monopoly power in product markets and high *ex ante* profit margins, which tend in time of increasing demand to become converted into very large realized profits and, in turn, into large wage settlements — so that product-market monopoly power appears to get incorporated in progressively higher wages rather than secularly increasing profit margins. Third, union wages have risen more rapidly than nonunion since the late 50s, even though the unionized fraction of the labor force has been declining,[6] and preliminary observations demonstrate a tendency, at least during the 1970s, for wages in regulated industries to rise markedly more, on the average, than in nonregulated.[7] And fourth, there is some tendency for these settlements to spill over into less concentrated and nonunionized industries, partly in conformance with what Arthur Okun characterized so graphically as "the invisible handshake."[8]

These seem to me the main components of what one might, appropriating Marshall's famous metaphor, refer to as the microeconomic blade of the stagflationary scissors. It takes both blades to create the policy dilemma we confront today, namely that fighting inflation with restrictive macroeconomic policies alone threatens to require severe and sustained recession.

Despite these various ways in which, as I see it, monopoly power plays an important role in the inflationary process, I find it difficult to subsume all of them under the heading of market structure, and even more difficult to look for a solution in reorganizing industries toward the pure-competition end of the spectrum. I will list some of the reasons.

First, the main problem, as I see it, is in labor, not product markets. And analysis of markets in terms of the structure-behavior-performance framework or the classical competition-monopoly axis makes much less sense for labor than product markets.

Second, the not-much-more-than 20 percent of American employees who are unionized and the few highly publicized key collective-bargaining agreements are too short a tail to wag the entire wage-structure dog. Arthur Okun's "invisible handshake" cannot be understood simply as an agreement to match union-wage increases. It seems, rather, to characterize a much broader and more fundamental change in wage policy on the part of the entire universe of employers. To be sure, the willingness and the ability of employers to pursue such a policy may well reflect some imperfections in either labor or product markets, which enable them either to refrain from short-term profit maximization or to set wages, in part, in order to forestall unionization of their employees.

In any event, however — and this is my main contention — the principal remedy, if we are ever going to find one that is not worse than the disease, is not likely to be an attempt to restore more effective competition in either labor or product markets. This is at least as much a political generalization on my part as an economic one. Instead, I see future policies to deal with the wage/wage and wage/price spirals evolving along such lines as:

1. Tax-based antiinflationary plans (TIPs), which use the tax system to induce restrained wage and price setting;
2. Prohibiting the incorporation of cost-of-living-adjustment clauses in collective bargaining agreements, as I understand they do in Germany;[9]
3. Requiring, as I understand they do in Japan,[10] that all contracts expire at the same time, which would bring us closer to
4. An arrangement under which wage policy is made more nearly on a national basis, in one comprehensive set of negotiations, rather than *seriatim,* as in the United States.

There is more to be said about these various possibilities, both pro and con, than I can say in this essay. Observe, however, that the first and second would leave market structures unchanged, and attempt instead to influence performance directly. The first would do so by providing incentives to produce less inflationary results. The second would break the automatic connection between wages and preceding changes in the CPI; also it would probably shorten contract lives, which would presumably make wages more responsive in the short run to macroeconomic developments.

The third and fourth suggestions, in contrast, would involve moving in a direction directly opposed to the implicit preference of industrial-organization economics. In recognition of the fact that wage setting is at least as much a political as an economic process, the notion would be to bring it to the center of the political stage. Mancur Olson has argued that the only way to introduce social responsibility into the bargaining process is to concentrate it and make it more nearly universal, rather than to disperse it even more, along competitive lines.[11]

There is much more that needs to be said about this proposal as well. Simultaneous, integrated negotiations do offer a hope of ending the process of successive attempted catch ups and leapfrogging. If, instead, everyone sits down at the table at the same time, it will become obvious that there is no way in which everyone can get a jump on everyone else. It may well be, however, that this proposal is no more feasible politically, and would raise fully as many practical difficulties as an attempt massively to restructure industry: who would represent the more than 75 percent of the labor force that is not organized in unions? How would changes in wage structure be determined? On the other hand, if chronic inflation and stagnation seem to continue to be our only available alternatives, I believe it highly likely that we will see periodic efforts by leaders of labor, business, and government to strike some sort of national accord or compact in which relaxation of macroeconomic restraint would be one part of the bargain, and wage and price restraint another.

Finally, while centralized, unified collective bargaining may offer the promise of freeing us from what I have referred to elsewhere as the tyranny of small decisions,[12] it would do so only at the cost of exposing us to the threat of massive breakdowns of negotiations and general strikes. Which only demonstrates, once again, that, just as inflation is a socio-political phenomenon, so a society's success or failure to contain it depends on the socio-political factors that determine its ability to reconcile competing income claims without conflict.

I do not mean to exaggerate. I can think of two kinds of market restructurings in the competitive direction that ought to be added to the foregoing list of possible remedies for the wage/wage and wage/price spirals. One would be elimination of multi-employer bargaining. This could weaken the power of unions, by removing their ability to pick employers off one by one, and by giving individual firms a greater incentive to resist wage increases. On the other hand, by fractionating the decision-making process and introducing the possibility of competition among unions and union leaders in an industry, it could result in even less socially responsible behavior. The other would be to dismantle cartel-producing regulation in situations where effective competition is achievable. The best hope for limiting above-average wages of the Teamsters and airline pilots in the future is trucking and airline deregulation. That is why they opposed it.

I return to my main argument, however: even though I see some relation between concentration or cartelization in product markets, on the one side, and the wage/price spiral on the other, I can conceive of no politically achievable restructuring of the former that would eradicate the latter. Instead, the relevant spectrum of public antiinflation policies runs, as I see it, from Thatcherism-Reaganism through TIPs, direct interventions into the bargaining process and social compacts, to mandatory controls — not, primarily, from monopolistic to competitive market structures.

Energy

Probably no industry has been subjected to more intensive and continuous study by industrial-organization economists than oil. I would be among the last to deny the important role that monopoly has played in presenting us with the massive energy problem that our country faces, and giving it its present shape. Whether we conceive of world oil markets as subject to an effectively functioning cartel or to dominant-firm monopoly, with Saudi Arabia playing the role that used to be played by Texas, I find it difficult to doubt, to put it mildly, that the production decisions of the exporting countries are substantially influenced by a consideration of their effect on the market price, that is, by monopoly power.

At the same time, I believe we must come to confront more and more directly the question of how different the price of oil would be today were the world's petroleum industry more competitively structured. In raising this question, I am influenced primarily by:

- Our tendency in the past, in thinking about how high a competitive price of oil would be, to look only to drilling and lifting costs in the Middle East, and to pay insufficient attention to user costs — the value sacrificed by producing and selling a barrel today rather than holding it for tomorrow. This consideration influences the production decisions even of a purely competitive producer, provided, of course, that he is free of the law of capture. Determining the level of user costs is, of course, an exercise in prognostication. All we can safely say, on the basis of the experience of the last ten years or so, is that it must be much higher in the estimation of the producers — which is what counts — than the one dollar or so a barrel that William Nordhaus estimated to be the royalty value of oil in the ground as little as a decade ago.[13]
- Our discovery that the availability of oil shales, heavy crudes, and synthetic gases and liquids from coal do not, as was once very widely believed, put an upper limit on the price of crude oil at a level of about five dollars a barrel. Translate that five-dollar figure into what I am now pleased to be able to refer to as Reagan dollars, and you still have those previously optimistic estimates of the point at which supply would turn sharply elastic off by a factor of three or four — and we still do not know where the ceiling really is.
- The disappointing results achieved by the sharply accentuated drilling activity of the last several years, suggesting in yet another way that the marginal cost curve is very steeply inclined.

The consequence of these considerations is to leave me reasonably certain that, even if OPEC were to disappear and the structure of the industry were to become markedly less oligopolistic than it is today, the price of oil would be closer to today's thirty-five-dollar level than to the three dollars of a decade ago.

Whatever the validity of this reasoning, it appears that making the American petroleum-producing industry more highly competitive is fairly close to irrelevant to our present situation (although I continue to be skeptical that U.S. refiners with large investments in domestic crude-oil production have the proper incentives with respect to the prices they pay for foreign crude, even with a large part of their foreign production properties nationalized). Instead, the most promising approaches have centered on:

- Deregulation of crude-oil and natural-gas prices;
- Ways of exercising monopsony power in world markets, individually, or in collaboration with other importing countries;
- Determining the proper degree and mix of government interventions to speed the development of alternative energy sources and encourage conservation;
- Reforming public-utility regulation to get prices closer to marginal costs both in the aggregate and by time of use; requiring interconnections among utility companies with cogenerators, solar, wind and small hydro installations; and eliminating the distortion — a case of Averch-Johnson in total reverse — created by the combination of automatic fuel adjustment clauses and rate awards that have systematically denied electric companies the ability to earn anything even close to their true cost of capital, which together have the effect of discouraging the making of any additional investments, however small, to realize savings in fuel costs, however large.

Regulation and Regulatory Reform

I have occasionally asked myself whether the acceptance by a confirmed microeconomist of the position of National Cheerleader in the fight against inflation made any sense at all. I justified it to myself at the time — apart, that is, from the all-but-sufficient consideration that the President asked me — on the grounds that, while responsibility for the all-important macroeconomic policies would rest elsewhere, regulatory reform and the improvement of microefficiency in the economy generally are important components in a longer-run effort to squeeze the underlying powerful inflationary pressures out of the economy. Whatever the validity of that view, there is no doubt inflation made it a good deal easier for us to achieve some very desirable regulatory reforms that might otherwise have been unachievable.[14]

I am satisfied that there are at least three ways in which a micro-policy effort of this kind does make sense as part of an antiinflation program.

First, social regulation — to protect the environment, public health, safety on the job — is one of the ways in which we place demands on the economy and thereby contribute to the imbalance between the sum-total of demands and aggregate supply that constitutes inflation. (I have already sketched the outlines of my rejoinder to the monetarists' denial that any such micro interventions could cause or explain inflation.)

Second, to the extent that cartel-like, protectionist regulation compels inefficiencies or interferes with the dynamic pressures that competition would otherwise exert, it has contributed to the stagnation of productivity, which has further aggravated this progressive imbalance in the last several years.

Finally, to the extent that economic regulation has, by creating and protecting monopoly power, contributed to the perverse behavior of wages and prices, then clearly it has contributed to the unresponsiveness of prices to macroeconomic restraint, which is one blade of our stagflationary scissors.

In the reform of strictly economic, industry-specific regulation, as well as in the struggle against such openly protectionist interventions by the government as the steel trigger-price mechanism, the proposed imposition of quotas on Japanese cars, and the application of the antidumping laws to perishable agricultural commodities, industrial-organization economics has had some of its most brightly shining hours; nor have those opportunities been exhausted. We will continue for a long time to be defining the circumstances and the ways in which it is preferable to rely on the unregulated market as the central organizing institution. More specifically, there remains a need for:

- Studying and assessing the future course of such largely deregulated industries as the airlines, motor carriers, financial markets and railroads, and combatting the efforts that have already begun to reverse the process.
- Designing the proper deregulatory course for communications, which includes answering extremely difficult questions about the kinds of structural arrangements necessary to permit franchised public utility monopolies like the Bell System to operate in competitive areas.
- Investigating the possibilities of introducing more effective competition into such areas as insurance, maritime shipping, and agricul-

tural marketing, which at present enjoy exemption from the antitrust laws.

- Learning to apply the antitrust laws to newly deregulated industries. To the extent that previously tightly regulated industries enter the domain of general antitrust, those laws and the issues surrounding their application — questions about the proper definition of predation, the optimum admixture of information and more direct consumer protections, the assessment of proposed mergers — become more important in our economy, not less.
- Evaluating the never-ending efforts of private interest groups to induce the government to protect them from competition.

In all these areas, and many others that will undoubtedly have occurred to you, industrial organization remains highly relevant.

In very large measure, however, I expect the emphasis of the regulatory reform movement to shift heavily in the months and years immediately ahead to the area in which, by general consensus, competition does not work. There is a very great deal of important work to be done, at both the general and specific levels, to develop criteria and regulatory techniques to introduce a more incisive economic calculus into what we might call social-protective regulation — probing the uses and limits of cost-benefit analysis, exploring the possible use of regulatory budgets and of innovative techniques that will maximize private incentives to achieve regulatory goals in the most cost-effective ways possible. This is clearly a very important task for microeconomics, but not, unless my imagination fails me, for the structure/conduct/performance analytical framework.

Productivity and Industrial Revitalization

Space and the complexity of the subject permit me to offer only a few observations about this very important set of problems.

First, our heavily advertised and widely deplored loss of industrial supremacy turns out, on examination, to be very much like the news of Mark Twain's death. I suspect that, unless you happen to have read the last *Economic Report of the President,* you will be surprised to know that during the last decade our industrial output increased more rapidly than did West Germany's or France's, and of course far far more than in Great Britain, though markedly less than Japan's.[15] The problems are heavily concentrated in automobiles and steel — the consequence of bad management, mistakes, inordinate wage settlements over the last decade translated complacently into ever-higher prices, a sudden shift in our energy situation, a concentration of environmental and other regulations (most of them long overdue), and, finally, an inevitable catching-up industrialization by countries like Japan, Taiwan, South Korea, and Brazil. (These industries, I am sure it will at once have occurred to you, would probably be performing better today if they were more competitive. The fact remains that they have never been effectively challenged by antitrust and I see no prospect that they will be.)

Second, however, while the sharp and disturbing decline in the measured rate of increase in productivity during the last decade has been partly the consequence of the erroneous way in which we measure productivity, so as to exclude the consumption of inputs the costs of which were previously external to the firm; and partly the temporary consequence of the sudden upsurge in the size of the labor force; and partly the result of historical changes — such as the slowing down in the shift of labor out of agriculture and the sharply increased real costs of energy — that appear irreversible, it is nevertheless a serious problem that we must confront.

Third, dealing with this problem is almost certainly going to force us to explore new methods of organizing and motivating economic activity — new forms of labor-management cooperation in reducing costs, ensuring and improving product quality, and reconciling industrial change with the preservation of security for the individual.

Fourth, I suspect the contribution of industrial-organization economics to these efforts is likely to be primarily negative — that is, to counteract proposals designed to insulate industries from competitive pressures — although that is important enough. It will be our function, for example, to

- Make clear to the public the negative consequences for productivity and inflation of protectionist government interventions and other such restrictions on competition.
- Cast a skeptical eye on glib references to the alleged success of government interventions in other countries in picking and supporting industrial winners, arguments that are being used to justify setting up monstrous Reconstruction Finance Corporations to speed the process of industrial revitalization. There is a very strong tendency of observers to see in foreign experience what they are looking for — a tendency from which I am not immune. There seems reason to believe, however, that the contributions of such interventions — let alone their transferability — have been greatly exaggerated. It appears, for example, that in Japan government intervention in the steel industry, commonly cited as an example of successful industrial policy, is a case in which, on the contrary, there seems to

have been a very serious waste of capital, with the improved competitive position of that industry being attributable primarily if not entirely to its earning a very low return on that capital; that the most successful Japanese industries, such as consumer electronics and automobiles, have had only very limited government support; and that other cases in which governments have attempted to pick winners have been conspicuously unsuccessful: aircraft in Great Britain, computers in France, the nuclear industry in Germany.[16]

- Be alert to the dangers of industry-wide labor-management cooperation, and even more of the setting up of tripartite boards representing business, labor, and the government becoming instruments for the comprehensive syndicalization of our economy.
- Resist any tendencies the new administration may show to weaken the antitrust laws, and to retard or reverse the process of economic deregulation.

I have everything prepared but a conclusion. Am I saying that industrial organization is moribund, as a field? No one could even glance through this book and reach such a conclusion.

Am I suggesting that we should relax our enforcement of the antitrust laws, or our efforts in other ways to make the economy more effectively competitive? Not at all: as I am pleased to argue facetiously in defending my own labors in the antiinflation vineyard, we can only surmise with horror how much worse matters would be today but for those efforts.

I guess what I am really urging is a continuation of the trend of closer integration of industrial organization with microeconomics and microeconomic policy generally; breaking out of the structure-behavior-performance box in the many situations where that framework seems not very useful; a recognition that the range of available micro policy instruments and the need for imaginative new institutional arrangements extends far beyond the various categories of competition and monopoly, and the range of policy instruments far beyond the antitrust laws.

Notes

1. See Edward S. Mason's Preface in Carl Kaysen and Donald Turner, *Antitrust Policy: An Economic and Legal Analysis* (Cambridge: Harvard University Press, 1959).

2. See our *Fair Competition, The Law and Economics of Antitrust Policy* (Ithaca: Cornell University Press, 1954).

3. Arthur M. Okun, *Equality and Efficiency: The Big Tradeoff* (Washington, D.C.: The Brookings Institution, 1975). I will devote no further attention to this last, increasingly pressing set of issues, because it is so clearly outside the scope of industrial organization

economics. (Even this generalization needs qualification in intriguing ways: consider the effect of product differentiation and the particular directions of industrial research, development, and innovation on our collective demand for various kinds of private and public goods.)

4. See, for example, the report by the General Accounting Office, with the neutral title *The Voluntary Pay and Price Standards Have Had No Discernible Effect on Inflation:*

> The rate of inflation is equal to the difference between the rate at which total spending is rising and the rate of increase in the total output of goods and services. From the third quarter of 1978 through the first quarter of 1980, total spending in the United States grew at an average yearly rate of 10.9 percent. This growth far exceeded the economy's capacity to increase its total output of goods and services. *Inflation was inevitable* (stress supplied).

PAD-81-02 (December 10, 1980) p. 42.

5. "Market Power Inflation: A Conceptual Framework," in *The Roots of Inflation* (New York: Burt Franklin, 1975) pp. 239-272. See also Harvey Leibenstein, "The Inflation Process: A Microbehavioral Analysis," *American Economic Review,* 76 (May 1981): 368-73; and Gardner Ackley, "Evaluation of Incomes-Policies Alternatives," presented at The Conference Board Colloquium on Alternatives for Economic Policy, Washington, D.C., June 1981.

6. See Daniel Mitchell, "Some Empirical Observations of Relevance to the Analysis of Union Wage Determination," *Journal of Labor Research* 1 (Oct. 1982): 193–215, and *Unions, Wages and Inflation* (Washington, D.C.: The Brookings Institution, 1980).

7. Milton Kafoglis and Oliver Grawe, "A Reconsideration of the Efficiency of Regulation," presented to American Economic Association (Association for the Study of the Grants Economy), December, 1979.

8. *Prices and Quantities: A Macroeconomic Analysis* (Washington, D.C.: The Brookings Institution, 1981) chapter 3. For amplification of these several points, see my "Market Power Inflation," note 4, above, and, for a particulary thoughtful and thorough survey, Douglas F. Greer, *Industrial Organization and Public Policy* (New York: Macmillan, 1980), chapters 21 and 22.

9. Lester C. Thurow, "Cut Wages 4 Percent — Everybody's," *New York Times* (January 11, 1981), III–2.

10. *Ibid.*

11. *The Rise and Decline of Nations: Economic Growth, Stagflation and Social Rigidities* (New Haven: Yale University Press, 1982), Chapters 3 and 4.

12. I referred there to the possibility that the sum total effect of a large number of small, individually optimizing decisions might not be optimal at all. The analogy to tandem or leapfrogging wage settlements ending up in mutual frustration is, I think, apt. "The Tyranny of Small Decisions: Market Failures, Imperfections, and the Limits of Economics," *Kyklos,* 19 (1966): 23–47.

13. "The Allocation of Energy Resources," *Brookings Papers on Economic Activity,* III (1973) 527–70.

14. See my "Regulatory Reform: Is It Politically Achievable" in Leroy Graymer and Frederick Thompson (ed.), *Reforming Social Regulation: Alternative Public Policy Strategies* (Los Angeles: Sage Publications, 1982), Part III, Chapter 12.

15. *Economic Report of the President,* Washington, D.C. (January 1981) p. 30.

16. I draw here upon unpublished papers prepared for the Carter Administration's Economic Policy Group, including Paul Krugman, "Foreign Experience with Industrial Policy: A Critical Review," draft, 1980 (otherwise unidentified).

2 THE ANTI-ANTITRUST MOVEMENT

Willard F. Mueller

We are in the midst of a new antitrust movement, but unlike those of earlier times, this one is an anti-antitrust movement. My objectives here are to place the current attack on antitrust in historical perspective, examine its origins, and comment on the arguments of the economist who has emerged as the most popular exponent of abolishing the antitrust law.

The antitrust laws were this nation's response to the *laissez-faire* capitalism that came into full flower after the Civil War. The new economic order, epitomized in the great trusts, created a feeling of unease among the people. Writing in 1911, Supreme Court Justice John M. Harlan characterized the mood that gave birth to the Sherman Act of 1890. "There was everywhere," said Harlan, " a deep feeling of unrest. . . the conviction was universal that the country was in real danger [from] the aggregations of capital in the hands of a few individuals and corporations controlling, for their own profit and advantage exclusively, the entire business of the country. . ."[1]

These feelings and fears gave rise to the Sherman Act of 1890. This act and the Clayton Act of 1914 were rooted primarily in the belief that excess corporate power must be restrained to assure fair competition, prevent exploitation of the consumer, and protect democratic institutions by preventing excessive centralization of economic power.

Until World War I there was continuing agitation for more vigorous enforcement and strengthening of the Sherman Act of 1890. In the 1912 presidential campaign each candidate — Roosevelt, Taft, and Wilson — spelled out an agenda for curbing excessive corporate economic power. The result was the enactment in 1914 of the Clayton Act and Federal Trade Commission Act. World War I changed abruptly the nation's agenda, and following that conflict, concern with these matters was set aside as the nation was promised a return to "normalcy."

During the 1920s there occurred the first concerted attack on the antitrust laws. Enforcement effort dwindled, many courts were openly hostile, and, for a time, the Federal Trade Commission (FTC) came under seige and was charged with harboring persons hostile to American capitalism. To many, a return to "normalcy" meant a return to the *laissez-faire* capitalism of the nineteenth century.

The most progressive senators, such as LaFollette and Norris, continued to support the FTC until the middle 1920s, when, in 1925, President Coolidge appointed William E. Humphrey, his former campaign manager and a lobbyist for Western lumber interests, to the chairmanship of the FTC. The new Humphrey-majority's anti-antitrust sentiments so alienated the progressives that some proposed abolishing the agency. Under Humphrey's aegis, the FTC was converted from an instrument for "preservation of fair methods of competition . . . into a device for limiting price competition itself."[2]

By the late 1920s and early 1930s many special-interest groups urged drastic changes, if not outright repeal, of the antitrust laws on grounds that these laws shackled business initiative and that their repeal was essential to economic recovery; many of the arguments were very similar to those used today.[3]

The most ambitious proposal for legitimizing a cartelized economy was the Swope Plan of 1931, formulated by General Electric President Gerald Swope. It called for coordinating production and consumption through legalized cooperation among corporations to stabilize "competitive methods and prices."[4] In 1932 both political parties were being urged to repeal or drastically weaken the antitrust laws. Leading members of the American Economic Association rallied to the defense of the antitrust laws. In a sharply worded "reaffirmation of the essential principle of fair competition," the economists urged both political parties to reject these attacks.[5]

The statement may have had some effect. The 1932 Republican platform was silent on the issue, though the chairman of the resolution committee favored a plank attacking the Sherman Act. The Democratic Party platform included a brief statement embodying the main features of the economists' statement.

Any satisfaction over this seeming victory was short-lived, however, since a centerpiece of one of the New Deal's first creations, the National Industrial Recovery Act (NIRA), repudiated the antitrust laws, replacing them with the codes of fair competition that businessmen had sought and FTC Chairman Humphrey had tried to give. Then, quite unexpectedly, at what seemed antitrust's darkest hour, a new era of antitrust began. In 1935 the National Recovery Administration (NRA), already economically ill, was given a death sentence by the Supreme Court. President Roosevelt, disturbed by the failures of his program to prevent a deepening of the depression in 1937–1938, turned his back — at least partially — on centralized NRA-type planning in favor of making competitive capitalism work more effectively. To accomplish this he appointed Thurmond Arnold to head a substantially enlarged Antitrust Division and called for a full-scale investigation into the way twentieth-century capitalism worked and how it could be improved.

During 1937–1942, a period many recall as the golden age of antitrust, Thurmond Arnold pursued an aggressive policy. In a single year he filed more Sherman Act cases than had been brought during the first 20 years of the Act. Perhaps the main legacy of these years was the demonstration that antitrust still had a meaningful role a half century after the Sherman Act was enacted. Although Arnold's big cases generally were stalled during the war years, the antitrust agencies rebounded strongly at war's end, and the big cases went forward.

While antitrust as a movement was dormant in the postwar decades, the enforcement effort did not wither as it had after World War I. The reason for this difference, as historian Richard Hofstadter persuasively argues, was that Arnold's regime had resulted in the institutionalization of the antitrust process: "Despite the collapse of antitrust feeling both in the public at large and among intellectuals, antitrust as legal-administrative enterprise [was] solidly institutionalized."[6]

The most important area of activity involved merger enforcement, which was given new life by the Celler-Kefauver Act of 1950. The Act amended and greatly strengthened Section 7 of the Clayton Act, which had been rendered totally ineffective by a series of Supreme Court decisions in the 1920s.

Following passage of the 1950 Act, the FTC and the Antitrust Division initiated an aggressive program of enforcement. Although it has been almost totally ineffective in dealing with conglomerate mergers, the Celler-Kefauver Act has been used effectively in challenging horizontal mergers, the type that most directly injures competition. A few statistics illustrate the immensity of the merger-enforcement effort. During 1951–1980 the antitrust agencies issued 500 merger complaints challenging 1,477 mergers. This effort was not merely a charade involving small acquiring companies, as Galbraith has asserted. The bulk of these complaints challenged large acquiring companies: 83 percent of all acquired assets were by companies with assets exceeding $1 billion and 95 percent by companies with assets exceeding $250 million.[7]

From my studies, I conclude that many American industries would definitely be much more concentrated were it not for this enforcement effort. Many large corporations seem to have insatiable appetites for growth by merger, even when it can be accomplished only by conglomerate acquistions that make little or no economic sense. It takes little knowledge of business behavior to realize that, without restraints on horizontal mergers, this merger appetite would be wholly unrestrained, leading to unacceptably high levels of concentration in many industries.

The Celler-Kefauver Act clearly has done very little about conglomerate mergers, but it might have been otherwise had the agencies followed through on the efforts begun in the late 1960s and early 1970s. The Supreme Court, under Chief Justice Earl Warren had upheld the government in all of the conglomerate merger cases to reach the highest court. The agencies, especially the Antitrust Division under Donald Turner (1966–1968) hesitated in following up on these victories. Then, in 1969, President Nixon appointed Richard W. McLaren to head the Antitrust Division. As a condition of accepting the appointment, McLaren had received Attorney General Mitchell's approval to test whether the Celler-Kefauver Act could be used to challenge successfully large conglomerate mergers, especially those involving acquisitions of dominant firms and those creating the potential for reciprocity. McLaren first laid out his game plan, and then began carrying it out expeditiously.[8] Although few observers believed McLaren would actually carry out his plan to challenge conglomerate mergers, during 1969 he brought suit to block three large acquisitions by ITT (Hartford Fire Insurance, Canteen Corporation, and the Grinnell Corporation), and two other large conglomerate mergers. This marked the zenith of the conglomerate-merger enforcement effort.

The counterattack came swiftly. While most business leaders merely criticized McLaren, ITT offiicals, headed by Board Chairman Harold Geneen, descended on Washington, perhaps encouraged by ITT's success in helping to topple the Allende government in Chile.[9] I have recounted the ensuing campaign at length elsewhere, though I did so without benefit of the subsequently released White House Watergate tapes.[10] These tapes demonstrate that Richard McLaren's policy was overruled by the President himself. A key day in these events was April 19, 1971. Several months earlier Richard McLaren had successfully petitioned the Supreme Court for permission to appeal the *ITT-Grinnell* case, and the Justice Department's appeal brief was ready by March, 1971. Under White House pressure, McLaren asked the court to postpone submission of the brief for one month, to April 20, 1971. On the afternoon of April 19, 1971, the President met with his chief aide, John Ehrlichman, and George Schultz, Director of the Office of Management and Budget. Their conversation was recorded by the President's secretly installed tape recorder.[11]

The conversation begins with Ehrlichman telling the President that the *ITT-Grinnell* appeal was being pursued despite his attempts to give the Justice Department signals to the contrary. The President (P) expressed outrage, and decided to call Deputy Attorney General, Richard G. Kleindienst (K), to give McLaren his marching orders.

P [Picks up the telephone] yeah.
K Hi, Mr. President.
P Hi, Dick, how are you?
K Good, how are you, sir?
P Fine, fine. I'm going to talk to John [Attorney General Mitchell] tomorrow about my general attitude on antitrust.
K Yes sir.
P And in the meantime, I know that he has left with you, uh, the IT & T thing because apparently he says he had something to do with them once.
K [laughs] Yeah. Yeah.
P Well, I have, I have nothing to do with them, and I want something clearly understood, and, if it is not understood McLaren's ass is to be out within one hour. The IT & T thing — stay the hell out of it. Is that clear? That's an order.
K Well, you mean the order is to — .
P The order is to leave the God damned thing alone. Now, I've said this, Dick, a number of times, and you fellows apparently don't get the me, the message over there. I do not want McLaren to run around prosecuting people, raising hell about comglomerates, stirring things up at this point. Now you keep him the hell out of that. Is that clear?

K Well, Mr. President —
P Or either he resigns. I'd rather have him out anyway. I don't like the son-of-a-bitch.
K The, the question then is —
P The question is, I know, that the jurisdiction — I know all the legal things, Dick, you don't have to spell out the legal —
K [Unintelligible] the appeal filed.
P That's right.
K That brief has to be filed tomorrow.
P That's right. Don't file the brief.
K Your order is not to file a brief?
P Your — my order is to drop the God damn thing. Is that clear?
K [Laughs] Yeah. I understand that.
P Okay.
K [Unintelligible]
[President hangs up]

After this conversation the President said to those gathered, "I hope he resigns. He may." Then follows an attempt by George Schultz to assure the President that he was following sound Chicago School economics in permitting conglomerate mergers. It must have comforted Nixon to learn that Schultz had "checked this over with my friend Stigler" who assured Schultz that mergers presented no problem.

But Nixon was too preoccupied with McLaren's independent behavior in the ITT case to sit silently and endure for long Schultz's lecture on Chicago School economics.

P . . . the problem is McLaren's a nice little fellow who's a good little antitrust lawyer out in Chicago. Now he comes in and all those bright little bastards that worked for the Antitrust Department for years and years and years and who hate business with a passion. . . have taken him over. . . . That was all right fifty years ago. Fifty years ago maybe it was a good thing for this country. It's not a good thing for the country today. That's my views about it, and I am not — we've been through this crap. They've done several of them already about — they raised holy hell with the people that we, uh, who — well Geneen [Chairman of ITT], hell, he's no contributor. He's nothing to us. I don't care about him. So you can — I've only met him once, twice — we've, I'm just uh — I can't understand what the trouble is.[12]

Presidential counsel John Erhlichman (E) then made a feeble effort to come to McLaren's defense.

E McLaren has a very strong sense of mission here.
P Good — Jesus, he's — get him out. In one hour.
E He's got a
P One hour.
E Very strong —
P And he's not going to be a judge either. He is out of the God damn government. You know, just like that regional office man in, in San Francisco. I put an order into Haldeman today that he be fired today.
E Yeah

Attorney General Mitchell subsequently discussed these matters with the President and advised him that it would be politically unwise to interfere with the ITT appeal. The President agreed to heed Mitchell's advice to permit the appeal to go forward after Mitchell assured him, "We can get rid of the ITT thing, I think".

Get rid of it they did. The Justice Department entered into a sham agreement with ITT settling all three ITT cases before the Supreme Court was given an opportunity to hear the *ITT-Grinnell* appeal.[13] Thus ended the assault on conglomerate mergers. Since 1971 no significant conglomerate mergers have been challenged.

The New Attack on Antitrust

It would be a mistake to single out the ITT affair as the origin of the current anti-antitrust movement. It was merely one scene in a hit play, "The Watergate Scandals," that ran well in Washington for two seasons. McLaren's assault on conglomerate mergers foundered, as Henry C. Simons might have said, on the orderly process of democratic corruption.

The new attack on antitrust began well before Watergate. The very success of antitrust and the consumer movement were partly responsible for galvanizing corporate America into action in the 1960s and 1970s.

From World War II until about 1973–1974, the enforcement effort was modestly aggressive, especially in the area of mergers, and the courts became increasingly sympathetic to strict interpretations of these laws. Private antitrust activity reached historic highs in the 1960s and 1970s. As historian Richard Hofstadter put it, whereas "once the United States had an antitrust movement without prosecution; in our time there have been antitrust prosecutions without a movement.''[14]

The Warren court played a central role in all this, as perhaps the only Supreme Court since 1890 that felt comfortable with vigorous enforcement of the antitrust laws. But the strong pro-antitrust era of the Warren court ended in 1973–1974, when in the words of associate Justice White, a ''new anti-trust majority'' emerged. One legal authority asserts that the Burger Court has a deep-rooted ''anti-antitrust'' bias.[15]

The changed composition of the Court reflected a broader conservative movement that had spread across the land, as special interests mobilized to change the antitrust laws as well as other aspects of our economic and political systems. It is a mistake to assume the new attack on antitrust flowered from seeds only recently planted. It germinated two decades ago and has been growing continuously ever since.

The Chicago School of economics has long provided the main intellectual resources for attacking the antitrust laws and their enforcement. But the views from Chicago did not have great influence on public policy until they became firmly implanted at a number of other universities, (for example, UCLA, Virginia, Rochester, and Texas A&M) and when they became generously endowed by industrial interests seeking intellectual legitimization of their objectives.

During the 1960s and 1970s business interests stepped up greatly their support of groups and individuals holding views compatible with those of business. The most obvious manifestations of corporate efforts aimed at shaping views toward modern capitalism are the American Enterprise Institute, the Hoover Institution, the Heritage Foundation, and other centers of conservative economic thought. The National Chamber of Commerce has supported academic researchers critical of the regulatory agencies.[16] Corporate philanthropists of the New Right have increasingly contributed generously to ''scholars''. The John M. Olin (of Olin Corporation) and Sarah Scaife Foundation (large holder of Gulf Oil securities), together reportedly have given $7.5 million to academics at places like the University of Chicago, UCLA, and the American Enterprise Institute.[17] The Heritage Foundation, launched just seven years ago with a $250,000 contribution by ultraconservative brewing tycoon Joseph Coors, last year had a budget of $5.3 million.[18]

The world's largest corporation, AT&T, has assumed responsibility for publishing the major professional journal in regulatory economics, the *Bell Journal of Economics*.[19] If this is a harbinger of how our professional journals will be sponsored in the future, perhaps IBM or Exxon will take over the financially troubled *Industrial Organization Review*.

The University of Miami's Law and Economics Center provides special two-week, all-expense-paid, cram courses in *laissez-faire* economics for the federal judiciary. The Center is financed almost exclusively by large corporations, in some cases, corporations (ITT and IBM) that have cases before the very judges attending the Center.[20] To date, nearly one-fifth of the federal judiciary has attended at least one of the Center's institutes. Upon returning home to their chambers, the judges receive monthly mailings from the Center on crucial economic issues like advertising. The anti-antitrust bias of the Center's faculty was probably pretty well summed up by Chicago School economist, Harold Demsetz, when he told the assembled judges, "My own personal view is that the place of the antitrust laws comes with explicit price collusion — and probably nowhere else."[21]

These various forces are subtly, and often not so subtly, influencing many people's views toward the antitrust laws. For example, Office of Management and Budget (OMB) Director David Stockman, an historian by training, reportedly gained most of his knowledge of regulatory economics by reading publications of the American Enterprise Institute. (Not too surprisingly, Stockman named Institute scholar, James Miller, to head regulatory matters within OMB.) This also likely explains Stockman's views on antitrust, which he put succinctly: "I disagree with the whole antitrust tradition."[22] It is hardly surprising, therefore, that, "the decision to push for an end to funding the Federal Trade Commission's competition bureau was made on the basis of a two page memorandum after less than a minute's deliberation by OMB Director Stockman."[23]

Ironically, the current critics of antitrust rely on the ideology of free markets. They object not to competition, they assert, but rather to the allegedly anticompetitive effect of the antitrust laws. Competition, in their view, already is very intense and would continue to be so in the absence of antitrust; and where competition is not working effectively, the problem more likely than not is to be found in some anticompetitive government-imposed policy. There is also much loose talk about the need for larger American corporations so that they can compete more effectively in foreign markets.

Rather than attempt to review all the critics, I shall examine in some detail the criticisms raised by Lester C. Thurow, Professor of Economics and Management at the Massachusetts Institute of Technology. I do so not out of personal malice. Professor Thurow has excellent academic credentials in his field of specialization, and I understand he is a pleasant and engaging young man.

I have chosen to discuss Thurow's views solely because nearly every recent criticism of antitrust appearing in the popular press and business magazines gives prominent play to his ideas.[24] Thurow has never bcen one to limit his views to the classrooom or to the professional literature. Although he has been commenting on antitrust policy for some time, he first moved to center stage by writing a piece for *The New York Times*, entitled, "Let's Abolish the Anti-trust Laws."[25] Since then his voice or written words are everywhere. In February 1981, he was interviewed at length by the executive editor of *Dun's Review*. *Dun's* titled the interview: "Abolish the Antitrust Laws," with the long subtitle, "That's the View of Top Economist Lester Thurow, A Liberal Democrat, Who was an Economic Advisor to George McGovern and Jimmy Carter."[26]

Methinks that much of Thurow's popularity with the business press is explained by the contents of the subtitle. Nothing so warms the heart of the conservative as criticisms of antitrust by liberal democrats who were former advisors to presidents or contenders for high office.

To avoid mistaken criticism, I shall comment only on statements made directly by Thurow, thus avoiding error that comes from misquotations or misinterpretations by the occasional unsophisticated or careless journalist.

I begin by examining his views as revealed in his latest book, *The Zero-Sum Society*.[27] In his review of *Zero-Sum*, my colleague, Professor Robert J. Lampman, predicts that the book "will interest undergraduate students in economics as well as the general reader."[28] Were they restricted to the narrower audience of professional economists, Thurow's errors would cause less mischief.

As with other matters, Thurow's views on antitrust are unequivocal: "The antitrust approach has been a failure," says Thurow, "The costs it imposes far exceed any benefits it brings."[29] He gives five reasons for these conclusions.

Free Trade Makes Antitrust Unnecessary

According to Thurow, in markets where international trade exists or could exist, "If they [the antitrust laws] do anything, they only serve to hinder U.S. competitors who must live by a code that their foreign competitors can ignore."[30] The assertion that U.S antitrust laws disadvantage American corporations in international competition is an old chestnut used to discredit the laws for decades. Yet there is no persuasive empirical evidence, nor does Thurow cite any, to support the claim. First, U.S. corporations generally are considerably bigger than their foreign competitors. Second, the main restraints on U.S. behavior in foreign markets are those forbidding participation in cartels. There are few, if any, respectable economic arguments that show how the inability to participate in a cartel reduces a company's ability to compete. On the contrary, the accepted economic wisdom, supported by considerable historical experience, is that firms outside a cartel have greater sales and profits than the cartel.

Thurow's other argument regarding international trade is that, "If competitive markets are desired, the appropriate policy should be to reduce barriers to free trade."[31] He cites as examples the actual trade barriers in steel and the proposed barriers in automobiles. Thurow's problem here is that he lacks historical perspective. We did have free trade in steel until the late 1960s. But, because competition was ineffective among domestic steel companies, they responded to imports by yielding market share rather than by cutting price. As a result, by the late 1960s they had surrendered such a large part of the market to foreign competitors that they placed in jeopardy the jobs of hundreds of thousands of workers and the capital of numerous investors. At this point the Johnson administration was persuaded to negotiate the first of a series of restraints on steel imports. The point here is that ineffective competition was the underlying reason for abandoning free trade in the first place.

I readily acknowledge that the antitrust laws have failed to keep the steel industry competitive enough, though they have accomplished much even here. The problem with the steel industry would not be improved by repealing the antitrust laws and permitting greater concentration, and certainly not be permitting complete cartelization as Thurow would permit in industries involved in international trade. The available evidence indicates that the largest steel companies have not been the most innovative and that greater size is not needed to make the leaders more efficient. Moreover, with or without free trade, buyers in middle America are totally dependent on domestic steel companies when buying many products and are protected only by competition among domestic sellers. Thus, free trade often promises much more than it delivers, and clearly merely being in favor of it in principle is not reason enough to warrant abandoning concern with competition among domestic competitors. As Frank Knight said many years ago, the free traders win the debates but the protectionists win the elections.

Monopoly for Breakfast?

Thurow next comes to the defense of monopoly by arguing that the general rise in income tends to greatly increase the relevant market in which firms compete. Most goods people buy today are not "physiological necessities but luxuries that could be substituted by other goods. . ."[32] The person considering the purchase of a Rolls Royce may substitute for it "a swimming pool, a summer home, or a wide variety of products." In Thurow's economic world all of these products are in the same market, so even if Rolls Royce has a monopoly it is not in a position to exploit it. Thurow then proceeds to use this economic argument to attack one of his favorite targets for ridicule, the Federal Trade Commission (FTC) case challenging the monopoly power of the leading makers of dry breakfast cereals. Thurow's defense of the industry exceeds in zeal — if not in economic rigor — that of the economists employed to defend the industry in court, for example, J. Fred Weston, Harold Demsetz, Lester Telser, Jesse Markham, and a gaggle of others.

Thurow concedes that a few sellers have power over the price of branded cereals. But this poses no problem in his view, "Since any individual consumer can, if he chooses, buy no-name brand corn flakes at a much lower price, the brand names must be yielding some psychic utility or brand-name corn flakes would not be sold."[33] Acknowledging that this psychic utility likely was created by advertising, Thurow asks, "So what?" After all, "most wants have been determined by some. . . form of advertising." And while this may lead some consumers to make "silly decisions," the government has no business stopping "people from making silly decisions that do not affect anyone but themselves." If one were to pursue similar logic on the subject of income distribution, an area in which Thurow professes expertise, one might reason that market failures that distorted income distribution were not the public's business so long as the resulting distortion created by, say, advertising affected only the individuals misled by it. It is generally acknowledged that the food-purchase decisions of the poor are more often distorted by advertising than are the decisions of the economically more fortunate. But Thurow's compassion for the poor evidently does not extend to situations where advertising misleads them into paying enormous monopoly overcharges; they are being justly punished for making "silly" purchase decisions.

This naive defense of advertising-created monopoly power is almost enough to make a Chicago School economist blush. Indeed, Thurow himself evidently is not entirely satisfied, for he proceeds to build other defenses for the industry. But instead of setting things right, he merely falls into new errors.

He considers the case where consumers do not have a lower price alternative to a powerful brand of corn flakes. Not to worry here either says Thurow: "If the brand premium gets too large, others can easily enter the no-name brand corn flakes market.'' After all, he sees no patent or other significant entry barriers. (He conveniently ignores the relevant entry barriers: trademarks of established brands, the huge promotion and advertising costs of launching new brands, and the difficulty of getting shelf space because of brand proliferation.) Of course, the very fact that branded corn flakes typically command a 20 percent premium over no-name brands is compelling evidence to most industrial-organization economists that there exist enormous barriers protecting the established brands. Thurow also is less than fair with his readers in selecting corn flakes as his example, since they, puffed wheat, and puffed rice are about the only cereal brands available under private label. Indeed all private-label brands of cereal make up less than 4 percent of total dry breakfast cereals. Markups on other dry cereals are considerably greater than on corn flakes. For example, Kellogg's Sugar Frosted Flakes are essentially corn flakes with sugar added. Scherer[34] reports that after adjusting for the added sugar costs, Sugar Frosted Flakes prices are 16 percent more than Kellogg's Corn Flakes, which in turn sell for 20 percent more than private-label corn flakes.

Thurow defends these high premiums on the grounds that consumers are better off because their psychic utility has been enhanced by the amount of the premium. This is the kind of silly reasoning that gives economists a bad name among people of common sense. The prices consumers pay in these circumstances are determined by the market power of sellers rooted in oligopoly and product differentiation created largely by advertising. Merely because some consumers are willing to pay the price asked does not automatically justify that price. Many consumers prefer skim milk to ordinary milk, and doubtless many would be willing to pay a premium for it, although its costs are less than for milk with higher butterfat content. The reason they pay less is that competition forces prices to reflect cost differences. This is the way prices behave in a market where competition is working. All this Thurow ignores.

Thurow closes his defense of breakfast cereal pricing by beseeching his readers not to fear even if cereal companies monopolize cereal sales. Even in this worst-possible-case the consumer is protected because ''there are still a great deal of other breakfast alternatives (bacon and eggs, no breakfast). These other products make the market a competitive market even if there is no competition within the dry cereals business.''[35]

Now, this is really too much. True, often substitute products place limits on the holders of market power, and one must be tolerant of laymen who conjure up all sorts of silly examples of substitutes that protect consumers against monopoly prices. But surely the American Economic

Association should expect better of its members. The computed cross-elasticity of demand between breakfast cereals and eggs is 0.01.[36] This means that a 100-percent increase in the price of breakfast cereals will result in a 1 percent increase in the consumption of eggs. I doubt if the cross-elasticity of demand between cereals and bacon is any higher. Thurow's other alternative for curbing the power of a cereal monopolist, namely to not eat breakfast, sounds like Marie Antoinette's advice to the poor of France, "Let them eat cake." Many Americans may go without breakfast, but their doing so has not curbed the power of the cereal companies. The simple fact is that 40 percent of consumers spend over 25 percent of their income on food, and 20 percent of consumers spend over 33 percent. Despite the affluence Professor Thurow sees all about him, most Americans are not indifferent to the billions of dollars in monopoly overcharges incorporated into their food bills.[37]

Conglomerates Make Antitrust Laws Unnecessary

Another phenomenon of modern capitalism dear to Thurow's heart is the huge conglomerate enterprise. It is not to be condemned but embraced because it so enhances competition as to make the antitrust laws unnecessary because "monopoly rents are inherently limited in an economy full of large conglomerate firms."[38]

This is so, says Thurow, because conglomerates are ever ready to enter oligopolistic industries where firms earn high profits: "Excessive rates of return attract competitors, and potential competitors have the ability to enter *all* those markets that are not natural monopolies."[39] Surely no serious student of industrial structure, much less the man of industry, can take this assertion seriously. And Thurow offers not one shred of evidence to support his assertion. In fact, he contradicts the views he expressed in an earlier work, *Generating Inequality*. In explaining why firms in low-profit industries do not invest in high-profit industries, Thurow said in 1975, "Barriers to entry are often high, and managers often do not have the specialized knowledge necessary to make profits in another industry. The existence of high profits in the cosmetics industry, for example, does not mean that iron and steel executives could earn profits there."[40]

Economists still differ over the competitive significance of growing industrial conglomeration. But none can ignore the growing evidence that continuing mergers among large firms are eliminating more and more potential competitors. Nor do conglomerates have a good track record of significant *de novo* entry in highly concentrated industries, for example, cereals, soft drinks, and so forth.

Finally, growing industrial conglomeration tends to dull the incentive for large conglomerates to enter one another's domains, recognizing that to do so is to invite hostile retaliation elsewhere.[41] I realize mine is still a minority view on this aspect of conglomerates. Many economists are blind to the problem because they ignore the available evidence and do not seek out evidence of their own. For believers and nonbelievers alike, I suggest reading the intriguing story of how AT&T and IBM have avoided direct competition for years because each believed it had more to gain from avoiding competition with the other than engaging in it.[42]

Antitrust Costs Exceed Their Benefits

Thurow next argues that "it is not obvious that anything of economic value is accomplished even if an antitrust case is won by the government."[43] As usual he chooses his own ground. In this instance, his argument rests almost exclusively on the IBM case — as he interprets it.

Thurow first supposes that if the government were to win the case, IBM might be broken into three or four firms. So what, he exclaims! "By now we should have enough experience to know that a three or four firm oligopoly does not act noticeably different from a one-firm monopoly faced with potential competition (the Japanese). . . ."

Not so. Most industrial organization economists, even those of a Chicago view, believe there is a significant difference. Also, Thurow's arithmetic is faulty. If IBM were broken up, the total number of U.S. mainframe-computer manufacturers would be ten or more. Equally important, were IBM to lose its dominant position, entry would be easier and existing firms could compete more effectively, especially since appropriate relief would also call for restraint on predatory conduct.

The truth, of course, is that neither Thurow, I, nor anyone else knows what relief will occur if the government wins. My candid opinion is that, at best, the new Assistant Attorney General for Antitrust, William Baxter, will end the case with an innocuous consent agreement, or worse still, abandon the case. But should this come to pass, it will not demonstrate any inherent defect in antitrust but a manifestation of the anti-antitrust movement's success in placing in high office persons who do not believe in much current antitrust doctrine.

Thurow also glibly asserts that any tampering with IBM's dominant position will undermine its efficiency, thereby giving aid and comfort only to our enemies, the foreign computer makers. This is another unsupported assertion for which there is much contrary evidence.[44]

Although Thurow concedes IBM's "dominant position" permits it to earn handsome profits, not to worry, because "this is not to say that it has been able to extract *crippling* monopoly rents from computer customers." This comment sheds much light on Thurow's value judgments concerning what constitute excessive profits. He apparently would tolerate all but those that are so excessive as to "cripple" consumers. This is like telling the thief he may commit grand larceny so long as he does not maim his victim.

After his *tour de force* demonstrating that antitrust provides no benefits, Thurow condemns the laws because enforcement "diverts scarce resources from the real problem, which is productivity."[45]

Thurow again turns to the IBM case as a perfect example of this waste of scarce resources. Economists in the IBM case, as Thurow understands it, wasted numerous resources debating over what constituted the relevant market in which to measure IBM's market power. He says that "if the market is large mainframe computers, then IBM's got 98% of it. . . . On the other hand, if IBM is in the office-equipment market, then the company has a small share of that market. So all of the testimony revolves around such issues as whether a typewriter is the same thing as a computer. Well, that's just a silly issue. . ."[46]

Silly indeed! So silly that I wonder where in the world Thurow got his unworldy impressions as to what the case is all about. True, relevant market is one important issue. But never did the government assert, nor did any economist testify, that IBM had 98 percent of any market. And even though some IBM economists engaged in flights of fancy in defining the breadth of the relevant market, none ever went so far as to include typewriters.

Thurow's unfamiliarity with actual cases has never prevented him from drawing important conclusions about antitrust matters. In response to the question of whether he could think of a single antitrust case that had been good for the economy he first replied, "I can't think of any off hand." But on reflection he cited the "Brown Shoe machinery case." He said the company involved "eventually fell on hard times and was merged out of existence. In a sense the government destroyed the company. But I don't think that's the purpose of the antitrust laws."[47]

Students of antitrust doubtless will be puzzled by this example, since there never was such a case. Apparently Thurow got the famous *Brown Shoe* case, involving Section 7 of the Clayton Act, confused with the famous *United Shoe Machinery* case, involving the Sherman Act. Both are precedent-setting cases. But there is no basis for Thurow's statement that the government's action caused the demise of either Brown Shoe or United Shoe Machinery. Both were ordered to divest certain properties, but the divested properties are still alive and well.

Nonprice Competition to the Rescue

Thurow's final objection to the antitrust laws is their preoccupation with price competition. Reminiscent of the New Competition literature of the 1950s, Thurow argues that "price is clearly only one of the many competitive weapons (advertising, product quality, and so forth) and in many areas not the most useful or used weapon."[48] True enough. But Thurow ignores two key points. First, if a firm is shielded from price competition, often the same shields protect it from other forms of competition. Second, some other forms of competitive rivalry, especially advertising, may be destructive of competition because they erect entry barriers and inflate costs. But Thurow dismisses this possibility by appeal to the standard *laissez-faire* rationalization that however a corporation chooses to compete must be in the public interest because private decision makers can be trusted to choose that which is best. As he sees it, "When industries do not engage in price competition they do so for the perfectly good reason [that] it simply isn't the most efficient way to compete."[49]

Now you have heard it all: Thurow's five reasons why we should abolish the antitrust laws. He asks his readers to accept his teaching on faith; he cites no authority for any of his assertions.

The Thurow Antitrust Act of 1980

Do not misunderstand me. Antitrust does have a place in his Zero-Sum Society. His antitrust act would consist of two basic propositions:

> The first would be a ban on predatory pricing. . . The second would be a ban on explicit or implicit cartels that share either markets or profits. Firms can grow by driving competitors out of business or by absorbing them, but they cannot agree not to compete with each other.[50]

There it is, "The Thurow Antitrust Act of 1980," clear, concise, and inconsistent. It would prohibit price fixing among all the firms in an industry, yet it would permit all firms in an industry to merge and form a monopoly. Apparently recognizing belatedly this inconsistency, Thurow is now willing to drop his rule against price fixing. When *Dun's Review* asked his views on price fixing, Thurow replied, "I don't think there's really very much of it going on."[51] When he then was asked whether he would "scrub the laws against price fixing too," he replied, "That's right. Congress would be standing by ready to write a new statute if a rash of price fixing took place. But my hunch is that it probably wouldn't be necessary."[52]

Evidently Thurow is unfamiliar with the hundreds of U.S. corporations that have been indicted for price fixing in recent years, or the rich historical literature documenting the propensity of businesses to engage in elaborate and pervasive price fixing schemes in nations without laws prohibiting such behavior. He even seems to have forgotten the words of his intellectual mentor, Adam Smith, who warned over 200 years ago that "people of the same trade seldom meet together, even for merriment and diversion, but the conversation ends in a conspiracy against the public in some contrivance to raise prices."

In sum, Thurow's case for repealing the antitrust laws rests on no more than his hunches, guesses, speculations, and erroneous interpretations of these laws.

After examining carefully Thurow's views, I think every fair-minded person will agree that there really is much less to Thurow's ideas than first meets the eye. His are not the statements of a scholar or even a well informed layman. Most professors expect better of their students in Economics 101.

Thurow's Empty Box

How to explain, then, the uncritical attention given Thurow's views? The answer is to be found in the anti-antitrust movement that is everywhere about us. All movements seek respectable spokesmen. When the movement has a conservative base, none is in greater demand than the liberal intellectual who embraces, in part at least, the conservative's creed. In this setting a man willing to lend his intellectual prestige to a movement, and be embraced by it in return, need not necessarily know whereof he speaks. And he may gain the limelight and popular applause for a time by wrapping his ideas in an attractive package. All this, it seems, Lester Thurow has done. But, alas, after we remove the wrappings on Thurow's package, nothing remains but an empty box.

Thus ends my epistle on Lester C. Thurow. Some may legitimately ask if there is anything in the antitrust box. To answer, I would begin with the confession that I have not been an uncritical champion of these laws or of the adequacy of their enforcement. These laws are imperfect instruments of social control. We must, therefore, continually appraise with open minds alternative means of ensuring that the enormous powers of the large modern corporation are used to serve the public good. But it is inconceivable to me that America would abandon the antitrust laws without putting in their place something far more substantial than the empty promise that their repeal will result in the rebirth of the world of Adam Smith.

These laws contain our only legal rules for bridling the modern corporation's enormous economic power in the marketplace. The main purpose of these laws has always been to maintain, so far as possible, a decentralized economic system and to place some restraint on the use of economic power. Justice William O. Douglas put it well:

> Industrial power should be decentralized so that the fortunes of the people will not be dependent on the whim or caprice, the political prejudices, the emotional stability of a few self-appointed men. The fact that they are not vicious men but respectable men is irrelevant.[53]

Neither have the people given those in the vanguard of the anti-antitrust movement a mandate to return to a system of nineteenth century *laissez-faire* capitalism; nor will the people tolerate such action, once the motives of the anti-antitrusters are more widely understood. There is today, much as in 1890, a feeling of unease and impotence in dealing with powerful corporations that, in the words of former ITT Chairman Harold Geneen, "have become the primary custodians of making our entire system work." This quite naturally raises questions about the legitimacy of their custodianship. A recent *Fortune* article reported that many Americans are questioning the legitimacy of the large corporation. *Fortune* found that 51 percent of Americans with incomes of $25,000 or more believed that "big business is becoming a threat to the American way of life."[54] The fact that a majority of the most fortunate beneficiaries of American capitalism hold this view should give pause to those who believe there exists no real concern among the people on these matters. Many businessmen, too, fear that unrestrained capitalism may destroy itself. A longtime student of our system, A. C. Hoffman, retired vice-president of Kraft, Inc., observed: "At the present rate at which American industry is being merged and consolidated, we will indeed reach that ultimate stage of *monopoly capitalism* which many predicted."[55]

I have expressed these concerns not to attack our system but to urge repudiation of false prophets who would destroy it in the name of saving it. My mentor, the late George W. Stocking urged that "capitalism must be saved from its friends."[56] Never has that advice been more sound than today.

Notes

1. *Standard Oil Company of New Jersey v. United States,* 221 U. S. 1, 83 (1911).

2. M. Fainsod and L. Gordon, *Government and the American Economy* (New York: W. W. Norton & Co, Inc., 1941) p. 520

3. The president of the American Bankers Association said, "the way to progressive success in all commercial and industrial efforts is through constant introduction of new economies, but against the institution of these economies there is often the menace of the Sherman Law interpretations. . . . Do not changing times call for a careful revision?" *The New York Times*, Section XX (October 12, 1930) p. 2.

In 1931, the National Chamber of Commerce included among its four recommendations for recovery, "Modification of the antitrust laws to make clear agreements intended to relate production to consumption." *The New York Times* (December 18, 1931) p. 15.

4. Fainsod and Gordon, *Government,* p. 569.

5. "The Economists Committee on Antitrust Policy," *American Economic Review* (September 1932) p. 464.

6. R. Hofstadter, "What Happened to the Antitrust Movement?" in E. F. Cheit, ed., *The Business Establishment* (New York: John Wiley & Sons, 1966) p. 116.

7. W. F. Mueller, *The Celler-Kefauver Act: The First 27 Years*, a study prepared for the use of the Subcommittee on Monopolies and Commercial Law of the Committee on the Judiciary. House of Representatives, 95th Congress, 2nd ses. (Washington, D. C.: U. S. Government Printing Office December 1978).

8. W. F. Mueller, "The ITT Settlement, a Deal with Justice?" *Industrial Organization Review*, 1, No. 1 (1973) pp. 67-86.

9. *The International Telephone and Telegraph Company and Chile*, Report to the Committee on Foreign Relations, U. S. Senate, by the Subcommittee on Multinational Corporations, June 21, 1973.

10. Mueller, "The ITT Settlement," op. cit.

11. The following quotations are from the transcript prepared by the Impeachment Inquiry Staff of the House Judiciary Committee from conversations recorded by President Richard Nixon, commencing 3:30 P.M. April 19, 1971.

12. February 29, 1972, columnist Jack Anderson broke the famous Dita D. Beard (a former ITT employee) story that alleged the ITT settlement was tied to a $400,000 political contribution by ITT to the Republican party.

13. Mueller, "The ITT Settlement," op. cit.

14. Hofstadter, "What Happened," p. 116.

15. H. R. Lurie, "Mergers Under the Burger Court: An Anti-antitrust Bias and Its Implications," *Villanova Law Review* (January 1978).

16. The National Chamber of Commerce financed a study of conglomerate mergers by Jesse M. Markham that was published as J. W. Markham, *Conglomerate Enterprise and Public Policy,* Division of Research, Graduate School of Business Administration, Harvard University, Boston, 1973.

A fascinating confidential memorandum was written for the Chamber by Supreme Court Justice Lewis F. Powell, Jr., "Attack on American Free Enterprise," August 23, 1971, shortly before his appointment to the Supreme Court. The memorandum was addressed to Eugene B. Syndor, Jr., Chairman, Education Committee, U. S. Chamber of Commerce. The memorandum is a blueprint for attacking, and perhaps silencing, those critical of any aspect of capitalism. It goes so far as to recommend that the Chamber establish a body of scholars that would review all textbooks in economics, sociology, and political science so as to encourage authors, publishers, and users to "return to a more rational balance." He likewise perceived as the most "fundamental problem" the ideological imbalance of many faculties. "Correcting this is indeed a long-range and difficult project. . . This is a long road and not one for the faint hearted." *Ibid.*, pp. 16, 17 and 19.

17. G. C. Staple, "Free Market Cram Course for Judges, *The Nation* (January 26, 1980) p. 79.

18. "Reagan's Think Tank" *Dun's Review* (April 1981) pp. 110-114.

19. This is not to imply that scholars publishing in the *Bell Journal* have compromised their intellectual principles by doing so. To me, this is not a question of whether or not the *Journal* is tendentious. As a basic principle, scientific journals should not be sponsored by the very interests that are the subject of inquiry. To me this seems self-evident, although many economists evidently feel otherwise. And not too surprisingly, a previous editor of the *Journal* has, publicly, taken exception to my views.

20. Staple, "Free Markets," p. 78. See also "Big Corporations Bankroll Seminars for U. S. Judges," *Washington Post* (January 20, 1980) p. A 1.

21. Staple, "Free Markets," p. 20.

22. Interview in *The Village Voice*, quoted by Federal Trade Commissioner Patricia P. Baily in a speech "Seventeenth Annual Symposium on Trade, Association Law and Practice," February 25, 1981. Republican Commissioner Baily reportedly had the inside track to become Acting Chairman of the FTC until she gave this speech.

23. *Ibid.*

24. See for example, "New Thunder from Economists on the Left," *Business Week*, (December 3, 1979) pp. 131–133: and "Antitrust Grows Unpopular," *Business Week* (January 12, 1981) pp. 90–93.

25. L. C. Thurow, "Let's Abolish the Antitrust Laws," *The New York Times*, October 19, 1980. He had written a piece attacking Senator Kennedy's Conglomerate Merger bill. "Bigness and Badness," *The New Republic* (April 28, 1979) pp. 10-12.

26. Interview of L. C. Thurow by Gerald R. Rosen, "Abolish the Antitrust Laws," *Dun's Review*, February 1981, pp. 72–74.

27. L. C. Thurow, *The Zero-Sum Society* (New York: Basic Books, 1980).

28. R. L. Lampman, "Review of *The Zero-Sum Society*," *Journal of Economic Literature*, 19, No. 1 (1981) pp. 91-92.

29. Thurow, *The Zero-Sum Society*, p. 146.

30. *Ibid.* p. 146.

31. *Ibid.* p. 146.

32. *Ibid.* p. 147.

33. *Ibid.* p. 147.

34. F. M. Scherer, "The Welfare Economics of Product Variety: An Application to the Ready-to-Eat Cereals Industry," *Journal of Industrial Economics*, Dec. 1979, p 127.

35. Thurow, *Zero-Sum*, p. 147.

36. P. S. George and G. A. King, *Consumer Demand for Food Commodities in the United States with Projections for 1980*, Giannini Foundation Monograph No. 26 (Berkeley, Calif.: Experiment Station, University of California) March 1971) p. 51.

37. R. Parker and J. Connor, "Estimates of Consumer Loss Due to Monopoly in the

U. S. Food-Manufacturing Industries,'' *American Journal of Agricultural Economics* (November 1979) pp. 626–639.

38. Thurow, *Zero-Sum,* p. 147.

39. *Ibid.,* p. 148 (emphasis added).

40. L. C. Thurow, *Generating Inequality* (New York: Basic Books, 1975) p. 147.

41. W. F. Mueller, ''Conglomerates, a Nonindustry,'' in W. A. Adams, ed., *The Structure of American Industry* (New York: MacMillan, 1977) pp. 461–467.

42. See for example, Merrill Brown, ''Backstage with Big Business,'' *The Washington Post*, February 1, 1981, pp. F1 and F4, and ''Litton Evidence Alleging AT&T Coerced IBM Will Be Permitted at Antitrust Trial,'' *Wall Street Journal*, Feb. 9, 1981, p. 5.

43. Thurow, *Zero-Sum,* p. 148.

44. See for example G. W. Brock, *The U. S. Computer Industry* (Cambridge, Mass.: Ballinger, 1975).

45. Thurow, ''Abolish the Antitrust Laws,'' *Dun's Review* (February 1981) p. 72.

46. *Ibid.*, p. 73.

47. *Ibid.*

48. Thurow, *Zero-Sum*, p. 149.

49. *Ibid.,* p. 150.

50. *Ibid.*

51. Thurow, ''Abolish,'' p. 72.

52. *Ibid.*

53. *U. S. v. Columbia Steel Co.*, 344 U. S. 495 (1948).

54. *Fortune* (March 26, 1979) p. 91.

55. A. C. Hoffman, ''Trends in the Food Industries and Their Relationship to Agriculture,'' Farm Foundation, Chicago, November 11, 1962, p. 2.

56. G. W. Stocking, ''Saving Free Enterprise from Its Friends,'' *Southern Economic Review* (April 1953) pp. 431-44.

3 ANTITRUST ENFORCEMENT: WHERE IT HAS BEEN; WHERE IT IS GOING

Oliver E. Williamson

Antitrust, which once enjoyed widespread support, has come under withering attack from a variety of quarters recently. Many of the critics regard antitrust as an anachronism, and openly counsel that it be abolished. But some hold the opposite view. They urge that antitrust enforcement be strengthened, and recall the Warren Court years with nostalgia.

Critics of the first kind appear to be dismayed over the difficulties experienced by U. S. auto, steel, and other industries as compared with the robust successes of the Japanese. A reshaping of the relations among firms and between business and government along the lines of the Japanese model is widely held to be attractive. The details of the Japanese model remain somewhat obscure, however, and its transferability to the U. S. scene is problematic. Until the model is more fully worked out, its net benefits assessed, and its transferability demonstrated, it would appear to be judicious to regard reforms along these lines as speculative. For the purposes of this paper therefore, my examination of antitrust will remain within the framework of U. S. experience.

A decade is a useful interval over which to observe and report on

Research on this paper was facilitated by a grant from the National Science Foundation.

antitrust developments. The 1960s, 1970s, and 1980s can each, I think, be usefully characterized as an antitrust era. Specifically, concentration and entry-barrier analysis flourished in the 1960s. Efficiency analysis gained ascendancy in the 1970s, and I expect the 1980s to be the period when the analysis of strategic behavior comes of age. Arguments that antitrust should be abolished would be easier to understand had there been no substantial progress during the seventies or if the problems of the eighties were inconsequential. Inasmuch, however, as antitrust made remarkable progress during the seventies and since difficult problems of strategic behavior remain unresolved, calls for the abolition of antitrust are premature if not uninformed.

Antitrust enforcement in the 1960s is briefly examined in the first section of this chapter. The reforms of the 1970s are reviewed next. Some of the concerns and recent developments relating to strategic behavior are then treated and unresolved enforcement dilemmas for the 1980s are addressed. Concluding remarks follow. I argue that, whereas reliance on entry-barrier arguments was excessive in the 1960s, much of this was redressed by a shift of attention to efficiency, in all of its forms, in the 1970s. Difficult strategic-behavior issues have, nevertheless, surfaced and this area is presently in great flux.[1] Considerable research resources have recently been directed at these issues — as a result of which there is a prospect for better resolution in the latter part of this decade.

The 1960s

The 1960s was the era when market-power analysis flourished. This was partly due to earlier theoretical, empirical, and policy studies in which entry barriers were prominent, but it was also because antitrust economics was sorely lacking in two other respects. First, there was a general undervaluation of the social benefits of efficiency. Second, there was a widespread tendency to regard efficiency very narrowly — mainly in technological terms. An awareness of transaction costs, much less a sensitivity to the importance of economizing thereon, had scarcely surfaced. Instead, the firm was held to be a production function to which a profit-maximization objective had been assigned. Subject to rudimentary economy-of-scale considerations, the efficient boundaries of firms were taken as given. Accordingly, efforts to reconfigure firm and market structures that went beyond these natural boundaries were assessed almost exclusively in market-power terms.

The intellectual basis for market-power analysis was provided by Joe Bain in the 1950s, especially in his book *Barriers to New Competition* (1956). Many of the antitrust ramifications of this approach to industrial organization were set out by Carl Kaysen and Donald Turner very shortly thereafter in their book *Antitrust Policy: An Economic and Legal Analysis* (1959). The decade of the sixties witnessed further applications of this line of reasoning and widespread adoption of entry-barrier arguments by the courts.

Illustrations of the success of entry-barrier reasoning are the *Procter & Gamble* and *Schwinn* cases, both of which were decided by the Supreme Court in 1967.[2] The first of these cases was anticipated by the Federal Trade Commission's opinion in *Foremost Dairies,* where the Commission ventured the view that the necessary proof of violation of Section 7 "consists of types of evidence showing that the acquiring firm possesses significant power in some markets *or* that its overall organization gives it a decisive advantage in efficiency over its smaller rivals."[3] Although Donald Turner, among others, was quick to label this as bad law and bad economics (1975, p. 1324) in that it protects competitors rather than promote the welfare benefits of competition, the Commission carried this reasoning forward in *Procter & Gamble* and linked it with barriers to entry in the following way:[4]

> In stressing as we have the importance of advantages of scale as a factor heightening the barriers to new entry into the liquid bleach industry, we reject, as specious in law and unfounded in fact, the argument that the Commission ought not, for the sake of protecting the "inefficient" small firms in the industry, proscribe a merger so productive of "efficiencies." The short answer to this argument is that, in a proceeding under Section 7, economic efficiency or any other social benefit resulting from a merger is pertinent only insofar as it may tend to promote or retard the vigor of competition.

This emphasis on entry barriers and the low regard accorded to economies also appears in the Supreme Court's opinion. Thus the Court observed that Procter's acquisition of Clorox may[5]

> . . .have the tendency of raising the barriers to new entry. The major competitive weapon in the successful marketing of bleach is advertising. Clorox was limited in this area by its relatively small budget and its inability to obtain substantial discounts. By contrast, Procter's budget was much larger; and, although it would not devote its entire budget to advertising Clorox, it could divert a large portion to meet the short-term threat of a new entrant. Procter would be able to use its volume discounts to advantage in advertising Clorox.

Thus, a new entrant would be much more reluctant to face the giant Procter than it would have been to face the smaller Clorox.

Possible economies cannot be used as a defense to illegality.[6]

The aforementioned insensitivity to transaction-cost economizing was coupled with a preoccupation with entry barriers in reaching the *Schwinn* decision. Donald Turner, who was then the head of the Antitrust Division, succinctly expressed the prevailing attitude toward nonstandard or unfamiliar business practices as follows: "I approach territorial and customer restrictions not hospitably in the common law tradition, but inhospitably in the tradition of antitrust law."[7] This view, which I shall refer to as the inhospitality tradition, was widely held among antitrust specialists during the 1960s. Rather than presume — or at least investigate the possibility — that vertical restrictions served affimative economic purposes, it was assumed instead that they were designed to enhance market power. Specifically, the government argued that "Schwinn's strenuous efforts to exclude unauthorized retailers from selling its bicycles suggest that, absent these restraints, there would be a broader retail distribution of these goods with the resulting public benefits (including lower price) of retail competition."[8] Since the government believed that it was "unnecessary to create quality images" because products that are objectively superior would be self-evident, and since product differentiation can adversely affect the condition of entry, Schwinn's efforts to effect differentiation were held by the government to be contrary to the public interest.

Accordingly, antitrust enforcement in the 1960s can be described as a period during which market-power concerns were virtually determinative. The benefits of economies were willfully disregarded, and the evidence of economies was narrowly restricted to those with technological origins. A series of reactions, many of which were needed correctives, was set in motion by the excesses to which this type of reasoning was given.

The 1970s

The reconceptualizing of antitrust issues that occurred during the late 1960s and early 1970s is sketched below. This mainly entailed a shift away from entry barriers to address economic organization from the standpoint of what economic purposes are being served. Two of the cases that were decided during the 1970s in which this shift is reflected will be briefly described.

Efficiency Analysis

The reforms of antitrust enforcement in the 1970s had their origins in critiques of the 1960s. These include (1) the insistence of the Chicago School that antitrust issues be studied through the lens of price theory; (2) related critiques of the entry-barrier approach; (3) application of the partial-equilibrium welfare-economics model to an assessment of the tradeoffs between market power and efficiency; and (4) a reformulation of the theory of the modern corporation whereby transaction-cost-economizing considerations were brought to the fore. An additional contributing factor was the reorganization of the economics staff of the Antitrust Division. Whereas previously the staff economists were used almost exclusively to support the legal staff in the preparation and litigation of cases, they were now asked to assess the economic merits of cases before filing.

The Chicago School approach has been set out by Richard Posner (1979) elsewhere. Although it is possible to quibble with Posner's rendition of Harvard versus Chicago (as these were viewed in the 1960s), it is nevertheless clear that the efficiency orientation favored by Aaron Director (and his students and colleagues) has stood the test of time rather well. Thus whereas Director's views on tie-ins, resale-price maintenance, and the like were widely regarded as suspect — "In some quarters the Chicago School was regarded as little better than a lunatic fringe" (Posner 1979, p. 931) — this approach enjoys wider respect today.[9] But Chicago, or at least the diehard branch, has, in the process of applying price theory to antitrust, insisted on an uncommonly narrow formulation. (Specifically, as discussed below, the diehard-Chicago approach to the study of strategic behavior is myopic and simplistic. This has a bearing, however, more on the enforcement issues of the 1980s than to those of the 1970s.)

Given Chicago's price-theory orientation, many of the criticisms of the entry-barrier approach understandably originated there as well. Objections of two kinds were registered. The first of these held that the basic entry-barrier model, as set out by Bain (1956) and elaborated by Franco Modigliani (1958), purported to be but did not qualify as an oligopoly model. As George Stigler put it, the entry-barrier model solved the oligopoly problem by murder: "The ability of the oligopolists to agree upon and police the limit price is apparently independent of the sizes and numbers of oligopolists" (1968, p.21). Put differently, the model did not address itself to the mechanics by which collective action was realized. Instead, it simply assumed that the requisite coordination to effect a limit-price result would appear. As discussed below, recent models in the entry-barrier tradition have avoided this problem by explicitly casting the analysis in a sitting monopolist-duopoly framework. Addressing the issues of entry in this more limited context has analytical advantages, but applications outside of the dominant-firm context are appropriate only upon a showing that the necessary preconditions to effect oligopolistic coordination are satisfied.

The other objection to entry-barrier analysis relates to public-policy misuses of entry-barrier reasoning. That the condition of entry is impeded is neither here nor there if no superior structural configuration — expressed in welfare terms — can be described. However obvious this may be on reflection, this was not always the case. Rather, there was a widespread tendency to regard barriers of all kinds as contrary to the social interest. But as Robert Bork has put it, "The question for antitrust is whether there exist *artificial* entry barriers. These must be barriers that are not forms of superior efficiency and which yet prevent the forces of the market. . .from operating to erode market positions not based on efficiency" (1978, p. 311; emphasis added).

The distinction between remediable and irremediable entry impediments thus becomes the focus of attention. Little useful public-policy purpose is served, and considerable risk of public-policy mischief results, when conditions of an irremediable kind are brought under fire. Mistaken treatment of economies of scale illustrates what is at stake. Thus, suppose that economies of scale exist and that the market is of sufficient size to support the larger of two technologies. Since superior outcomes will be attributable to the less efficient technology only under very unusual conditions, net social benefits ought presumably to be attributed to these scale-economy conditions. To describe such economies as barriers to entry, however, does not invite this conclusion; to the contrary, mistaken welfare judgments are encouraged. Many of the enthusiasts of entry-barrier analysis have been reluctant to concede such hazards.

That efficiency benefits were held in such low regard in the sixties is partly explained by the widespread opinion that, as between two structural alternatives — one of which simultaneously presents greater market power and greater efficiency than the other — the more competitive structure is invariably to be preferred. This view was supported by the implicit assumption that even small anticompetitive effects would surely swamp efficiency benefits in arriving at a net valuation. The FTC opinion that "economic efficiency or any other social benefit. . .[is] pertinent only insofar as it may tend to promote or retard the vigor of competition"[10] — where competition is defined in structural terms — is a clear indication of such thinking.

Application of the basic partial-equilibrium welfare-economics model to an assessment of market power versus economies trade-offs disclosed that to sacrifice economies for reduced market power came at a high cost (Williamson 1968). Although the merits of this framework remain open to dispute (Posner 1975, p. 821), the general approach, if not the framework itself, has since been employed by others. Bain was among the first to acknowledge the merits of an economies defense in assessing mergers (1968, p. 658). Wesley Liebeler (1978), Robert Bork (1978), and Timothy Muris (1979) have all made extensive use of the partial-equilibrium trade-off model in their insistence that antitrust enforcement that proceeds heedless of trade-offs is uninformed and contrary to the social interest.

A common argument against trade-off analysis is that the courts are poorly suited to assess economic evidence and arguments of this kind (Bok 1960). In fact, a simple sensitivity to the merits of economies is sufficient to avoid the inverted reasoning of *Foremost Dairies;* and although errors of the *Schwinn* kind are avoided only upon recognizing that economies can take transaction cost as well as technological forms, the mistakes of the inhospitality tradition also become less likely once this step has been taken.

Whereas technological innovations were easily accommodated within a production function framework (and economists have devoted considerable attention to these matters) organizational innovation is alien to this framework (and, as of the early 1960s, had been generally neglected). The publication of Alfred Chandler's book *Strategy and Structure* (1962) represented the opening wedge in an effort to develop a deeper understanding of the importance of organizational innovation and its relation to the study of the modern corporation. Chandler focused on the shift from the traditional hierarchical structure (or unitary form) to the multidivisional (or M-form) structure. This innovation first appeared in the 1920s and was imitated and widely adopted thereafter. Chandler argued that the new structure had deep rationality properties that permitted the firm to realize superior results in both strategic and operating respects. It was uninformed and untenable to argue that internal organization was a matter of indifference after the appearance of Chandler's book.

Independently, Armen Alchian (1969) and Richard Heflebower (1960) also recognized that organization form had an important bearing on economic performance. They advanced the proposition that corporations were discharging functions ordinarily associated with the capital market. The internal-resource allocation, incentive, and control attributes of the modern corporation were subsequently discussed and developed by others (Williamson 1970, 1975). This in turn led to a more general study of firm and market structures whereby the issue of mediating transactions was addressed not as a datum but as an economizing issue. Although this insight owes its origins to Ronald Coase's classic 1937 paper, it was not until the 1970s that the issues were operationalized.

Whereas both the production function approach and inhospitality tradition regarded markets as the natural, hence efficient, way by which to mediate transactions between technologically separable entities, this presumption was unacceptable once firms were described not as production functions but as governance structures. Whether transactions should be mediated by markets, hierarchies, or mixed modes was thus an issue to be investigated by assessing the transaction-cost ramifications of each. Such a comparative institutional undertaking involved (1) dimensionalizing transactions, (2) describing alternative governance structures, and (3) recognizing that transaction costs would be economized by matching governance structure with transactions in a discriminating way (Williamson 1971, 1975, 1979b).

This approach to the study of economic organization disclosed that many nonstandard or unfamiliar business practices that were, at best, puzzling, when assessed in technological terms, were in fact the outcome of rational transaction-cost-economizing efforts. Vertical integration, vertical market restrictions, and aspects of conglomerate and multinational organization were all reexamined to advantage. Organizational innovations that had hitherto been regarded as presumptively unlawful, under the inhospitality tradition, were thus accorded greater sympathy. Indeed, subject to the condition that certain structural thresholds (mainly high concentration coupled with barriers to entry) are not exceeded, a presumption that organizational innovations have the purpose and effect of economizing on transaction costs is warranted.[11] This is a rather drastic departure from the mistaken views of the 1960s.

Two Cases

It is a credit to the growing sophistication of antitrust that the 1970s witnessed a shift away from asserted, but often only imagined, entry-barrier effects to consider the affirmative purposes served by new business configurations. This occurred both with respect to mergers-for-economies as well as vertical market restrictions (and other nonstandard business practices). The 1975 decision of the Federal Trade Commission to vacate the administrative law judge's order and dimiss the complaint in the *Budd Company* case illustrates the shift in mergers-for-economies thinking.[12] The complaint had stressed Budd's importance as a potential entrant into narrowly defined lines of commerce and held that the benefits conferred by Budd on the acquired firm (Gindy) disadvantaged small rivals. The Commission rejected the complaint counsel's narrow definition of the market and regarded the acquisition as procompetitive — in that the acquisition relieved Gindy of financial and other handicaps that it had experienced previously. The upside-down valuation of economies in *Foremost Dairies* and *Procter* was thus recognized as a perversion of sound antitrust economics.

The Supreme Court's decision in 1977 in the *GTE-Sylvania* case also corrected mistaken reasoning of the sixties, specifically that of *Schwinn.* Contrary to *Schwinn,* the Court held that[13]

> [vertical] restrictions, in varying forms, are widely used in our free market economy. As indicated above, there is substantial scholarly opinion and judicial authority supporting their economic utility. There is relatively little authority to the contrary. Certainly there has been no showing in this case, either generally or with respect to Sylvania's agreement, that vertical restrictions have or are likely to have a "pernicious effect on competition" or that they "lack. . .any redeeming virtue". . . .Accordingly, we conclude that the per se rule in *Schwinn* must be overruled.

The 1960s preoccupation with competition, often amounting to no more than a concern over competitors coupled with a naive view of the modern corporation, was thus substantially redressed.

Strategic Behavior: A Progress Report

The main issue on the research agenda for industrial organization during the next decade is the study of strategic behavior — by which I mean efforts by established firms to take up advance positions or respond contingently to rivalry in ways that discipline actual and discourage potential competition. Whether such behavior exists, what forms it takes, how widespread each type is, and what antitrust ramifications attach thereto, are all open to dispute.

Although a great deal of research talent has been directed to these issues in the past few years and real progress has been made, we still have a long way to go before the main issues can be thought to be settled. Unlike efficiency analysis, where industrial organization could draw upon applied welfare economics for assistance, the study of strategic behavior poses puzzles that are quite novel. The need for new theory has not gone unnoticed and a number of applied theorists have been developing new models designed to answer these requirements.

Although this work is progressing rapidly, it is still in early stages of development. As matters stand presently, established firms have considerable latitude in responding defensively to new rivalry. Unlike the entry-barrier era of the sixties, where courts were quick to find anticompetitive purpose lurking behind innocent and efficient practices, the courts in the seventies have been very cautious in evaluating claims of predation and strategic abuse by dominant firms.[14] This is partly because agreement is lacking on criteria for discerning admissible from excessive competitive replies to new rivalry. Additionally, there are problems in translating proposed criteria to operational measures that the courts can apply with confidence. Related to both of these is the hazard, to which the courts have been alert, that firms that complain they are subject to predatory pricing (and other unlawful practices) may, in fact, be seeking protectionist relief from legitimate, albeit complex, rivalrous behavior. Also, the enforcement ramifications of some of the new models have yet to be worked out.

Diehard Chicago

The distinguishing characteristic of what Posner has referred to as "diehard Chicagoans" (1979, p. 932) is a reluctance to confront strategic behavior in any but a very narrow context. The favored approach, as illustrated most recently by the commentary of John McGee (1980), has been to insist upon studying strategic behavior issues in myopic terms.[15]

Predatory Pricing. McGee's survey of the recent predatory-pricing literature is mainly negative with one conspicuous exception. McGee advises readers that "Robert Bork's formulation of the problem commands attention" (1980, p. 293) and concludes that, "In his masterful analysis of the U. S. antitrust laws, Robert H. Bork shows why predatory price cutting would be rare or nonexistent even if there were no legal rules against it" (1980, pp. 316-317). Although I agree that Bork has made important contributions to the study of antitrust,[16] McGee and I differ on our assessment of Bork's treatment of strategic behavior in general and predatory pricing in particular.

Thus Bork poses the problem of predatory pricing by considering a firm with an 80-percent market share that "wishes to kill a rival with 20 percent in order to achieve the comforts and prerogatives of monopoly status'' (1978, p. 149). He concludes, upon examining the rationality of such an undertaking, that predatory pricing of this kind is ''most unlikely to exist'' (1978, p. 155). But the case that Bork considers is a very special and relatively uninteresting kind. As discussed below, the full ramifications of predatory pricing are not disclosed by focusing on a dominant firm's efforts to destroy a rival that has already committed itself by investing in specialized human and physical capital (and hence needs only to recover its variable costs to remain viable during the predatory seige).

McGee is nevertheless attracted to this formulation and therefore regards predatory pricing as insignificant. Indeed, his preferred legal rule on predatory pricing is to ignore it altogether (McGee 1980, p. 317). Upon recognition, however, that some rule must be adopted, McGee understandably endorses the most permissive predatory-pricing rule that has yet to be proposed: the Areeda-Turner marginal-cost-pricing rule.[17] In fact, this rule has found favor in many courts. But as Paul Joskow has explained, this has occurred because of a pressing need to fill a void and ''not because of the triumph of economic efficiency considerations in the interpretation of antitrust statutes'' (1980, p. 202).

Voids can be filled, of course, in many ways. One of the reasons the courts were attracted to a marginal-cost-pricing rule, I conjecture, is that they perceived the dangers that more stringent rules would encourage protectionist abuses and accordingly favored a very permissive standard. In the process, however, of reducing the risk of what Joskow and Alvin Klevorick (1979, p. 223) refer to as ''false positive'' error — that is, incorrectly declaring something predatory that in fact is efficient — the courts have accepted a huge risk of ''false-negative'' error — that is, allowing behavior that is, in fact, predatory to continue.

Although a consensus on this issue has not yet developed, there is widespread concern that a marginal-cost-pricing standard is defective.[18] A basic problem with this criterion is that it appeals to static-welfare-economics arguments for support while predatory pricing is unavoidably an intertemporal issue. As William Baumol succinctly puts it, static analysis of the kind in which Areeda and Turner rely is ''inadequate. . .because it draws our attention from the most pressing issues that are involved'' (1979, p. 2). The ''nub of the problem. . .[is] the intertemporal aspect of the situation'' (1979, p.3)

The Condition of Entry. As a result of persistent criticism, much of it originating with Chicago, it is now widely recognized that the entry-barrier arguments of the 1960s were much too sweeping. But such a demonstration does not establish that this entire tradition should be rejected. The possibilities that remediable impediments to entry might arise, and that such circumstances are identifiable, ought to be considered. Consistent with his neglect of strategic factors, Bork seems unwilling to entertain such possibilities. This unwillingness is due chiefly to his implicit assumption that labor and capital markets operate frictionlessly, so that every market outcome is presumptively a merit outcome and further discussion is pointless. Once transaction costs are admitted, however, the assumption of frictionlessness no longer applies, the possibility of introducing strategic impediments to entry arises, and the main argument needs to be qualified. To be sure, the exceptions may not be numerous and the difficulties of informed or efficacious intervention may be great. Such defects might better be tolerated, therefore, rather than made subject to public-policy review and attempted rectification. But this is a separate argument. Neither Bork nor others of the antientry-barrier belief have addressed the entry-barrier issues on these grounds. Since the frictionlessness assumptions on which Bork implicitly relies are unacceptable to many students of antitrust, continuing dispute over the nature and importance of entry barriers is to be expected.

Recent Headway. Objections that have or could be leveled at early entry-barrier models and related applications to predatory pricing include: (1) the structural preconditions are not carefully stated; (2) whether it is more attractive to bar rather than accept entry is assumed but not demonstrated; (3) attention is focused on total costs, but the composition of costs and the characteristics of assets matter crucially and have been neglected; (4) the incentives to engage in predation are weak; and (5) cost asymmetries between established firms and potential entrants are asserted but rarely addressed. Recent work has made headway with each of these issues.

Structural Preconditions. As discussed above, the early entry-barrier models purported to be oligopoly models. But the question of how oligopolists managed to achieve effective concurrence of market action — with respect to price, output, investment, and so forth — was not addressed. The relevance of those models outside of the dominant firm context was thus questionable.

Recent models in the entry-barrier tradition have essentially abandoned the oligopoly claim. The issues are posed instead in a duopoly context between a sitting monopolist and a potential entrant. Those who would apply these models to oligopoly presumably have the heavy burden of demonstrating their applicability.

Similar care has been taken in assessing claims of predation. The hazard here is that the legal process will be misused to discourage legitimate rivalry. There is growing agreement that the structural preconditions that must be satisfied before claims of predation are seriously entertained are very high concentration coupled with barriers to entry (Williamson 1977, pp. 292-293). Joskow and Klevorick (1979, pp. 225-231) and Ordover and Willig (1981) concur and propose a two-tier test for predatory pricing. The subset of industries for which strategic behavior warrants public-policy scrutiny would thus appear to be the following: (1) the sitting monopolist-duopolist situation; (2) regulated monopolies; (3) dominant-firm industries; and (4) what William Fellner has referred to as "Case 3 oligopoly" (1949, pp. 47–49) — which is an industry where an outside agency (for instance, a union) enforces collective action.[19]

Rationality of Preentry Deterrence. In principle, entry can be deterred in any of three ways: (1) by expanding output and investment in the preentry period, thereby discouraging the incentive to enter; (2) by threatening aggressive postentry responses; and (3) by imposing cost disadvantages on rivals. The second of these is addressed below. The first is in the spirit of Bain and Modigliani and has been dealt with more recently by Avinash Dixit, who models the entry problem in a duopoly context (1979, 1980). This permits him simultaneously to display and assess the profitability and feasibility of having the sitting monopolist adopt any of three postures: (1) behave in an unconstrained-monopoly fashion; (2) expand output and investment so as to deter entry; and (3) accept entry by taking up a Stackelburg-leadership position in relation to the entrant. Dixit demonstrates that entry deterrence is optimal when fixed costs are of intermediate degree; the complaint that entry deterrence is an imposed, rather than derived, result can be dismissed if the requisite conditions are satisfied.

Costs, Assets, and Credibility. The standard entry-barrier model assumes that potential entrants have access to the same long-run average total cost curve as do established firms. But the composition of costs between fixed and variable is ignored. This poses the following anomaly: extant firms and potential entrants are indistinguishable if all costs are variable. The only effective entry-deterring policy in circumstances where all costs are variable is setting price equal to total cost, which is to say that entry deterrence is without purpose. The crucial role of fixed costs in entry deterrence is evident from an examination of Dixit's (1979) formulation of the entry problem.

Even granting that entry deterrence sometimes is optimal, another question arises as to how large a monopoly distortion can develop by reason of temporal asymmetry (the sitting monopolist has assets in place at the outset) and fixed-cost conditions. Schmalensee has recently addressed this issue and shows that the preentry present value of excess profits that can be realized by established firms "cannot exceed the capital (start-up) cost of a firm of minimum efficient scale," and that scale economies are therefore of little quantitative importance from a welfare standpoint (1980, pp. 3, 8). This result is questionable, however, because it ignores the reputation-effect incentives discussed below.

A related issue that has come under scrutiny is the matter of credible threats. This goes to the issue of what postentry behavior is appropriately imputed to the sitting monopolist. As Curtis Eaton and Richard Lipsey observe (1980, p. 721), both credible and posturing threats take the same form — "If you take action *X*, I shall take action *Y*, which will make you regret *X*." But credible and noncredible threats are distinguishable in that the party issuing the threat will rationally take action *Y* only if credibility conditions are satisfied. If the Nash response to *X* is indeed to take action *Y*, the threat is credible. But if, despite the threat, *X* occurs and the net benefits accruing to the party issuing the threat are greater if he accommodates (by taking action *Z* rather than *Y*), then the threat will be perceived as posturing rather than credible. Since such threats will be empty, Eaton and Lipsey have urged that analysis of strategic behavior focus entirely on threats for which credibility is satisfied. The translation of this argument into investment terms discloses that the sitting monopolist must invest in durable, *transaction-specific assets* if he is to successfully preempt a market and deter entry.[20]

Reputation Effects. Bork's original assessment of the benefits of predation, McGee's commentary thereon, the Areeda-Turner criterion for assessing predation, Schmalensee's measure of welfare distortion, and the Eaton and Lipsey treatment of credible threats all address the issue of entry and predation in a very narrow context. A large, established firm is confronted with a clearly defined threat of entry and its response is assessed entirely in that bilateral context. The rationality of killing a rival (Bork 1978) or of deterring an equally efficient firm (which has not yet made irreversible commitments) becomes the focus of attention (Eaton and Lipsey 1980, 1981). If, however, punitive behavior carries signals to this and other firms — in future periods, in other geographic areas, and, possibly, in other lines of commerce — such analyses may understate the full set of effects on which the would-be predator relies in his decision to discipline a rival. Assessing this requires that the issue of predation be addressed in a teaching and learning context — which, since teaching and learning models are not well developed, is not easy, and is somewhat speculative.

Recognition that reputation effects can be important has nevertheless been growing and there has been some headway in dealing with the issues. The general point has been made by Christian von Weizsacker in the context of what he refers to as the extrapolation principle (1981, pp. 72–73):

> One of the most effective mechanisms available to society for the reduction of information production cost is the principle of extrapolation. By this I mean the phenomenon that people extrapolate the behavior of others from past observations and that this extrapolation is self-stabilizing, because it provides an incentive for others to live up to these expectations. . . . By observing others' behavior in the past, one can fairly confidently predict their behavior in the future without incurring further costs. . . .
>
> [This] extrapolation principle is deeply rooted in the structure of human behavior. Indeed it is also available in animal societies. . . . The fight between two chickens does not only produce information about the relative strengths in the present, but also about relative strength in the future.

Whereas Eaton and Lipsey and others have emphasized that only credible threats will effectively deter rivals and that credibility is realized by making preemptive investments, reference to reputation opens up the possibility that behavior matters. If, however, all of the objective factors pertinent to rivalry are fully disclosed, what is it that a firm can credibly do to alter preceptions?

The answer to this puzzle, as to many others in economics, is that the fiction of complete knowledge facilitates analysis, but sometimes obscures the core issues. Obscuration is a special hazard where competition of a small-numbers kind with repeat play is involved.

David Kreps and Robert Wilson have addressed the issues by observing that the general problem with so-called noncredible threats is that "the competitor realizes that if faced with a *fait accompli* of entry, the monopolist will find it optimal to accept this entry. Thus the believability of the threat is tenuous; perhaps the competitors will simply call the monopolist's bluff and enter" (Kreps and Wilson 1980, p. 2). But while others terminate the analysis here, Kreps and Wilson go on to pose the following dilemma: "if the monopolist carries out the [noncredible] threat, then he will become known for being tough, and this will deter subsequent challenges and therefore be to his long-run advantage. Today's entrant, realizing that the monopolist will meet today's challenge in order to deter challenges in the future, believes that the threat is credible and thus does not enter'' (1980, p. 2).

Kreps and Wilson evaluate the behavioral aspects of credibility by considering a series of examples of noncooperative games. The two crucial features are (1) there must be uncertainty regarding the sitting monopolist's payoffs, and (2) the game involves repeated play. While the specific source of uncertainty is not important, they nevertheless offer several possibilities: ''There may be uncertainty concerning the monopolist's production function. The monopolist may derive nonpecuniary benefits from fighting, or he may gain pecuniary benefits indirectly in another of his activities. He may simply be irrational . . . , [or there may be] uncertainty about the monopolist's discount rate'' (p. 24).

With respect to repeated play, they observe that ''the play of early rounds may be overwhelmingly influenced not by immediate payoffs but by considerations of what information is being transmitted'' (p. 58). This incentive to develop a reputation for toughness is especially great where the sitting monopolist ''plays against a sequence of different opponents, none of whom [has] the ability to foster a reputation'' (p. 58). Accordingly, whereas credible-threat conditions must be fully satisfied in a full-information game, quasi-credibility may do if there is payoff uncertainty and repeat play.[21]

Applications pose the question of whether the circumstances where reputation-effect incentives are strong can be recognized. An important consideration is whether local entry is being attemped into a small sector of the total market in which the established firm enjoys dominance. Exploratory entry into a local geographic market, or into one or a few products in a much broader line of related products, would presumably enhance the appeal of a teaching response. The likelihood that the observed behavior is strategic is increased in the degree to which (1) the response is intensively focused on the local disturbance (is carefully crafted to apply only to the market where entry is attempted) and (2) goes beyond a simple defensive response (for example, holding output unchanged in the face of entry) to include a punitive aspect (for example, increasing output as the reply to entry).

Cost Asymmetries. Areeda and Turner (1975) and, more recently, Ordover and Willig (1981, pp. 13-14) take the position that the predatory impact of a price reduction by a dominant firm can be judged by whether such a reduction will exclude an equally efficient rival. As I have argued elsewhere, this is a peculiar criterion for assessing the welfare benefits of contingent increases in output — ''now it's here, now it isn't, depending on whether an entrant has appeared or perished'' (Williamson 1977, p. 339). I did not, however, comment on the costs incurred by the entrant except in passing (1977, pp. 296, 303-304). This is a regrettable oversight, since Ordover and Willig, like Areeda and Turner before them, argue that whenever an incumbent's costs are lower than the entrant's, ''a price just below the rival's cost does earn the incumbent some profit, . . .and therefore induces exit without violation of our standard of predation'' (1980, p. 14). Inasmuch as they make no reference to the contrary, Ordover and Willig appear to have reference to the full pecuniary costs experienced by the rival. In consideration of the series of strategic-cost disadvantages that an entrant experiences or may be made to bear in relation to an established firm, this is surely a dubious criterion.

There are two points here, the first of which is that history matters in assessing costs. Temporal cost differences can arise in operating cost, cost of capital, and learning-curve respects. The second point is that the established firm may, by its own actions, be responsible for cost differences of the first two kinds and may contribute to the third.

Operating-Cost Asymmetries. The possibility that a potential entrant experiences cost disadvantages by reason of strategic-forward integration into distribution has been addressed by Bork (1978, pp. 156-158). Thus suppose that the dominant firm experiences identical costs whether its product is distributed by integrated or independent dealers. Forward integration may nevertheless be attractive because this has the effect of raising the costs to potential rivals. If potential entrants that would otherwise enjoy cost parity (say in terms of manufacturing costs) must, because of foreclosure, simultaneously create a distribution capability to effect entry, and if *additional* costs are incurred in creating a side-by-side distribution network that would be avoided by utilizing (or expanding) existing, but nonintegrated, distribution capacity, forward integration may be presumed to have been undertaken for the purpose of creating strategic operating-cost asymmetries.

Capital Cost Differentials. Assume, for the purposes of the argument here, that the potential entrant would experience identical distribution costs to that of the established firm if it were to enter both manufacturing and distribution stages rather than manufacturing alone. Suppose also, however, that the would-be entrant has demonstrated competence only at the manufacturing stage. Two-stage entry thus requires it to raise funds for an unfamiliar second stage to which the capital market can be expected to attach a risk premium (Williamson, 1975, pp. 110–112; 1979b, pp. 962–964). Accordingly, cost parity between established firm and potential rival can be upset by capital cost differentials.

The capital costs of would-be entrants can further be increased if established firms can quasi-credibly threaten to engage in postentry predation. If the "suppliers of capital to [potential] entrants perceive that the risks in the particular markets are greater than they had previously thought them to be, the cost of capital to new entrants will rise" (Joskow and Klevorick 1979, p. 231).

Learning Effects. The proposition that costs are a function not merely of the scale and scope of a firm's activity but also of the cumulative output was set out by Armen Alchian in 1959. Only recently, however, have the strategic ramifications been addressed. One of the complications that is introduced by learning effects is that the test of remunerative pricing by dominant firms in early-stage growth industries is much more difficult (Williamson 1977, p. 323). Current costs need to be reduced by the discounted effect on future costs in making the assessment. As Michael Spence puts it, "When there is a learning curve, the short-run output decision is a type of investment decision. It affects the accumulated output, a stock, and through it, future costs and market position" (1981, p. 1).

But there is more to it. First and foremost, the established firm, which enjoys the benefits of lower costs by reason of accumulated output, will never be confronted with an equally efficient rival if costs comparisons are made in the immediate postentry period and learning curves are important. Second, out of recognition of the intertemporal cost effects, the established firm may have an incentive to engage in aggressive pricing designed to "reduce the return to competitors investing in expanded market shares" (Spence 1981, p. 41). Additionally, the established firm may upset efforts to achieve cost parity by threatening (perhaps with good cause) to bring law suits should the entrant attempt to shorten the learning period by hiring away key employees.

The upshot is that the *equally efficient rival criterion is primarily suited to static circumstances where historical differences and contrived cost asymmetries may be presumed to be absent.* This scenario is evidently favored by those who take a narrow view of predation and advocate a marginal cost pricing standard. To the extent, however, that actual circumstances are not accurately described in this way, allowance for cost differences may be necessary if an informed assessment of predation is to be realized.[22]

Unresolved Dilemmas

The study of strategic behavior has made remarkable progress during the past five years. A number of troublesome problems nevertheless remain. These include: (1) whether efforts to curb predation should focus primarily on price and output, or if other aspects of rivalry should be included; (2) inasmuch as rules governing predation set up incentives for established firms to preposition, should allowance be made for prepositioning in assessing the merits of alternative rules; and (3) whether victims of mistaken predation should be accorded protection.

Dimensions

Although they are not independent, the study of strategic behavior is usefully split into ex ante and ex post parts. Ex ante behavior takes the form of preentry investment (in capacity, research and development (R&D), promotion, the offer of multiple brands, and so on) while ex post behavior involves specific adaptations by dominant firms contingent upon entry. As between the two, aggressive strategic behavior in ex post respects is widely believed to be the more reprehensible, but there are complicating factors here as well.

Christian von Weizsacker's work on innovation is instructive in this regard. He distinguishes between progressive and mature industries and observes that the positive externalities of innovation are especially strong in a progressive industry due to the "possibility of generating the next innovation" (1981, p. 150). A welfare assessment of the intertemporal incentives to engage in innovation in a progressive industry leads von Weizsacker to conclude that "a pricing action by an incumbent, which by reasonable standards is not considered a predatory action in a nonprogressive industry, [*a fortiori*] cannot be called a predatory action in a progressive industry" (1981, p. 210).

A somewhat different aspect is emphasized by Ordover and Willig, who, in an important paper, contend that ex post "manipulation of the product set can frequently be more effective than price cutting as an anticompetitive tactic" (1981 p. 18). Two types of tactics are examined. The first entails "the introduction of a new product that is a substitute for the products of the rival firm and that endangers its viability by diverting its sales. The second tactic is employed in the context of systems rivalry. It consists of the constriction in the supply of components that are vital to consumers' use of the rival's product, coupled with the introduction of systems components that enable consumers to bypass their use of the rival's products'' (p. 19). Although both their criterion for assessing predation as well as the practicability of implementing their rules for assessing strategic R&D and the upward repricing or withdrawal of preexisting components complementary to a rival may be disputed, the issues have nevertheless been structured in a useful way. Follow-on studies will surely make use of this framework.

But what should be done in the meantime when the law is confronted with problems that run well ahead of the theory? SCM Corporation asked for compulsory licensing relief in its complaint that Xerox had excluded SCM from the plain-copier market,[23] and Berkey Photo argued that unannounced product innovations by Kodak placed it at an unfair disadvantage.[24] The FTC has also brought some rather ambitious strategic behavior suits. A collusive strategy of brand proliferation formed the basis of its complaint against the principal producers of ready-to-eat cereals (Kellogg, General Mills, General Foods, and Quaker Oats),[25] and the FTC subsequently charged duPont with making preemptive investments in the titanium-dioxide market.[26]

Except for cases that are patently protectionist (and some of these have a protectionist flavor), there are no happy choices. Put differently, trade offs proliferate and our capacity to evaluate them is very primitive. Thus, although some reject these suits with the observation that ''Plaintiffs arguments in the high-technology cases of the 1970s rest implicitly on an atomistic theory of competition which posits an organized economy with no changes in technology, no shifts in consumer tastes, no change in population — and no future that is essentially different from the past'' (Conference Board 1980, p. 18), this is really a red herring. Strategic behavior is an interesting economic issue *only* in an intertemporal context where uncertainty is featured. The high-technology cases are plainly of this kind, and arguably involve strategic calculations in which private and social valuations differ. The courts have understandably been cautious in moving ahead in this area. Assuming that these are matters that can be reexamined as a deeper understanding of the issues and a capacity to make informed trade offs develops, this would appear to be the responsible result.

Prepositioning

A primary focus on ex post price and output behavior does not, however, mean that ex ante investments should be ignored entirely. Indeed, if comprehensive comparisons of the welfare ramifications of alternative predatory-pricing rules are to be attempted, differential ex ante consequences, if they exist, should presumably be included.

The ways by which firms will preposition in relation to different rules have been addressed by Spence (1977), Salop (1979), Dixit (1979, 1980), and Eaton and Lipsey (1980, 1981) in relation to entry deterrence in general and by Williamson (1977) as entry deterrence applies to predation. The general argument here is that an "established firm can alter the *outcome* to its advantage by changing the initial conditions. In particular, an irrevocable choice of investment allows it to alter its post-entry marginal cost curve, and thereby the post-entry equilibrium" (Dixit 1980, p. 96). This line of reasoning has been applied to the study of predation with the following result: each predatory pricing rule predictably gives rise to "pre-entry price, output, and investment adjustments on the part of dominant firms whose markets are subject to encroachment. To neglect the incentives of rules whereby dominant firms made *pre-entry adaptive responses of a strategic kind* necessarily misses an important part of the problem" (Williamson 1977, p. 293).

There is less than unanimity, however, over whether these prepositioning effects should be taken into account. Recent supporters of the marginal cost/equally-efficient-rival pricing rule (McGee 1980, Ordover and Willig 1981) ignore the prepositioning ramifications of alternative rules. Whether this is because they believe them to be unimportant or beyond the purview of responsible analysis is unclear. For the moment, the matter of prepositioning incentives and their relevance for rule assessment is under dispute.

Mistaken Predation

A troublesome question arises where predatory pricing is attempted in circumstances where the structural preconditions described previously are not satisfied. I will refer to this class of events as "mistaken predation," in that even if the predator is successful in driving a rival from the market it will fail to realize anything but very transient market-power benefits. A significant excess of price over cost cannot be supported for any but a short period of time where rivals are many and entry is easy. Where this obtains, an attempt at predation is mistaken because a correct assessment of the net benefits will disclose that they are negative.

The fact that attempted predation is mistaken does not, however, guarantee that it will never occur. Where it does, should the victims be entitled to relief by bringing suit and recovering damages? The application of the type of reasoning employed by Joskow and Klevorick would suggest a negative answer. The hazard is that many of the suits brought by firms in competitive industries would have the purpose of relieving these firms from legitimate rivalry rather than attempted predation. Since mistaken predation will presumably be rare or, at least, not repeated, the "false positive errors — that is, . . . errors that involve labeling truly competitive price cuts as predatory" (Joskow and Klevorick 1979, p. 223) would appear to be high and augur against allowing suits of this kind. Some firms would be victimized as a result, however, and other students of predation may assess the hazards differently.

Conclusion

The 1960s was a decade when antitrust was preoccupied with measures of concentration and entry barriers. Such a narrow formulation facilitated easy enforcement — to the extent that Justice Stewart was moved to observe that "the sole consistency that I can find under Section 7 is that the government always wins"[27] — but sometimes at the expense of an informed welfare assessment of the issues. Three factors contributed to this condition. First, it was widely believed that oligopolistic collusion was easy to effectuate. Second, wherever entry barriers were discovered they were held to be anticompetitive and antisocial, there being a great reluctance to acknowledge trade-offs. And third, the business firm was thought to be adequately described as a production function to which a profit-maximization objective had been assigned.

These views had two unfortunate consequences. For one thing, anything that contributed to market power — offsetting benefits notwithstanding — was held to be unlawful. Second, nonstandard or unfamiliar business practices that departed from autonomous market contracting were also held to be presumptively unlawful. If the natural way by which to mediate transactions between technologically separable entities is through markets, surely any effort by the firm to extend control beyond its natural (technological) boundaries must be motivated by strategic purpose.

Matters changed in the 1970s, as a greater appreciation for efficiency benefits developed, and as the conception of the firm as a governance structure took hold. The perverse hostility with which efficiency differentials were once regarded gave way to an affirmative valuation of efficiency benefits,[28] and business practices that were previously suspect, because they did not fit comfortably with the view of the firm as a production function, were reinterpreted in a larger context in which — implicitly, if not explicitly — transaction-cost economizing was introduced. As a consequence, antitrust errors and enforcement excesses of the 1960s were removed or reversed in the 1970s.

Despite progress with these matters, antitrust cannot settle back to a quiet life. Other difficult antitrust issues relating to strategic behavior have recently surfaced, and existing criteria for assessing the lawfulness of strategic practices are actively under dispute. Significant headway with a number of strategic-behavior issues has nevertheless been made and more is in prospect. The study of strategic behavior has been clarified in the following significant respects: (1) severe structural preconditions in both concentration and entry-barrier respects need to be satisfied before an incentive to behave strategically can be claimed to exist; (2) attention to investment and asset characteristics is needed in assessing the condition of entry — specifically, nontrivial irreversible investments of a transaction-specific kind have especially strong deterrent effects; (3) history matters in assessing rivalry — both with respect to the leadership advantage enjoyed by a sitting monopolist as well as in the incidence and evaluation of comparative costs; and (4) reputation effects are important in assessing the rationality of predatory behavior.

This last has a bearing on two crucial aspects of the strategic-behavior issue. For one thing, those who argue that strategic behavior can be disregarded unless credible threat conditions are fulfilled have overstated the case. This is not to suggest that the study of credible threats cannot usefully inform the analysis of strategic behavior. But if knowledge is imperfect then dominant firms can alter expectations by posturing (as well as by objectively fulfilling credibility conditions), in which event precommitments need not be as extensive as the credible threat literature would indicate. Second, myopic assessments of strategic behavior understate the incentives to engage in predation. Those who focus on the incentive to kill a specific rival are ignoring what may often be the stronger incentive — that is, to develop a reputation that will subsequently help to deter this and other firms in later periods, in other geographic markets, and in other lines of commerce.

Among the issues actively under dispute in the study of strategic behavior are the following: (1) whether the equally efficient rival criterion is a useful one;[29] (2) whether the assessment of predatory pricing rules should make allowance for prepositioning incentives;[30] (3) whether strategic behavior should focus primarily on ex post contingent responses or can also be responsibly extended to include ex ante investments;[31] and

(4) what remedies should be sought.[32] Clarification on these as well as sharpening of the issues enumerated in the preceding paragraph can be expected as the 1980s progress. I expect that antitrust enforcement regarding strategic behavior will be in much better shape at the end of the decade as a result of intervening scholarship. I furthermore anticipate that the continued need for antitrust will be demonstrated — and, alarmist cries for the abolition of antitrust will be discredited — in the process.

Notes

1. A shift of the traditional entry-barrier approach in the direction of strategic behavior was signaled by the influential paper of Richard Caves and Michael Porter (1977).

2. *Federal Trade Commission* v. *Procter & Gamble Co.*, 386 U. S. 568 (1967); *United States* v. *Arnold Schwinn & Co.*, 388 U.S. 365 (1967).

3. *In re* Foremost Dairies, Inc., 60 F.T.C. 944, 1084 (1962), emphasis added.

4. Quoted from Bork (1978, p. 254).

5. *Federal Trade Commission* v. *Procter & Gamble Co.*, 386 U. S. 568, 574 (1967).

6. Although perverse applications of economies reasoning are much less common today, occasional aberrations nevertheless appear. See note 28, for an example.

7. The quotation is attributed to Turner by Stanley Robinson 1968 N. Y. State Bar Association, Antitrust Symposium, p. 29.

8. Jurisdictional Statement for the United States at 14, *United States* v. *Arnold Schwinn & Co.* 388 U. S. 365 (1967). For a discussion, see Williamson (1979a, pp. 980–985).

9. The recent Areeda and Turner antitrust treatise is an example. See Posner (1979, pp. 933–938) for a discussion of the earlier Kaysen and Turner book as compared with the Areeda and Turner treatise.

10. See note 4.

11. Developing this takes us beyond the scope of the current paper, but it has been addressed elsewhere (Williamson 1981). Among the leading organizational innovations during the past 150 years that have important transaction-cost economizing attributes are (1) the appearance of managerial hierarchies in the railroads in the 1860s; (2) selective forward integration out of manufacturing into distribution that occurred at the end of the nineteenth century; (3) the invention of the multidivisional structure in the 1920s and its subsequent diffusion following World War II; (4) the extension of multidivisionalization to manage diversified lines of commerce (the conglomerate); and (5) the further application of this to promote technology transfer in the multinational enterprise.

12. Budd Co., [1973–1976 Transfer Binder] Trade Regulation Reporter CCTT, para 20, 998 (FTC No. 8848 Sept. 18, 1975).

13. *Continental T.V. Inc. et al.* v. *GTE Sylvania Inc.* 433 U.S. 36, 45 (1977).

14. For references to the relevant cases, see Ordover and Willig (1981, p. 70, n. 2).

15. Although McGee was not among those identified by Posner as being a member of the diehard school, McGee has since volunteered that he qualifies for membership (1980, p. 292, n. 15).

16. See my review of Bork's book in Williamson (1970a).

17. This rule is mainly associated with the 1975 paper of Phillip Areeda and Donald

Turner. McGee, however, observes that he originated the rule ten years earlier (McGee, 1980, p. 290).

18. Janusz Ordover and Robert Willig, in a recent paper, develop cost based criteria that they contend are in the spirit of Areeda and Turner (Ordover and Willig, 1981, pp. 9, 16). In fact, however, their double test — the price exceeds both average and marginal cost — is much more stringent, and they nowhere propose average variable cost as a suitable surrogate, the operational result at which Areeda and Turner arrive.

19. It has been argued that the United Mine Workers performed this function in the bituminous-coal industry (Williamson 1968).

20. Asset specificity can take three forms: site specificity, physical asset specificity; and human asset specificity. For a discussion of these issues in transaction-cost terms and an assessment of their organizational ramifications, see Williamson (1979b).

21. Assessing investment behavior is made more complex as a consequence. Thus even if a firm is "unable to use excess capacity or a highly developed sales network profitably, . . . *if* its opponents think that the firm might be able to use that capacity/sales network to engage in profitable predation, then the firm may wish to develop that capacity/sales network" so as to confirm the fear (Kreps and Wilson 1980, p. 61).

22. F. M. Scherer observes that "Entry at or near the minimum optimal scale into significant oligopolistic markets is [rare] . . . . Indeed, it is sufficiently rare that it usually receives considerable attention in the relevant trade press" (1980, p. 248). Many models of predatory pricing ignore this and argue that only output that is produced by an equally efficient rival is socially valued.

23. *SCM Corp.* v. *Xerox Corp.* (DC Conn 1978) 1978–2 Trade Cases, Par. 62, 392.

24. *Berkey Photo, Inc.* v. *Eastman Kodak Co.* (DC NY 1978) 1978–1 Trade Cases, par. 62, 092.

25. *FTC* v. *Kellogg et al.*, Docket No. 8883.

26. *FTC* v. *E. I. du Pont de Nemours & Co.*, Complaint, Docket No. 9108, April 5, 1978 CCH Trade Regulation Reporter, transfer binder, Federal Trade Commission Complaints and Orders, 1976–1979, Par. 21, 407.

27. Dissenting opinion in *U. S.* v. *Von's Grocery, Inc.* 384 U. S. 270 (1966).

28. Vigilance is, nevertheless, necessary lest retrogression occur. Thus the government's lead attorney advised the court in *U. S.* v. *Occidental Petroleum* (Civil Action No. C–3–78–288) that the acquisition of Mead by Occidental was objectionable because it would permit Mead to construct a large "Greenfield plant, which was the most efficient and cost-effective investment," and that this would disadvantage Mead's rivals.

29. Lest there be any doubt, I regard this as a seriously flawed criterion.

30. I believe that they should, though this complicates the analysis.

31. My own view is that antitrust is best advised to focus — at least for the present — on ex post contingent behavior. Behavior that goes beyond being merely defensive to include a punitive aspect is especially reprehensible and, arguably, is also the easiest to assess. Accordingly, contingent behavior that is directed not merely at the immediate rival but has a teaching-and-learning aspect is properly made the principal focus of antitrust enforcement against predation — at least until the state of the art for modelling and assessing strategic behavior is significantly advanced from where it stands presently.

32. Not only are welfare assessments of ex ante entry-deterring behavior very subtle (von Weizsacker 1980, 1981), but meaningful relief for ex ante investments may be difficult to fashion. Unless, therefore, a clear showing of welfare losses is made and efficacious relief can be devised, caution would appear to be warranted before pressing antitrust to hold that ex ante investments are unlawful.

References

Alchian, A. A., "Costs and Outputs," in M. Abramovitz et al., *The Allocation of Economic Resources: Essays in Honor of Bernard Francis Haley* (Stanford, Calif.: Stanford University Press, 1959) 23–40.

Alchian, A. A., "Corporate Management and Property Rights," in H. G. Manne, ed., *Economic Policy and Regulation of Corporate Securities* (Washington, D. C.: American Enterprise Institute for Public Policy Research, 1969) 337–360.

Areeda, P. and D. F. Turner, "Predatory Pricing and Related Practices Under Section 2 of the Sherman Act," *Harvard Law Review* 88 (February 1975): 697–733.

Bain, J. S., *Barriers to New Competition* (Cambridge, Mass.: Harvard University Press 1956).

Bain, J. S., Industrial Organization (2nd ed.) (New York: John Wiley & Sons, 1968).

Baumol, W. J., "Quasi-Permanence of Price Reductions: A Policy for Prevention of Predatory Pricing," *Yale Law Journal,* 89 (November 1979): 1–26.

Bok, D., *Section 7 of the Clayton Act and the Merging of Law and Economics, Harvard Law Review,* 74 (December, 1960): 226–355.

Bork, R. H., *The Antitrust Paradox,* New York: Basic Books 1978.

Caves, R. E. and M. E. Porter, "From Entry Barriers to Mobility Barriers," *Quarterly Journal of Economics,* 91 (May 1977): 241–262.

Chandler, A. D., Jr., *Strategy and Structure* (Cambridge, Mass.: MIT Press 1962).

Dixit, A., "A Model of Duopoly Suggesting a Theory of Entry Barriers," *Bell Journal of Economics,* 10 (Spring 1979): 20–32.

Dixit, A., "The Role of Investment in Entry Deterrence," *Economic Journal,* 90 (March 1980): 95–106.

Eaton, B. C. and R. G. Lipsey, "Exit Barriers are Entry Barriers: The Durability of Capital," *Bell Journal of Economics,* 11 (Autumn 1980): 721–729.

Eaton, B. C. and R. G. Lipsey, "Capital, Commitment, and Entry Equilibrium," *Bell Journal of Economics,* 12 (Spring 1981).

Fellner, W., *Competition Among the Few,* (New York: Alfred A. Knopf, Inc. 1949).

Heflebower, R. B., "Observations on Decentralization in Large Enterprises," *Journal of Industrial Economics,* 9 (November 1960): 7–22.

Joskow, P. L., "The Political Content of Antitrust: Comment," in O. E. Williamson, ed., *Antitrust Law and Economics,* (Houston, Tex.: Dame Publishers 1980) 196–204.

Joskow, P. L. and A. K. Klevorick, "A Framework for Analyzing Predatory Pricing Policy," *Yale Law Journal,* 89 (December 1979): 213–270.

Kaysen, C. and D. F. Turner, *Antitrust Policy: An Economic and Legal Analysis,* (Cambridge, Mass.: 1959).

Kreps, D. M. and R. Wilson, "On the Chain-Store Paradox and Predation: Reputation for Toughness," GSB Research Paper No. 551, (June 1980), Stanford, Cal.

Liebeler, W. C., "Market Power and Competitive Superiority in Concentrated Industries," *UCLA Law Review,* 25 (August 1978): 231–1300.

McGee, J. S., "Predatory Pricing Revisited," *Journal of Law and Economics,* 23 (October 1980): 289–330.

Modigliani, F., "New Developments on the Oligopoly Front," *Journal of Political Economy,* 66 (June 1958): 215–232.

Muris, T. J., "The Efficiency Defense Under Section 7 of the Clayton Act," *Case Western Reserve Law Review,* 30 (Fall 1979): 381–432.

Ordover, J. A. and R. D. Willig, "An Economic Definition of Predatory Product Innovation," in S. Salop, ed., *Strategic Views of Predation,* (Federal Trade Commission, Washington, D. C. 1981).

Posner, R. A., "The Social Costs of Monopoly and Regulation," *Journal of Political Economy,* 83 (August 1975): 807–825.

Posner, R. A., "The Chicago School of Antitrust Analysis," *University of Pennsylvania Law Review,* 127 (April 1979): 925–948.

Salop S., "Strategic Entry Deterrence," *American Economic Review* (May 1979): 335–338.

Scherer, F. M., *Industrial Market Structure and Economic Performance,* (Chicago: 1980).

Schmalensee, R., "Entry Deterrence in the Ready-to-Eat Breakfast Cereal Industry," *Bell Journal of Economics,* 9 (Autumn 1978): 305–327.

Schmalensee, R., "Economies of Scale and Barriers to Entry," Sloan Working Paper No. 1130–80 (June 1980), Cambridge, Mass.

Spence, A. M., "Entry, Investment and Oligopolistic Pricing," *Bell Journal of Economics,* 8 (Autumn 1977): 534–544.

Spence, A. M., "The Learning Curve and Competition," *Bell Journal of Economics,* 12 (Spring 1981).

Stigler, G. J., *The Organization of Industry,* (Homewood, Ill.: 1968.)

Turner, D. F., "Conglomerate Mergers and Section 7 of the Clayton Act," *Harvard Law Review,* 78 (May 1965): 1313–1395.

von Weizsacker, C. C., "A Welfare Analysis of Barriers to Entry," *Bell Journal of Economics,* 11 (Autumn 1980): 399–421.

von Weizsacker, C. C., *Barriers to Entry,* (New York: Springer-Verlag 1981).

Williamson, O. E., "Wage Rates as a Barrier to Entry: The Pennington Case in Perspective," *Quarterly Journal of Economics,* February, 1968, *82,* 85–116.

———, "Economies as an Antitrust Defense: The Welfare Tradeoffs," *American Economic Review, 58* (March 1968), 18–35.

———, *Corporate Control and Business Behavior,* Englewood Cliffs, N.J., Prentice-Hall, 1970.

———, "The Vertical Integration of Production: Market Failure Considerations," *American Economic Review 61* (May, 1971), 112–123.

———, *Markets and Hierarchies: Analysis and Antitrust Implications,* (New York: Free Press 1975).

———, "Predatory Pricing: A Strategic and Welfare Analysis," *Yale Law Journal,* 87 (December 1977): 284–340.

———, "Bork, The Antitrust Paradox: A Policy at War with Itself," *University of Chicago Law Review,* 46 (Winter 1979a): 526–531.

———, "Assessing Vertical Market Restrictions," *University of Pennsylvania Law Review,* 127 (April 1979b): 953–993.

———, "Williamson on Predatory Pricing II." *Yale Law Journal,* 88 (May 1979c): 1183–1200.

———, "The Modern Corporation: Origins, Evolution, Attributes," *Journal of Economic Literature,* 19 (December 1981): 1537–68.

4 AN EVALUATION OF HORIZONTAL MERGER ENFORCEMENT

David B. Audretsch

In 1950 President Harry S Truman signed the Celler-Kefauver Act into law. This statute did much more than eliminate a loophole based on a legal technicality; it symbolized renewed congressional concern and vigorous commitment to the preservation of competitive markets and the prevention of monopoly power. As a result of the 1950 amendment one commentator was moved to write, "Thus, over 40 years after the enactment of the Clayton Act, it now becomes apparent for the first time that Section 7 has been a sleeping giant all along."[1]

Yet satisfaction with the antimerger law has been far from universal among economists. John Kenneth Galbraith argues that because the Act "exempts those who possess the market power and concentrates on those who would try to possess it," its enforcement "defends and gives legitimacy to a charade."[2]

Is enforcement of the Celler-Kefauver Act, along with the broader purposes of antitrust policy, a charade, an anachronism in a complex industrial society? This chapter investigates one aspect of the antitrust laws — horizontal-merger enforcement of the Clayton Act — and attempts to answer that question. By comparing the benefits with the costs of undertaking horizontal-merger cases, an evaluation of Celler-Kefauver enforcement is possible.

The Goals of Antitrust

What are the basic goals underlying antitrust policy? What did Congress have in mind when enacting the various antitrust statutes? These questions are as important as they are difficult to answer; without a clear conception of the purpose of the antitrust laws it is impossible to identify the social benefits from their enforcement. Despite this importance, the goals of antitrust remain elusive. F. M. Scherer, who was Director of the Bureau of Economics at the Federal Trade Commission from 1974 to 1976, found congressional intent "muddled and often contradictory." He observed, "I frequently felt that if we only knew precisely where we're to go, we could proceed there in a more orderly fashion. But clear objectives were a luxury we seldom enjoyed, ambiguity was our guiding star."[3]

Despite, or because of this confusion, considerable attention has been devoted to identifying the congressional intent behind the antitrust laws. Robert H. Bork[4] and Richard A. Posner,[5] for example, are convinced that allocative efficiency was not only the dominant, but the sole consideration of Congress in enacting the antitrust statutes. According to Bork, "Though an economist of our day would describe the problem of concern to [Senator] Sherman differently, as a misallocation of resources brought about by a restriction of output rather than one of high price, there is no doubt that Sherman and he would be thinking the same thing."[6]

Not all economists agree about the single-mindedness of Congress in passing the antitrust laws. Leonard W. Weiss[7] interprets the primary intent of Congress as concern over the redistribution of wealth resulting from monopoly power. According to Weiss, Congress was more interested in preventing large capital gains to the organizers of monopolistic cartels and mergers than avoiding losses in allocative efficiency.

Willard F. Mueller attributes broader, noneconomic as well as economic goals to congressional motivation underlying the Celler-Kefauver Act: "while Congress spoke much about broad economic, social and political consequences of economic power, when it wrote a statute to cope with these problems it applied an economic concept, the probable lessening of competition within particular geographic and product markets. It is important to keep in mind this distinction between the objective of the act and the statutory language."[8]

The goal of antitrust is apparently multidimensional. It includes the prevention and elimination of monopoly prices and restricted output, the redistribution of wealth away from monopolistic power, and the diffusion and decentralization of aggregate concentration of economic resources in society. This chapter operationalizes the goals of antitrust as two widely respected economic and social values: (1) the redistribution of wealth, and (2) allocative efficiency. It should be remembered, however, that the gain to society from antitrust enforcement may extend beyond these two categories of benefits.

Benefit Estimation

Based on two of the major social and economic values implicit in the antitrust laws — the redistribution of wealth and allocative efficiency — this section establishes a framework for estimating benefits within which an evaluation of the Celler-Kefauver Act and its subsequent enforcement may be made.

Redistribution of Wealth

Why do certain horizontal mergers redistribute wealth from consumers to firms with monopoly power? One explanation is based on evidence from a plethora of studies relating the four-firm concentration ratio to price-cost margins.[9] An acquisition or consolidation by one of the four largest firms in an industry implies an increase in the four-firm concentration ratio and a subsequent increase in the price-cost margin. This increase represents a transfer of wealth from consumers to firms and a reduction in allocative efficiency.

The gain from prohibiting such a merger can be algebraically derived. Excluding other variables, Norman R. Collins and Lee E. Preston[10] found the relationship between the price-cost margin and four-firm–concentration ratio to take the form

$$\frac{VS - CM - W}{VS} = a + bCR_4 \tag{4.1}$$

where VS is the value of shipments, CM is the cost of materials, W is the wage cost, and CR_4 is the four-firm–concentration ratio. If the acquiring firm is among the largest four in the industry, a horizontal merger will increase concentration by

$$\triangle CR_4 = \frac{VS_a}{VS}$$

where VS_a is the value of shipments of the acquired firm. Since

$$b \cdot CR_4 = b \cdot \frac{VS_a}{VS}$$

it follows that

$$\frac{\triangle(VS - CM - W)}{VS} = b \cdot \frac{VS_a}{VS}.$$

By prohibiting the merger, the gain to consumers is

$$\triangle(VS - CM - W) = b \cdot VS_a. \tag{4.2}$$

The benefit to consumers must be adjusted by three factors. The distributive effect applies only to a firm's net income after taxes. The tax revenues could, theoretically at least, be returned to consumers, nullifying part of the redistribution. Although there is ample evidence suggesting that Congress placed a high value on preventing wealth flowing from consumers to firms as a result of monopoly power, no such congressional concern was registered regarding a similar transfer from consumers to the public sector. Thus, only the share of VS_a representing net income accrues a direct benefit.

Similarly, no direct gain from preventing a merger exists until the divestiture of the acquired firm, or an equivalent remedy, occurs. Such relief is not usually simultaneous with a court decision favoring the government. Kenneth Elzinga[11] found that, of the merger cases occurring between 1950 and 1960, effective relief was not obtained in many because of the length of time required to achieve divestiture. Clearly, if a merger causes a redistribution of wealth because it increases market concentration, and, therefore, the price-cost margin, redistribution will not cease until the source of the effect — the increased concentration resulting from the merger — is eliminated. Direct benefits are zero until relief is effected.

The direct gain measured by equation (4.2) occurs over N future years. But this annual flow of benefits must be adjusted to reflect the valuation of future benefits in the period in which the case is undertaken. Thus, the direct gain in each future year must be discounted to calculate the net present value.

Adjusting equation (4.2) for these three qualifications yields the net direct benefits from the redistribution of wealth, B_{qd},

$$B_{qd} = \sum_{n=0}^{N} \frac{(1 - tr)}{(1 + d)^n} \cdot b \cdot VS_a \cdot V_n \tag{4.3}$$

where tr is the corporate tax rate of 48 percent and b, whose value was estimated in the study by Collins and Preston, is 0.144. V_n is included to represent the period in which effective relief was procured. If n^* is the year of divestiture, then $V_n = 0$ for $n < n^*$, and $V_n = 1$ for $n \geq n^*$. That is, there is no direct gain from a horizontal-merger case until relief has been achieved.

Data for the value of shipments of the acquired firm in the relevant market were gathered from a variety of sources — the *Merger Case Digest*, [12] *The Celler-Kefauver Act: The First 27 Years*,[13] and the *Statistical Report: Value of Shipments Data by Product Class for the 1,000 Largest Manufacturing Companies of 1950*.[14] In the paper previously cited, Elzinga provided a classification of antitrust enforcement prior to 1960 that identified merger cases where adequate relief was not achieved. Those cases that Elzinga included in the category of "unsuccessful relief," based on the independence and viability of the rechartered firm, were assigned zero direct benefits.

Elzinga's study, along with information from the above sources, was used to identify the number of years between the filing date of a case and the accomplishment of divestiture, n^*. A rate of 10 percent was used to discount the benefits accruing in the years following the date a case was filed.

Based on equation (4.3), the net direct-redistribution benefits for the seventy cases between 1954 and 1974 for which data was available are listed in appendix 4A. Not all of the cases contributed wealth-redistribution benefits. Some cases, as explained previously, did not achieve effective relief. There were eleven cases in which there was no viable remedy. Similarly, other cases were assigned zero direct benefits because they involved a merger that did not increase the four-firm–concentration ratio. There were seven cases with zero direct benefits because the merger presumably had no effect on the price-cost margin in the relevant market.

Based on all seventy cases, the average net direct-redistribution benefit is \$12.70-million per case. The exclusion of those cases not obtaining effective relief raises the average to \$15.06-million of direct-benefits per case. If only those cases that attained some positive level of benefits are included, each case contributed an average of \$17.09-million.

A horizontal-merger case not only provides the direct gain measured by equation (4.3); it also provides an indirect benefit, because future acquisitions do not occur as a result of the case. Deterrence from a horizontal-merger case is defined as mergers that would have occurred in the absence of antitrust enforcement. In fact, some researchers feel that deterrence may be the major source of benefits. According to Jesse W. Markham, "it is relevant to inquire into the effect Section 7 has had on the volume of mergers it presumably was designed to prohibit. In any society governed by law it is generally expected that the law's principal effect is to be found in its observance rather than its breach."[15]

Measurements of the deterrent effect have been estimated elsewhere.[16] Based on two different procedures, average-deterrence-per-case was estimated as 10.58. That is, on the average, each case prevented about eleven concentration-increasing horizontal mergers from occurring. Further, it was found that the deterrent effect was strongest immediately following a court decision, and then declined in subsequent years.

Using the value of shipments in a merger case to approximate the size of the deterred mergers, the net indirect wealth redistribution benefits, B_{qi}, can be measured by

$$B_{qi} = \sum_{n=0}^{N} \frac{DVS_a}{(1 + d)^n} \cdot b \cdot (1 - tr) \tag{4.4}$$

where the value of the deterred mergers, DVS_a, is formed from

$$DVS_a = MD \cdot VS_a$$

and MD is average-deterrence-per-case, adjusted for a diminishing effect over time.[17]

As shown in appendix 4A, all cases contributed a positive amount of benefits resulting from deterrence. This result obtained because the direct benefits are conditional upon effective relief and the effect the merger has on the four-firm–concentration ratio, while estimation of the indirect benefits is based solely on the size of the acquired firm.

Allocative Efficiency

A horizontal-merger case also provides an improvement in allocative efficiency. The direct gain is the deadweight loss avoided by prohibiting the merger. As discussed previously, a merger increasing the four-firm–concentration ratio has the effect of changing the price-cost margin. Such an increase in the price-cost margin leads to a reduction in allocative efficiency, W, which can be expressed in terms of a price-cost markup

$$W = \frac{1}{2}\left(\frac{VS + VS_a - (CM + W)}{VS + VS_a} - \frac{VS - (CM - W)}{VS}\right) \cdot VS \cdot \eta$$

where η is the elasticity of demand in the relevant market. Since

$$\frac{VS + VS_a - (CM + W)}{VS + VS_a} - \frac{VS - (CM + W)}{VS} = b \cdot \Delta CR$$

and

$$b \cdot \Delta CR = b \cdot \frac{VS_a}{VS}$$

the allocative gain from a successful merger case is

$$W = \frac{1}{2}\left(b \cdot \frac{VS_a}{VS}\right)^2 \cdot VS \cdot \eta$$
$$= \frac{1}{2} b^2 \cdot \frac{VS_a{}^2}{VS} \cdot \eta .$$

The net direct benefit from the gain in allocative efficiency, B_{fd}, is

$$B_{fd} = \sum_{i=0}^{N} \frac{\frac{1}{2} b^2 \cdot (VS_a{}^2/VS) \cdot \eta \cdot V_n}{(1 + d)^n} \tag{4.5}$$

where VS_a is the value of shipments of the acquired firm, VS is the total value of shipments in the relevant market, b is 0.144, and η, the elasticity of demand, is assigned a value of one. As in equation (4.2), $V_n = 0$ for $n^* > n$, and $V_n = 1$ for $n^* \leqslant n$.

Using the *Merger Case Digest* to identify the relevant market in each case, and *The Celler-Kefauver Act: The First 27 Years* along with the *Special Report Series: Concentration Ratios in Manufacturing*, [18] to measure the magnitude of VS, accurate information indicating the total value of shipments in the relevant market was obtained for 59 cases. Based on equation (4.5), the net direct allocative efficiency benefits were derived and are listed in appendix 4B.

Like the redistribution benefits, the major allocative-efficiency gain is the result of the deterrent effect. The net indirect benefit from preventing a deadweight loss because of deterrence, B_{fi}, is

$$B_{fi} = \sum_{i=0}^{N} \frac{\frac{1}{2} b^2 \cdot MD \cdot (VS_a{}^2/VS) \cdot \eta}{(1 + d)^n} \tag{4.6}$$

where *MD* is the average-deterrence-per-case adjusted for a diminishing effect over time.

Benefit-Cost Analysis

In the previous section the direct and indirect redistribution and allocative-efficiency benefits were estimated. A measure of the costs incurred from enforcing the Celler-Kefauver Act has been estimated elsewhere.[19] The average cost to the government of bringing a successful horizontal merger case was $604,000 in 1979. This measure includes administrative and other overhead expenses as well as litigation costs. The average private expenditure in a horizontal-merger case was estimated as $3,020,000. Thus, the total cost-per-case in 1979 dollars was $3,624,000.

Appendix 4A lists the benefit-cost ratios (in real dollars) based on the distributive gain from each case. Even though the primary motivation behind the antitrust laws appears to be the distributive effect, it should be remembered that a dollar redistributed is not strictly comparable to a dollar of public expenditure. That is, the benefits measured by B_q do not represent an increase in national output; there has been no net increase in production resulting from this redistribution.

A useful interpretation of the benefit-cost ratios in appendix 4A is that they indicate the amount of redistribution benefits accruing from each dollar spent on the case. This provides a guideline for decision makers who must choose a standard for the minimum amount of wealth redistributed from one dollar's worth of enforcement for the case to be economically efficient. For example, suppose that the subjective weight for one dollar of redistributed wealth, α, is 5 percent. Such a criterion states that of each dollar of benefits only five cents represents a gain in social welfare. Thus, for each dollar expended there must be twenty dollars, or $1/\alpha$, redistributed for the case to be economically efficient. Any case with distributive benefits less than twenty times the cost incurred in undertaking that case represents a waste of public resources.

The distribution of benefit-cost ratios over a wide range is shown in table 4-1. This summary information facilitates some evaluation of the economic efficiency of horizontal-merger enforcement. For example, if the subjective weighted value of one dollar redistributed, α, is 10%, then about one-fifth (21.4%) of the cases filed were an undesirable use of government resources, on the sole basis of redistribution benefits. If $\alpha = 2\%$, then almost one-half (45.7%) of the cases were inefficient. If $\alpha = 100\%$, then all of the cases represented an economically desirable public investment.

Table 4-1. The Size Distribution of Benefit-Cost Ratios, Based on the Distributive Effect

Benefit-Cost Ratios	*Number of Cases*	*Percentage*
1–10	15	21.4
11–50	17	24.3
51–100	12	17.1
101–150	10	14.3
151–200	6	8.6
201–250	4	5.7
251–300	4	5.7
301–400	2	2.9
Total	70	100.0

Summing direct and indirect allocative efficiency benefits, $B_f = B_{fd} + B_{fi}$, and then dividing by the average cost of merger enforcement in the appropriate year, yields the benefit-cost ratios shown in appendix 4-B. Total allocative-efficiency benefits exceed the cost of enforcement in 16 of the 59 cases. This implies that 25 percent of the horizontal-merger cases analyzed represented a net gain to society, disregarding all redistribution benefits. The size distribution of benefit-cost ratios based on the allocative efficiency gain is shown in table 4-2.

The appropriate benefit-cost measure for analyzing the effectiveness of a horizontal merger case is $(B_f + \alpha B_q)/C$, where C represents the enforcement costs. The difficulty in evaluating antitrust activity is that the

Table 4-2. The Size Distribution of Benefit-Cost Ratios for the Allocative-Efficiency Gain

Benefit-Cost Ratios	*Number of Cases*	*Percentage*
0.01–.50	31	53
0.51–1.00	13	22
1.09–1.50	8	14
1.51–2.00	2	3
2.01–2.50	1	2
2.51–3.00	3	5
3.01–3.50	1	2
3.51–4.00	0	0
Total	59	101

benefits on which Congress and some economists place primary importance cannot be simply added and compared to the expenditure of resources invested to achieve those benefits — the distributive effect must be subjectively weighted, making the benefit-cost analysis normative.

However, it is possible to indirectly compare the benefits and costs from horizontal merger enforcement. By identifying the minimum value of α that yields a benefit-cost ratio of unity, α^*, an economic evaluation of horizontal-merger enforcement is feasible. That is, α^* is defined as the value of α such that

$$\frac{B_f + \alpha^* B_q}{C} = 1.$$

For all $\alpha > \alpha^*$, the benefits exceed the cost; for all $\alpha < \alpha^*$, the benefits are less than the cost. Thus, α^* is the lower-bound subjective valuation of one dollar redistributed required to render the case economically efficient.

The value of α^* varies from 0.00 in those cases where the allocative-efficiency gain exceeds the cost, to 0.2991 in the *Hat Corporation of America* case. The implication is that if a policymaker is willing to spend at least one dollar for \$3.34 of wealth redistributed, the *Hat Corporation* case was an economically efficient use of public resources; the social welfare gained as a result of the case exceeded the opportunity cost of the resources invested.

Table 4-3 provides a summary evaluation of horizontal merger enforcement.

Given a level of α, the number of economically efficient cases consists of all cases where $\alpha^* < \alpha$. This is shown more clearly in figure 4-1, which is a cumulative-density function for the percentage of economically efficient cases for increasing levels of α^*. The intercept indicates the percentage of cases that were unequivocally economically efficient — 25 percent. Even if redistribution benefits are considered socially worthless, that is $\alpha = 0$, one quarter of the cases still yielded a net social gain on the basis of their allocative-efficiency benefits.

As larger levels of α^* are selected, the greater is the number of efficient horizontal-merger cases. For example, 46 percent of the cases were efficient for $\alpha^* = 0.5$ percent. This means that if \$200 of redistributed wealth is required for every dollar of expense incurred in an antitrust case, about half of the cases were economically efficient. If \$100 of redistribution is required for each dollar spent, 85 percent of the cases represented a net social gain. If \$3.33 of redistribution must occur for a case to be efficient, then all of the horizontal-merger cases analyzed represented an appropriate use of public resources.

Table 4-3. The Size Distribution of α^*

Range of α^*	*Number of Cases*	*Percentage*
0	15	25
.0001–.005	12	20
.006–.010	5	9
.011–.050	12	20
.051–.100	6	10
.101–.150	5	9
.151–.200	0	0
.201–.250	2	3
.251–.300	2	3
Total	59	99

α^* is the minimum of α yielding a benefit-cost ratio of one.

Conclusion

Have the benefits from horizontal-merger enforcement justified the costs? Is the Celler-Kefauver Amendment merely a charade, a futile effort by the antitrust agencies succeeding only in wasting society's resources? The purpose of this paper was to evaluate horizontal-merger enforcement made feasible by the Celler-Kefauver Act and provide some insight into these questions.

The relationship between concentration and price-cost margins estimated by Preston and Collins was used to measure the redistribution of wealth and allocative-efficiency gains from preventing a horizontal merger. The number of economically efficient cases based on these benefits depends upon the normative valuation of a dollar redistributed.

If the distributive effect is highly valued, almost all of the cases represented a net economic gain. If, for example, one dollar of public expenditure is equated with 100 dollars of redistribution, almost 90 percent of the cases were economically efficient.

Of course, to the degree that the distributive effect is discounted, the fewer were the number of economically efficient cases. If one is at odds with congressional intent, the number of economically efficient cases that were undertaken conceivably could be as low as 25 percent. However, if even a low value is placed on the distributive effect, the majority of cases yielded a net economic gain.

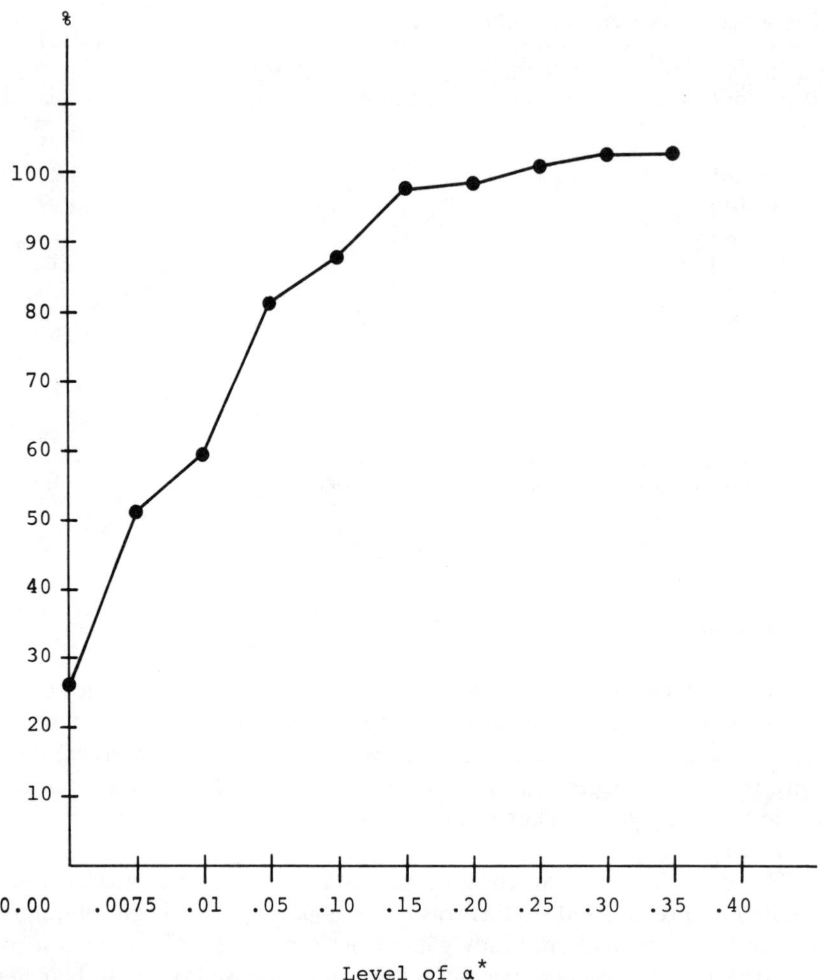

Figure 4-1 Percentage of Economically Efficient Cases for Increasing Levels of α^*

Based on two major social and economic values implicit in the antitrust laws — the redistribution of wealth and allocative efficiency — it appears that horizontal-merger enforcement has been remarkably successful. It can be concluded, therefore, that the Celler-Kefauver Act and its subsequent enforcement have enhanced social and economic welfare in this society.

Appendix 4A
Direct and Indirect Benefits and Benefit-Cost Ratios from Wealth Redistribution (Millions of Dollars)

Date of Complaint	Company Challenged	Direct Benefits B_{qd}	Indirect Benefits B_{qi}	Benefit-Cost Ratio
1954	Crown Zellerbach Corp.	.41	9.36	6.56
1955	Schenley Industries, Inc.	0.00**	109.62	72.12
1955	General Shoe Corp.	0.00**	369.08	242.82
1955	Union Bag and Paper Company	16.20	132.21	97.64
1955	A. G. Spalding and Brothers, Inc.	3.41	60.59	42.11
1956	Scovill Manufacturing	0.00**	4.41	2.81
1956	Vendo Company	0.00**	38.56	24.56
1956	Gulf Oil Corporation	0.00**	550.88	350.88
1956	American Radiator and Standard	24.23	273.23	189.46
1957	National Sugar Refinery Company	20.52	231.37	155.49
1958	National Alfalfa Dehydrating & Milling Co.	1.15	20.38	13.05
1958	Anheuser-Busch	4.69	47.38	31.56
1959	Diebold, Inc.	0.00***	55.09	32.79
1959	National Homes	15.26	154.25	102.73
1960	Simpson Timber Co.	10.56	211.54	132.20
1960	Continental Baking	21.80	220.35	141.61
1961	Koppers Co., Inc.	1.28	10.47	6.87
1961	Kaiser Aluminum and Chemical Corp.	11.72	132.21	84.17
1963	Richfield Oil	0.00*	511.72	293.59

Appendix 4A (continued)

Date of Complaint	Company Challenged	Direct Benefits B_{qd}	Indirect Benefits B_{qi}	Benefit-Cost Ratio
1963	Ingersoll-Rand Co.	15.59	127.25	80.25
1963	High Voltage Engineering Corp.	.87	13.77	8.22
1963	Diamond Alkali Co.	3.13	35.26	21.57
1963	Frito-Lay	25.09	396.63	236.92
1964	American Brake Shoe Co.	4.85	68.31	40.42
1964	Georgia-Pacific Corp.	0.00**	271.03	149.74
1964	Joseph Schlitz Brewing Company	57.68	423.62	265.91
1964	Crown Textile Manufacturing Co., Inc.	3.17	25.89	16.06
1964	Monsanto Company	20.71	209.33	127.09
1964	American Pipe and Construction Co.	1.95	27.54	16.29
1965	Hat Corp. of America	.61	5.51	3.31
1965	Russell Stover Candies	13.65	123.95	10.36
1965	Pennzoil Company	33.21	271.03	164.45
1965	Heff Jones	.79	7.16	4.30
1965	Pittsburgh Brewing Co.	0.00*	163.61	91.90
1965	Dean Foods Company	37.91	427.48	251.56
1966	Schenley Industries, Inc.	6.41	90.34	50.65
1966	Reed Roller Bit Co.	1.82	14.87	8.74
1967	Eversharp Inc.	68.16	688.59	384.14
1967	Cooper Industries, Inc.	0.00*	33.05	1.55
1967	Foremost Dairies, Inc.	30.10	245.69	139.99
1967	Bendix Corporation	12.89	203.82	110.01

Appendix 4A (continued)

Date of Complaint	Company Challenged	Direct Benefits B_{qd}	Indirect Benefits B_{qi}	Benefit-Cost Ratio
1967	Rexall Drug and Chemical Company	49.95	407.65	232.28
1968	Swingline, Inc.	4.54	51.23	27.07
1968	Stanley Works	6.34	100.26	51.75
1968	Vulcan Materials Co.	0.00*	30.30	14.71
1968	Occidental Petroleum	37.76	381.16	203.36
1968	Work Wear Corporation	0.00*	19.28	9.36
1968	Diamond International	24.75	181.79	100.26
1969	Burlington Industries	0.00**	372.94	172.66
1969	Avnet Inc.	5.25	66.11	33.04
1969	Papercraft Corp.	8.30	93.65	47.20
1969	Litton Industries	0.00**	286.45	132.62
1969	Chemetron Corp.	0.00**	137.72	63.76
1969	Iowa Beef Packers, Inc.	24.74	391.12	192.53
1970	P. R. Mallory and Co.	3.00	22.04	10.98
1970	Combustion Engineering	6.92	69.96	32.17
1970	Occidental Petroleum	0.00**	512.84	224.93
1971	North American Rockwell	23.60	266.07	121.20
1971	St. Joe Minerals Corp.	19.20	141.02	67.04
1971	Leggett and Platt, Inc.	1.85	29.20	13.62
1972	United Foam Corp.	2.62	33.05	14.33
1972	Converse Rubber Corp.	20.49	264.42	114.62
1972	Marathon Enterprises	2.03	14.87	6.74
1973	Guardian Industries	0.00*	3.31	2.02
1973	American Technical Industries, Inc.	1.20	8.81	3.79

Appendix 4A (continued)

Date of Complaint	Company Challenged	Direct Benefits B_{qd}	Indirect Benefits B_{qi}	Benefit-Cost Ratio
1973	Goodyear Tire & Rubber Company	40.87	412.46	171.98
1973	Firestone Tire & Rubber Company	21.79	220.35	91.72
1973	Liggett & Meyers, Inc.	12.11	152.59	62.39
1974	Walter Kidde & Co.	0.00**	26.44	9.14
1974	Leggett and Platt, Inc.	.83	10.47	3.91

*Merger did not increase four-firm concentration ratio.
**Merger did not obtain any relief.
***Both of the above.

Appendix 4B
Net Direct and Indirect Allocative Efficiency Benefits and Benefit-Cost Ratios (Millions of Dollars)

Company Challenged	Direct Benefits B_{fd}	Indirect Benefits B_{fi}	Benefit-Cost Ratio
Crown Zellerbach Corp.	.0063	.1422	.98
Schenley Industries, Inc.	0	.1189	.12
General Shoe Corp.	0	1.8135	1.19
Union Bag & Paper Corp.	.0209	.1891	.13
A. G. Spalding & Bros.	.0592	.7397	.53
Vendo Company	0	1.0065	.64
Gulf Oil Corp.	0	.5877	.37
American Radiator & Standard	.2725	2.9825	2.54
National Sugar Refining Company	.1072	1.9152	1.29
National Alfalfa Dehydrating Company	.0108	.1907	.12
Anheuser-Busch	.0780	.7869	.52
Diebold, Inc.	0	1.3263	.79
National Homes	.2680	2.7084	1.77
Simpson Timber Co.	0	1.3425	.79
Continental Baking	.0325	1.4567	.87
Koppers Co., Inc.	.0089	.0836	.05
Kaiser Aluminum	.0198	.2234	.14
Ingersoll-Rand	.0906	.7382	.47
High Voltage Engineering	.0176	.2778	.17
Diamond Alkali Co.	.0649	.7295	.45
Frito-Lay, Inc.	.2171	3.4256	2.05

Appendix 4B (continued)

Company Challenged	Direct Benefits B_{fd}	Indirect Benefits B_{fi}	Benefit-Cost Ratio
American Brake Shoe Co.	.3076	4.3281	2.55
Joseph Schlitz Brewing Co.	.1481	1.0856	.68
Monsanto Company	.2244	2.2647	1.38
American Pipe and Construction	.0432	.6080	.36
Hat Corp. of Amercia	.0017	.0150	.01
Russell Stover Candies	.1246	1.1286	.68
Pennzoil Company	.1377	1.1218	.68
Heff Jones	.0028	.0257	.02
Dean Foods Company	.0992	1.1162	.66
Schenley Industries, Inc.	.0133	.1875	.11
Reed Roller Bit Co.	.0378	.3078	.18
Foremost Dairies, Inc.	.1505	1.2258	.70
Rexall Drug and Chemical Co.	.2091	1.7028	.98
Swingline, Inc.	.0314	.3534	.19
Stanley Works	.1994	3.1468	1.62
Vulcan Materials Co.	0	.0836	.04
Occidental Petroleum	.0931	.9399	.50
Diamond International	.7045	5.1637	2.85
Burlington Industries, Inc.	0	.9818	.45
Avnet, Inc.	.0064	.0802	.04
Papercraft Corp.	.1951	2.1964	1.11
Litton Industries, Inc.	0	3.2358	1.50
Chemetron Corp.	0	1.5113	.70
Iowa Beef Packers, Inc.	.1710	2.6980	1.33

Appendix 4B (continued)

Company Challenged	Direct Benefits B_{fd}	Indirect Benefits B_{fi}	Benefit-Cost Ratio
P. R. Mallory & Co., Inc.	.1203	.8818	.44
Combustion Engineering	.0823	.8301	.40
Occidental Petroleum	0	3.5115	1.47
North American Rockwell	.1915	2.1548	.98
Leggett and Platt, Inc.	.0130	.2058	.09
United Foam Corp.	.0363	.4560	.20
Converse Rubber Corp.	.5657	7.1123	3.08
Marathon Enterprises	.0325	.2385	.11
American Technical Industries	.0070	.0511	.02
Goodyear Tire & Rubber Co.	.2272	2.7970	1.15
Firestone Tire & Rubber Co.	.0482	.4867	.20
Liggett and Myers, Inc.	.0330	.4160	.17
Walter Kidde & Co.	0	.0603	.02
Leggett & Platt, Inc.	.0613	.2055	.08

Notes

1. Harbeson, Robert H., "The Clayton Act: Sleeping Giant of Antitrust?" *American Economic Review*, (March 1958), p. 92.

2. Galbraith, John K., *The New Industrial State*. (Boston: Houghton Mifflin Co., 1967) pp. 187 and 197.

3. Scherer, F. M., "The Posnerian Harvest: Separating Wheat from Chaff," *Yale Law Review* 86 no. 974–1002 (April 1977): p. 977.

4. Bork, Robert H., "Legislative Intent and the Policy of the Sherman Act," *Journal of Law and Economics*, 60 (October 1966): 7–48.

5. Posner, Richard A., *Antitrust Law: An Economic Perspective*. (Chicago: University of Chicago Press, 1976).

6. Bork, p. 16.

7. Weiss, Leonard W., "The Concentration-Profits Relationship and Antitrust," in Harvey J. Goldschmid, H. Michael Mann, and J. Fred Weston, eds., *Industrial Concentration: The New Learning*. (Boston: Little, Brown and Company, 1974).

8. Mueller, Willard F., *The Celler-Kefauver Act: The First 27 Years*, a staff report to the Subcommittee on Monopolies and Commercial Law, 95th Congress, 2nd Sess. December 1978, p. 18.

9. See Weiss.

10. Collins, Norman R. and Lee E. Preston, "Price-Cost Margins and Industry Structure," *Review of Economics and Statistics*, (August 1969): 271–312.

11. Elzinga, Kenneth, "The Antimerger Law: Pyrrhic Victories?" *Journal of Law and Economics*, 12, no. 1 (April 1969): 43–78.

12. American Bar Association, Section of Antitrust Law, *Merger Case Digest*. (Chicago, Illinois: American Bar Association, 1972) p. 627.

13. Mueller, pp. 125–183.

14. U. S. Federal Trade Commission, *Statistical Report: Value of Shipments Data by Product Class for the 1,000 Largest Manufacturing Companies of 1950*. (Washington, D. C.: U. S. Government Printing Office, 1972).

15. Markham, Jesse W., "Mergers: The Adequacy of the New Section 7," in Almarin Phillips, ed., *Perspectives on Antitrust Policy*. (Princeton, N.J.: Princeton University Press, 1965) p. 166.

16. Audretsch, David B., *An Evaluation of Horizontal Merger Enforcement*, Ph.D. Dissertation, University of Wisconsin-Madison, 1980.

17. The structure of deterrence was found to decay gradually over time. This took the form

Years Following Case-Filing Date (n)	*Average Number of Mergers Deterred* (MD)
1	3.60
2	2.52
3	1.80
4	1.24
5	0.86
6	0.60

18. U. S. Bureau of the Census, Census of Manufacturers, 1972, *Special Report Series: Concentration Ratios in Manufacturing, MC 72 (SR)–2*. (Washington D. C.: U. S. Government Printing Office, 1975).

19. Audretsch, pp. 144–186.

5 TOWARD A BROADER CONCEPT OF COMPETITION POLICY

Robert E. Smith

This chapter consists of four parts. First, market power is defined generally and, while three types of market power are identified (long-run, short-run and rival-oriented market power), the focus is exclusively on the first two. In addition, interrelationships between long-run and short-run market power are described. The reach of antitrust policy with respect to the two types of market power is discussed in the second section. This consists of recasting Professor Machlup's argument in order to establish that the reach of antitrust policy with special reference to interfirm coordination in the exercise of the market power is limited. The third part presents a matrix depicting the relevance of antitrust policy to the exercise of the three options associated with short-run market power. The resulting gaps provide an opportunity to relate instruments of persuasion (for instance, incomes policy, administrative guidance) or direct control to antitrust in the development and coordination of a broader concept of competition policy.

Finally, in a partial defense of persuasion and controls, given their

---

Table 5-1 and figures 5-1 and 5-2 were previously presented in Smith, Robert E., "A Theory for the Administered Price Phenomenon," *Journal of Economic Issues* (June, 1979).

generally bad reputation, it is suggested that such policies have usually been applied at the wrong point on the Phillips loop. Logically, the effectiveness of an incomes policy is cyclically sensitive.[1]

Types of Market Power

Market power is defined as a constrained set of conduct options. In this context, types of market power can be differentiated in terms of different sets of conduct options and different constraint systems that determine the nature and the reach of the options. In addition, differences can be identified according to the type of social problems presented, the relevant policy instruments, and the targets. Table 5-1 summarizes the differences in these five dimensions that warrant the identification of long-run, short-run, and rival-oriented market power as distinct types of market power (Smith 1979). The focus here is on the first two types.

Two conditions are necessary for the exercise of long-run market power: the possession of a long-run market-power base and the ability to internalize or coordinate investment decisions and related price and production decisions. Each condition is necessary and neither is sufficient.

The long-run base is represented by the entry conditions of the industry that allow the range of price and profit options. In other words, entry conditions can determine the range of price elasticities of demand over which the industry must operate. Such conditions, for example, can force an industry to price over the inelastic portion of its demand curve.[2] Industries with barrier conditions less complete than blockaded entry are price-range takers. In this sense, barriers to entry, along with the price elasticity of industry demand, are the determinants of the range of price and profit options that characterize the long-run market power base of an industry (Modigliani 1958).

In addition to the possession of a long-run base, the exercise of long-run market power involves investment and related price decisions that must be coordinated if the available price and profit options are to be exploited fully. The constraint system that determines the available coordination or internalization options is described by transaction costs and benefits usually associated with such conduct.

Inability or failure to coordinate critical investment and related decisions can prevent the full realization of the price and profit options allowed by the long-run base. This failure usually manifests itself as excess capacity. Investment may have been rivalrous or herd-like in nature; in any event, it was not orderly.[3]

Table 5-1. The Four Components of Market Power

	Options	*Determinants*	*Social Problem*	*Policy Instrument*	*Target*
Long-run Market Power Base (LRMP)	1. Price level 2. Profit level 3. Price discrimination	1. Barriers to entry 2. Price elasticity of demand	1. Allocation inefficiency 2. Production inefficiency 3. Equity issues	1. Antitrust 2. Direct regulation	1. Buyer
Short-run Market Power Base (SRMP)	1. Stabilize price/ excess capacity 2. Stabilize profit/ increased costs 3. Stabilize price/ decreased costs	1. Nature of product 2. Break-even point	1. Inflation 2. Allocation inefficiency	1. Antitrust 2. Direct regulation 3. Incomes policy	1. Buyer
Internalization as a Facilitator of Market Power	1. Substitution of internal processes for external market processes	1. Nature of transaction costs 2. Benefits	1. Effectuates a. LRMP b. SRMP c. R-OMP	1. Antitrust	1. Buyer 2. Rival 3. Supplier
Internalization as an Additional Power Base: Rival-oriented Market Power (R-OMP)	1. Cross-subsidization 2. Reciprocity 3. The squeeze 4. Tapered integration 5. Ties	1. Form of the firm 2. LRMPB	1. No-problem school 2. Problem school a. Increase barriers to entry b. Foreclosure c. Predation	1. Antitrust	1. Direct effect: rival 2. Direct effect: supplier 3. Indirect effect: buyer

The coordination failure represented by such excess capacity provides a reason for the exercise of short-run market power. Simple observation informs us that firms frequently prefer to stabilize price against excess capacity rather than accept a price decline; that firms prefer to stabilize or protect profit margins against cost increases by raising prices; and that firms prefer to stabilize price against increased productivity.[4] These three stabilization options are the conduct options that identify short-run market power. They represent the options of making more profitable short-run adjustments to changes in demand and costs.

The ability to exercise these short-run options does not exist as uniformly over industries as the desire to exercise them; consequently, it is useful to inquire as to the determinants of that ability (for a fuller discussion, see Smith 1979a). The short-run power base involves the ability to stabilize price against excess capacity and depends upon a product that can efficiently be put into inventory, or upon a relatively low break-even point that facilitates a cutback of production. The latter constraint depends, in turn, upon the long-run power base and the flexibility of the short-run cost function (that is, the cost elasticity of supply). And flexibility is dependent on the significance of fixed to variable costs, as well as upon the addability, adaptability, interruptibility, and convertibility of the basic production-unit in the production process.

Possession of a short-run base is not sufficient to assure effective exercise of such power. Firms must also be able to coordinate the relevant inventory, price, and output decisions. As in the case of long-run market power, firms must possess both the power base and the ability to coordinate the relevant decisions.

If firms find price stabilization against excess capacity more profitable than a price decline, the relevant short-run supply function of the firm and, aggregated, for the industry will be the kinked SRS_m in figure 5-1.

The lower the break-even point and the greater the long-run market power, the longer is the plateau of price stabilization and the more powerful the short-run base. It is simple to demonstrate that price stabilization is the more profitable option[5] when the industry is operating over the inelastic portion of the industry-demand curve: To decrease price is also to decrease total revenue and to increase quantity supplied which, in turn, increases total costs. Operation over the elastic portion of industry demand involves a more complex relationship between price elasticity of demand and cost elasticity of supply.

In a very conventional context, figure 5-1 represents the interrelationship between long-run and short-run market power: long-run market power is represented by the $P_B P_C$ range of price and profit options and

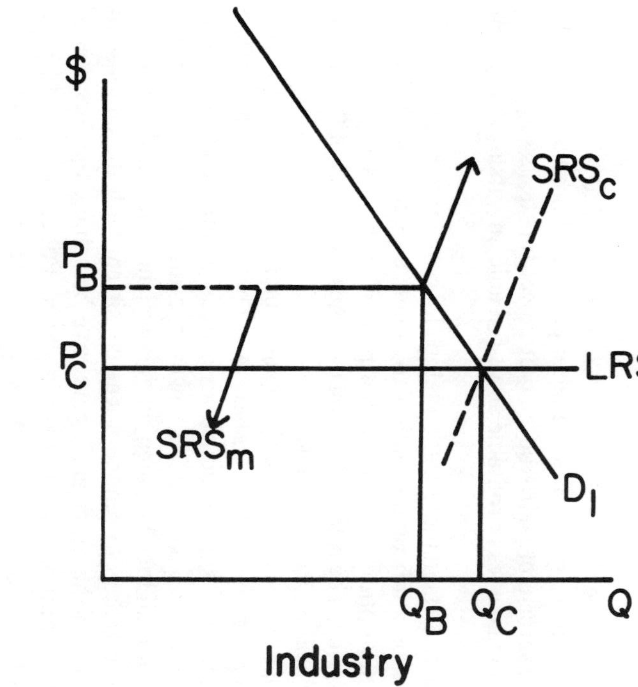

Figure 5-1 Long-run and Short-run Market Power

Key

P_B, Q_M = barrier price and quantity associated with long-run market power

P_C, Q_C = competitive price and quantity

SRS_m = short-run supply curve with short-run market power

SRS_C = short-run supply curve with competition

LRS = long-run supply curve at industry level

$SRATC$ = short-run average total cost curve at firm level

short-run market power by the kinked SRS_m as opposed to SRS_c. Briefly, long-run market power goes to the level of prices and profits and, given that level, the exercise of short-run market power functions to protect it from the need to make less profitable short-run adjustments to changes in demand and costs.

In the context of stagflation or the Phillips loop, the relevant short-run option is a combination of the option to stabilize price against excess capacity and the option to stabilize the margin against rising costs by increasing the price. The relevant option becomes the ability of the firm to increase price against excess capacity.

The third option to stabilize price against increased productivity involves the completed installation of new, more productive, facilities. The increased profitability should induce an increased rate of utilization or attract new entry and expansion. If, however, firms try to stabilize price, they invite a potential race between, in the one lane, entry and expansion the function of which is to reduce prices consistent with the increase in productivity and, in the other lane, collective bargaining the function of which may be to capture that increase for labor. Prices that should have fallen may not fall.

The exercise of short-run market power is capable of making more difficult the control of inflation and, more generally, the development of aggregate-demand policy. To stabilize price against either rising excess capacity or rising productivity is to increase the probability that prices that should have fallen do not fall, or fall more slowly. To stabilize the profit margin against rising costs is to be able to raise, with greater speed and certainty, prices today that would not have gone up until tomorrow. The exercise of short-run market power, however, is probably not a potent initiating force; it is a cost-push, not a demand-pull factor. As such, its exercise is reactive although it contributes to the outward, stagflationary looping as well as to the general upward spiral of prices and costs. Furthermore, it is possible that the difficulties associated with the exercise of short-run market power increase with the gravity of the stagflation condition, thereby reducing its effectiveness.

Professor Friedman has questioned the existence of any relationship between inflation and the exercise of market power. His analysis assumes the existence of only one type of market power: that of the traditional monopolist who is always maximizing profits. The argument is simple: if those with market power are always maximizing their profits, their pricing can contribute to inflation only if and when their market power is increasing. "Insofar as market power has anything to do with possible inflation, what is important is not the level of market power, but whether the market power is growing or not'' (Friedman 1966, p. 57). This argument overlooks the contribution of the distinction between long-run and short-run market power and, in so doing, overlooks the role of the latter with respect to inflation. The critical point is not whether the long-run market base is or is not cyclically sensitive (Friedman's point) but that the use of the short-run market power base, involving stabilization options, can be cyclically sensitive.

Because the determinants of long-run and short-run market power differ significantly, it is possible that an industry might have significant long-run market power and insignificant short-run market power.[6] If such an industry were also cyclically sensitive or tended to experience occasional overinvestment, its profit performance could well lack luster despite its concentrated structure.

The Limited Reach of Antitrust Policy

This section briefly considers the application of antitrust policy to the three components of market power: the two power bases and the ability to internalize. The focus will be primarily on the short-run power base and the ability to coordinate.

With respect to the long-run market power base, antitrust policy focuses on barriers to entry in a variety of ways. These cases involve industrial property, monopolization, certain types of merger cases (excluding the straight horizontal cases)[7], and certain types of predatory or exclusion cases. In these cases the authorities attempt to reduce the effects of barriers to entry or expansion. The issues, however, do not include the relationship between the exercise of market power and inflation.

The short-run market power base is not a recognized category in antitrust law and may not even be one in economics.[8] Nor is it likely that the short-run base will become an operative legal category; it will be difficult to reduce the base because of its technical and relatively objective characteristics. It is likely that the application of antitrust policy to the exercise of short-run market power will have to be limited to the need to coordinate the various stabilization decisions.

The ability to coordinate the relevant decisions is the third component, and it is common to the exercise of both long-run and short-run market power. To strike at either the ability to or the act of coordination is to strike at the exercise of both types of power. Antitrust policy strikes at both the act of coordination (collusion cases) and the structural conditions of the ability to coordinate (merger cases). This has been the major focus of government cases, at least in terms of numbers. To frustrate the ability or act of coordination can be expected to decrease the price and profit implications of the options that would otherwise be allowed by the long-run and short-run bases.[9]

Two recent empirical studies have made some interesting findings that suggest a limited reach of antitrust policy with respect to interfirm coordination. Professors Fraas and Greer concluded in an empirical study of the relationship between market structure and price collusion:

> . . . the evidence indicates that as the number of parties increases and/or as the structural conditions become increasingly complex, conspirators must increasingly resort to arrangements of more elaborate design or greater efficiency if they are to achieve their joint profit maximizing objectives . . . formal cartels arise more often where the structural conditions are not particularly favorable to collusion. (Fraas and Greer 1977, pp. 42–43)

In a study of the profitability of colluding and noncolluding firms in the United States, Professors Asch and Seneca found that collusive firms were consistently less profitable than noncolluders. They offered, in effect, four explanations, one of which is consistent with the analysis given below:

> It may be that, within the range of firm and market structures examined, broadly collusive behavior is the rule, . . . but that antitrust prosecution centers largely on the *unsuccessful* manifestations . . . [because of] the possibility that overt agreement, which is clearly more vulnerable to prosecution, is itself a response to conditions that are not conducive to the success of collusion. (Asch and Seneca 1976, p. 8)

Professor Machlup considered the relationship between the degree of ability to coordinate and the form or forms that coordination might take. In this analysis he differentiated between the "degree of collusion" and the "form of collusion" (1966, p. 439). We interpret the degree of collusion to be the measure of the probable success by which rivals achieve horizontal interfirm coordination[10] and, therefore, to be determined by the transaction costs that characterize the environment of different industries. On the vertical axis of figure 5-2, these various sets of transaction costs are ranked in the ascending order of their respective probability of successful coordination;[11] industries with the most favorable environments would be at the top.

Machlup saw the forms of collusion as ranging from the formal and direct to the informal and indirect — from written agreements, private or with public sanctions, to informal expressions of opinions about the

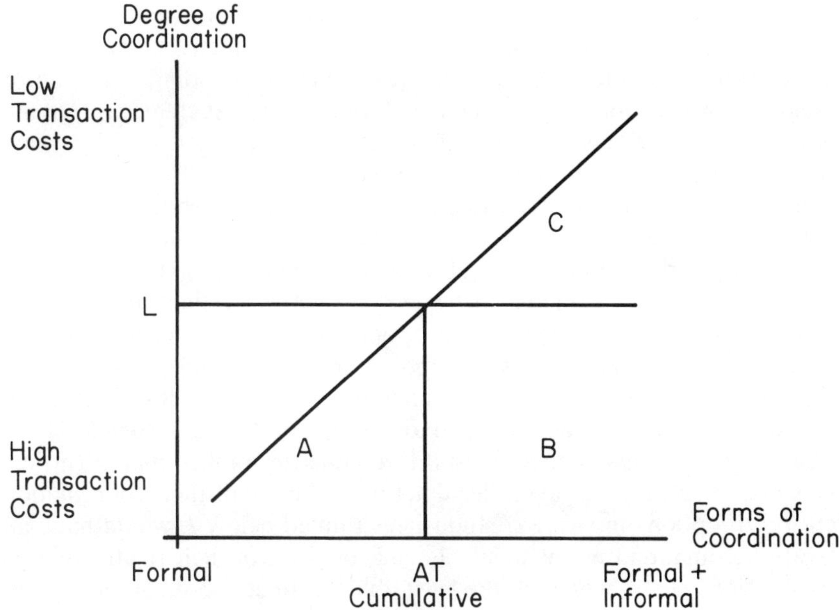

Figure 5-2 Degree and Forms of Coordination

fairness or ethics of certain practices with an implication of compliance (Machlup 1952, pp. 440–442). Accordingly, the forms of coordination are distributed along the horizontal axis of figure 5-2, moving right from the more formal and direct arrangements to the more informal and indirect. It is stressed that this is a distribution of sets of accumulated organizational options; movement to the right retains all previous options and adds the more informal, tacit arrangements. This latter ranking suggests that, when in the same set, these options are effective, though not necessarily perfect, substitutes for one another. It may well be that, within the same set, the more formal and direct options are somewhat more efficient than the more informal and indirect arrangements.

There exists a positive relationship (figure 5-2) between the ranked sets of transaction costs and the sets of accumulated options.[12] This relationship suggests the following two propositions: (1) industries with the least favorable environmental conditions (for example, high transaction costs of agreement) are limited to the most formal and structured organizational options; (2) industries with more favorable environmental conditions (for example, low transaction costs) enjoy a full set of similarly effective options that range from the formal to the informal. These two propositions pose an anomaly with respect to the exercise of horizontal interfirm coordination. Industries most able to coordinate effectively can use the more informal and less direct techniques, thereby avoiding detection or escaping prosecution because the law does not reach such means. On the other hand, those least able to collude effectively are restricted by transaction costs to the more formal and direct techniques. These tend to be more vulnerable legally. The anomaly lies in the tendency for antitrust law to concentrate on those industries least able to coordinate effectively and to fail to reach those more able to coordinate effectively.

This anomaly is depicted in figure 5-2 by the *AT* line; antitrust law holds all accumulated coordination options to the left of *AT* to be illegal. Line *L* indicates that these same options in the accumulated sets to the right of *AT* are also illegal. There remains, however, the less formal and less structured options above *L* and to the right of *AT* that are legal. These legal options are available only to those industries ranked on the vertical axis above *L*; they can avoid legal action if they limit their coordination efforts to options in space *C*. Industries ranked below *L* would have no legal coordination options available and, because of their relatively high transactions costs, would be the least able to effect coordination. Anticipated benefits euphemistically associated with high felt-need may well, however, induce them to try coordination regardless of high transaction costs and legal vulnerability. As long as the favored industries, on the other hand, exercise options in space *C*, antitrust enforcement would seem to concentrate on losers.

A Supplementary Role for Policies of Persuasion

In this section we combine the concept of legal and illegal sets of coordination options with the three stabilization options associated with short-run market power. The purpose is to identify potential gaps in the enforcement process and suggest a possible, supplementary role for policies of persuasion (for instance, incomes policies and administrative guidance) or control. In fact, we have officially utilized three policy instruments for the exercise of short-run market power: antitrust policy, incomes policy, and price controls.

Figure 5-3 forms the three stabilization options in columns and the legal and illegal sets of coordination options in rows. The resulting matrix can be used to compare the reach of antitrust and incomes policies. The former policy applies to all three short-run options as long as the coordination techniques fall within the illegal set;[13] it is equally illegal to agree to

Antitrust Sets \ SRMP Options	Stabilize Price Against		Stabilize Profits Against Increasing Cost
	Excess Capacity	Increasing Productivity	
Illegal Set	Antitrust	Antitrust Incomes	Antitrust Incomes
Legal Set		Incomes	Incomes

Figure 5-3 Matrix of Antitrust and Incomes Policies

raise, lower, or stabilize price. The effective reach of antitrust policy in the exercise of stabilization options decreases as the significance of industries with exempt coordination options increases in the economy.

Incomes policy, on the other hand, applies to a different combination of options and sets. On the basis of U. S. experience, incomes policy has been used primarily to allow a price increase where relative cost increases are due to below-average productivity increases, or to require some cost absorption when cost increases are due to generalized inflationary pressures. The latter function restricts the ability of a firm to stabilize profit margin against a cost increase. A secondary, and quite unsuccessful, function was to force prices to fall in those industries with above-average productivity increases. Such an incomes policy applies to the above two stabilization options whether the coordination efforts belong to the legal or illegal set. Accordingly, a combined antitrust-and-incomes policy covers five of the six possibilities in figure 5-3. Only the short-run option of price stabilization against excess capacity by legal efforts is entirely beyond the purview of the combined policies. And this is, of course, a potentially significant loophole.[14]

The Cyclical Sensitivity of an Incomes Policy

While the previous section suggests a supplemental role for policies of persuasion (and controls) in the exercise of short-run market power,[15] the use of such policies does not enjoy much support among economists. It is worthwhile, however, to point out that such policies may not have been given a fair chance to succeed, because they were usually applied at the wrong point in the stagflation or the Phillips looping process.[16] We shall argue that the probable effectiveness of an incomes policy increases when it is used in conjunction with deflationary macro policies, rather than with expansionary macro policies. In brief, the effectiveness of an incomes policy depends, in part, upon the stage of the Phillips loop at which it is applied — probable effectiveness increases if the authorities apply an incomes policy at the topside, clockwise looping rather than at the bottom of the loop.[17]

We assume these two conditions: (1) the effectiveness of an incomes policy decreases with the passage of time, and (2) the effectiveness of demand management (monetary and fiscal policies) increases with the passage of time. Effectiveness is defined as an increasing probability that the policy will realize expectations. It is expected that an incomes policy will maintain or decrease the rate of inflation, and that an expansionary policy will decrease the unemployment rate and will eventually increase the inflation rate. On the other hand, it is expected that a deflationary demand policy will increase the unemployment rate and will eventually decrease the inflation rate.

At the outset it must be stressed that an incomes policy is only a supplement to, not a substitute for, an appropriate aggregate-demand policy. In addition, it is suggested that the linkage of an incomes policy with a deflationary demand policy is more likely to succeed than the linkage of an incomes policy with an expansionary demand policy. The first linkage could have as its purpose the more efficient and rapid wind down of the economy. The rationale behind the inflationary linkage has been to curb the inflationary impact of an expansionary demand policy. U. S. policy has almost invariably involved an inflationary linkage.

Deflationary Linkage. In figure 5-4, E measures the effectiveness of a policy instrument in terms of the probability of realizing its purpose; Ey measures the effectiveness of an incomes policy and indicates that its capacity to curb price increases declines with time; and EM measures the effectiveness of a deflationary macro policy and indicates that its effectiveness is an increasing function of time — it bites harder as time passes. The net effectiveness (NE) of the deflationary linkage (NF_D) is measured by Ey and Em; it is a horizontal line. At a, for example, Em is pa, which, when added to Ey (or na), gives an NE at a of ma. The horizontal NE_D suggests that a deflationary linkage will have a sustained effectiveness in turning the economy down. The effectiveness of the incomes policy decreases as that of the deflationary macro policy increases. They supplement one another.

Expansionary Linkage. When the authorities, faced with high unemployment, decide to adopt an expansionary macro policy, its effectiveness in

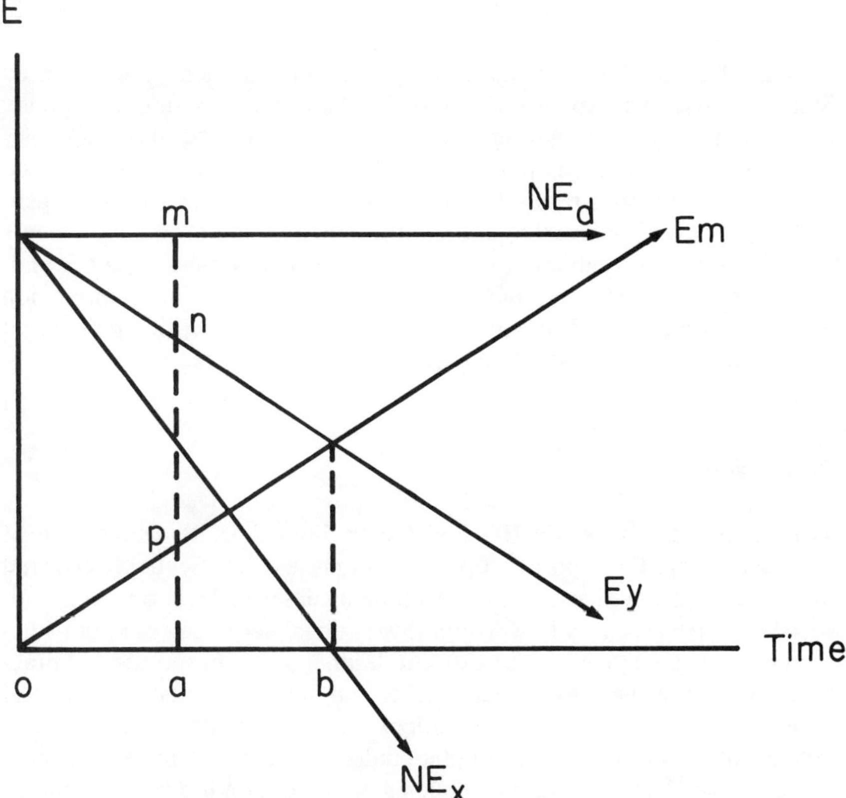

Figure 5-4 Net Effectiveness of Deflationary and Inflationary Linkages

reducing unemployment and increasing inflation is also represented by E_m. It should be stressed, however, that in this linkage E_m indicates the increasing probability of inflation with the passage of time, not of deflation as in the deflationary linkage. The net effectiveness of a linkage of an incomes policy (designed to curb the anticipated effects of an expansionary macro policy) and that macro policy is measured by $E_y - E_m$. The NE_x slopes down and to the right, intersecting the horizontal axis at b. This sloping suggests that incomes policy cannot contain an expansionary macro policy as that policy picks up steam. In this context, a negative NE means rising inflation or even a price explosion. In sum, the incomes policy fails in an expansionary linkage because its effectiveness in curbing inflation decreases when it is needed the most (that is, when the expansionary policy begins to generate inflationary pressure).

With the possible exception of our recent experience, the United States has used an expansionary linkage. The verdict is simple: a policy instrument used at the wrong time is wrong policy. The above analysis suggests that an incomes policy applied at the right time might be good policy; consequently, properly utilized, an incomes policy or, more generally, policies of persuasion and control might be effective supplements to antitrust in the regulation of the use of short-run market power and, consequently, to the use of macro stabilization policies. This combination of micro policies would constitute a broadening of competition policy as it is applied to the exercise of market power.

Conclusion

Two elements can be identified in the traditional U. S. conception of antitrust policy. First, antitrust policy establishes, for effectively covered industries and practices, a fairly well-defined set of legal options; and, second, management is free within this residual set to select options according to its own private interests. Additional policy proposals and practices exist, however, to reduce further this antitrust-constrained set of options. Historically, these practices and proposals have included policies of persuasion (for example, guidelines, administrative guidance) and controls.[18] The function of policies of persuasion has been to induce management to substitute within this residual set of options some public-interest considerations for their private considerations. This has been especially true in the area of inflation control.

These practices and proposals suggest a broadening of our competition policy beyond the traditional boundaries of antitrust policy. When applied to product markets, this broadened concept of competition policy would include antitrust policy, policies of persuasion, and direct controls. If the goal of competition policy is to approximate a competitive solution, such an expanded policy would be arguably more effective.

Policies of persuasion can supplement the negative regulation of antitrust policy in two ways. First, they can reduce further the residual options allowed by antitrust policy, thereby moving closer to a competitive solution. This is usually done by specifying the conduct desired. Second, policies of persuasion can be used in those industrial and conduct areas not effectively reached by conventional antitrust action. In addition, policies of persuasion may be more expeditious in operation.

Notes

1. At this point I would like to emphasize that I am not presenting a full defense of either persuasion or controls as antiinflationary instruments. I am simply trying to present such policies in a different light, and relate them to antitrust policy. It is conceivable that such policies might appear attractive again within the next four years. It is not inconceivable that complex problems require complex solutions.

2. According to this reasoning, sales maximization, in the sense of pricing at unit elasticity of industry demand, is available only to industries with entry conditions allowing the unit point in their set of available options. In the other cases, sales maximization means something else.

3. We have no received body of theory that describes the conditions of efficient coordination as we have for efficient allocation. The closest that we come is the rather suspicious phrase "orderly marketing" — suspicious because it is producer-oriented rather than consumer-oriented. In addition, it should also be noted that excess capacity may also be the result of imperfect information.

4. This last preference is represented by the standard of the 1962 guidelines that required that those industries with above-average productivity gains must reduce prices accordingly.

5. We assume, at this juncture, that entry conditions present a price increase because costs have not increased.

6. The opposite relationship is also possible, for example, the steel industry.

7. Straight horizontal-merger cases are excluded because they are based on a theory of enhanced interfirm coordination rather than on a theory of enhanced barriers to entry.

8. Professors Joskow and Klevorick (1979, p. 225) used the expression "short-run monopoly power" in their analysis of predatory pricing. Arthur Okun used the phrase "short-run market power" in an analysis of inflation (1981, p. 341). This is not to suggest, however, that they view short-run market power in the same way as developed above. Note is made only of their use of the term in specialized contexts.

9. We may be able to test for the antitrust significance of short-run market power (as opposed to the more conventional long-run market power) by charting either the cyclical nature of price-fixing cases or the proportion of cases in which excess capacity is a significant factor. It may well be that antitrust policy is, in fact, more concerned with the exercise of short-run than of long-run market power.

10. Machlup defined the degree of collusion in terms of the "*contents* of the expectations which sellers entertain regarding the behavior of their rivals or the *confidence* with which they entertain these expectations." (Machlup 1952, p. 440. Emphasis in the original.)

11. This assumes given market-power bases.

12. Machlup found no positive correlation between the form and degree of collusion. "Collusion of a relatively high degree may be most informal, based on nothing but tacit understanding. On the other hand, a rather elaborate apparatus is sometimes established to accomplish collusion of a relatively low degree. This lack of positive correlation between form and degree is due chiefly to the presence of other essential variables, especially the number of cooperating firms in the group." (Machlup 1952, p. 440) His conclusion resulted from the fact that he did not accumulate the form options moving toward the right on the horizontal axis. Without accumulation, there could be no positive relationship because, in his terms and consistent with the thrust of his argument, a high degree of collusion was associated with a full range of forms of collusion.

13. This is not to suggest that the Antitrust Division selects and prosecutes collusion

cases explicitly to cope with either the exercise of short-run market power or the associated aggravation of macro stabilization policies. To the extent, however, that challenged coordination efforts are implemented to realize any of the three stabilization options, antitrust policy operates more against the exercise of short-run than of the more conventional long-run market power. This is a fact that can be determined; see note 7.

14. In the context of short-run market power, direct regulation takes the form of direct price controls. Although, theoretically, direct controls can apply to all six possibilities in Figure 5-3, practically speaking, they are usually employed to control price increases.

15. Such policies may also have an indirect or spillover effect on long-run market power.

16. The Phillips curve is generally well-known and, in some quarters, controversial. It assumes that, as expansionary macro policies lower the unemployment rate, inflation increases. A further, though implicit, assumption is that, as macro policies turn deflationary because of concern over inflation, the curve is reversible. In other words, the policy assumption has been that deflationary policies will simply back us down the curve we have just climbed. History, however, has not been that kind. The Phillips curve has not proved to be reversible. Instead, deflationary policies at the end of an expansionary period loop us out and to the right in a clockwise circle. We soon experience continually rising inflation and rising unemployment. We have the worst of both worlds; we have stagflation. This is the Phillips loop. See Phillips 1958, p. 297.)

17. Not all policies of persuasion need be cyclical in nature. Their application should be cyclically sensitive if their purpose is to reduce the Phillips loop. On the other hand, some persuasion policies, such as administrative guidance, serve a more comprehensive set of social purposes.

18. "Competition policy . . . should be carried into effect in accordance with the norms of economic policy used in coherence with the other instruments used to realize these norms. In that regard we pointed to the flexibility required in its application and the necessity of using political means (persuasion in various forms and ways) rather than applying fixed rules in a strict manner." Other "political elements" include "appearing in the form of hearings, recommendations, advice, negative clearances with conditions attached and informal cartel policy." DeGaay Fortman 1966, p. 301.

References

Asch, Peter, and J. J. Seneca, "Is Collusion Profitable?" *The Review of Economics and Statistics* (February, 1976).

De Gaay Fortman, Bastiaan, *Theory of Competition Policy* (Amsterdam: North-Holland Publishing Company, 1966).

Fraas, Arthur G, and Douglas F. Greer. "Market Structure and Price Collusion: An Empirical Analysis," *The Journal of Industrial Economics* (September, 1977).

Friedman, Milton, "Comments," in *Guidelines, Informal Controls, and the Market Place*, George P. Schultz and Robert Z. Aliber, eds., (Chicago: The University of Chicago Press, 1966).

Joskow, Paul L., and Alvin K. Klevorick. "A Framework for Analyzing Predatory Pricing" *The Yale Law Journal*, 89. no. 2 (December, 1979): pp. 213–270.

Machlup, Fritz, *The Economics of Sellers' Competition* (Baltimore, Md.: The Johns Hopkins Press, 1952).

Modigliani, Franco, "New Developments on the Oligopoly Front," *Journal of Political Economy* (June, 1958).

Okun, Arthur, *Prices and Quantities* (Washington, D. C.: The Brookings Institution, 1981).

Phillips, A. W., "The Relation between Unemployment and the Rate of Change of Money Wage Rates in the United Kingdom, 1861–1957," Economica (November, 1958).

Smith, Robert E., "A Theory for the Administered Price Phenomenon," *Journal of Economic Issues* (June, 1979).

Smith, Robert E., "Economic and Political Characteristics of Cartel and Cartel-like Practices," in Schacter, Oscar and Hellawell, Robert, Editors, *Competition in Internal Business*, Columbia University Center for Law and Economic Studies, Columbia University Press, New York (1981), pp. 179–239.

II CONCENTRATION AND BEHAVIOR

6 The Notion of a Critical Region of Concentration: Theory and Evidence

Ralph M. Bradburd
and
A. Mead Over, Jr.

In the thirty years since Joe Bain's seminal study (1951), many economists have attempted to determine whether or not there exists a critical level of market concentration at which a discontinuity occurs in the relation between industry concentration and profitability. In this chapter we develop and test a more general model, based on organization costs, that posits the existence of two critical levels of market concentration: one at which an existing cooperative equilibrium will break down, and one at which a cooperative equilibrium will be attainable for the first time in a previously competitive industry. We show that the standard critical-level-of-concentration model can be regarded as a special case of our more general model, and also that there is a statistically significant difference in fit, in favor of the more general model.

We begin with a brief review of some of the previous literature in this area, and then develop an analytical model predicting two critical levels of concentration. We present the specification and estimation of the model

---

A version of this chapter previously appeared in *The Review of Economics and Statistics* and appears here with the permission of the North-Holland Publishing Company.

and we interpret our results as well as present conclusions and some policy implications of our findings.

Previous Empirical Research

For the most part, studies of the relation between concentration and profitability have focused on three issues. Is the relation positive? Is the relation a continuous one? If not, what is the level of concentration at which a discontinuity occurs? Because there is such an abundance of these studies, and because several excellent survey articles have been written on the topic,[1] we do not attempt a detailed review of previous studies, but instead confine our discussion to a general review of methodology and of the results of a few of the better known or more recent studies.

Bain (1951) found that rates of return were significantly higher in those industries in which the eight-firm–concentration ratio was greater than 0.70. Mann (1966) and Schwartzman (1959) also found evidence of a discontinuous relation between concentration and profitability. Kamerschen (1969), Kilpatrick (1967), and Collins and Preston (1968), on the other hand, all found evidence of a continuous relation between concentration and their respective measures of profitability.

Several further studies of the concentration-profitability relationship have recently been published. Meehan and Duchesneau (1973) and Dalton and Penn (1976) tested both for the existence of a critical level of concentration and for differences in slope of the relationship between the above- and below-critical-level groups. The results of both studies support the hypothesis that the relationship between the concentration ratio and profitability is discontinuous. They also indicate that increases in concentration beyond the critical level do not produce significant increases in profitability. Meehan and Duchesneau find four- and eight-firm critical levels of concentration of 0.55 and 0.70 respectively, while Dalton and Penn find levels of 0.45 and 0.60.

White (1976) and Sant (1978) both used switching-regression techniques to search for a critical level of concentration. White found evidence of a critical point at a concentration level between 0.56 and 0.59; and Sant found a critical level of 0.47.[2]

In another recent study, John Kwoka (1979) used data on the individual market shares of the ten largest firms in each industry to compare the explanatory power of continuous and discontinuous models, and also to investigate the roles of individual market shares of the top four firms in determining price-cost margins. Kwoka found that a discontinuous model performed better than a continuous one, and also that the market share of the third largest firm was negatively related to price-cost margins, a surprising result that was not obtainable from census data because of the confidentiality of market share data.[3]

In sum, the empirical results of these studies can best be described as mixed, with somewhat greater support for the hypothesis of a discontinuous rather than continuous relation between concentration and price or profitability.[4]

As Weiss (1974) points out, the search for a critical level of concentration is consistent with, if not always explicitly motivated by, the oligopoly theory proposed by Chamberlin (1956). Chamberlin maintained that, whatever their number, as long as firms recognize their interdependence and expect rivals to meet their price, the monopoly price will result. When the number of firms becomes just sufficiently large enough that firms no longer expect rivals to react to their actions, the industry price level would drop to one consistent with a more competitive equilibrium.[5]

Bain (1951) was the first to suggest that the drop in profitability might occur discontinuously at a given concentration ratio, and to search empirically for such a concentration ratio. All of the other cited studies have followed Bain's methodology rather closely, searching for the partition of industries at a chosen critical level of concentration that would maximize some function of the ratio of the within-group to the between-group variances in a measure of profitability.

The relevance of this theoretical and empirical work derives almost exclusively from its implications regarding the behavior of individual industries. It implies that a single industry whose concentration ratio increases from below to above the critical level could be expected to experience a discontinuous upward shift in profitability. Conversely, the theory and empirical methodology imply that an industry whose concentration ratio decreases from above to below the critical level could be expected to experience a sudden drop in profitability. However, despite these strong implications for the behavior of individual industries over time, the studies cited above have all used cross-section regression techniques that ignore any motion of given industries over time.[6]

Once one begins to view the concept of a critical level of concentration as a theory of the behavior of individual industries over time, one is troubled by another aspect of the cited studies — their unanimous assumption that the level of concentration at which a monopoly price equilibrium will collapse to a more competitive equilibrium is exactly the same as that at which an industry in competitive equilibrium will abruptly jump to a monopoly price equilibrium. In other words, the traditional studies ignore the possibility that patterns of behavior may exhibit stability.

As an illustration of the problem, imagine that the critical level of concentration is actually 0.5. Suppose that, after years of existence at a profitable monopolistic equilibrium with a concentration ratio above 0.5, a given industry's ratio drops to just below 0.5 and remains there for a few years. If we believe the theory of the critical-level-of-concentration, we would expect that the industry's profitability and prices would fall rather quickly to those consistent with a new more competitive equilibrium. Now suppose that, after a few years at the lower value, the concentration ratio of this same industry increases to a level only marginally greater than 0.5. The standard theory of a critical-level-of-concentration implies that the industry would immediately begin to readjust to the higher levels of price and profit that typify a monopolistic equilibrium. To us, this second adjustment seems quite unlikely.

As an alternative, we suggest that once the industry's concentration ratio decreases below the critical level and its profitability falls to the new lower level, the new equilibrium will exhibit a certain stickiness or stability with respect to marginal changes of the concentration ratio. Thus it is our view that the concentration ratio of the industry described in the example would have to rise appreciably above 0.5 before it would be reasonable to expect that the industry would again exhibit a monopoly equilibrium. Then, once attained, we would expect the new monopoly price equilibrium to also be sticky with respect to small changes in the industry's concentration. In the next section, we develop our theory of stable or sticky industry-equilibria in more detail.[7]

A Simple Model of Sticky Industry-Equilibria

In order to capture the concept of a stable or sticky industry equilibrium, we begin by defining two critical levels of concentration: the *integrative* critical level, at which a previously price-rivalrous industry will achieve a cooperation equilibrium; and the *disintegrative* critical level of concentration, at which a cooperative equilibrium will collapse and price-rivalrous behavior commence.

The integrative critical level of concentration is assumed to be higher than the disintegrative level, and together the two define a critical region of concentration within which industry pricing behavior cannot be predicted solely on the basis of current concentration. Figure 6-1 illustrates our hypothesis. Let us measure the degree of industry cooperation (or the

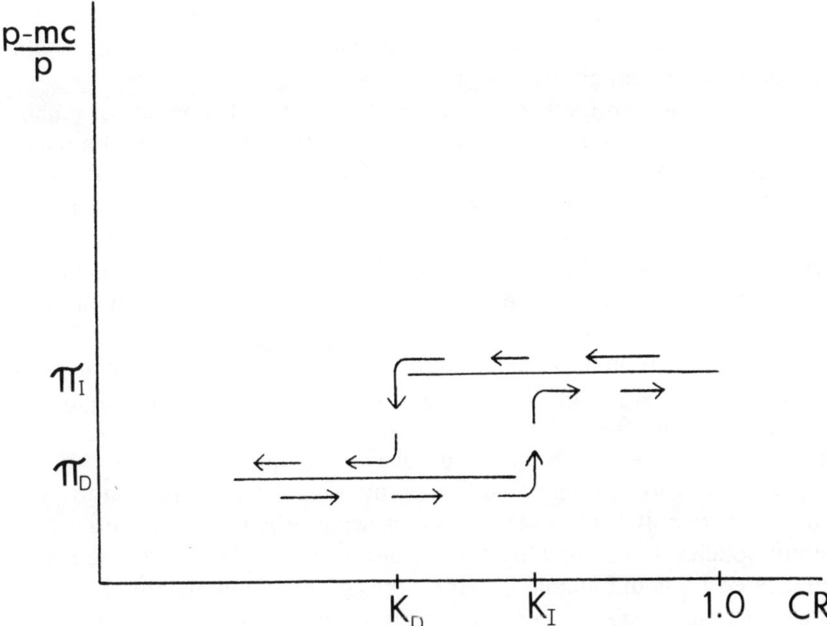

Figure 6-1 Two Critical Levels of Concentration

inverse of the degree of price-rivalry) by a price-cost margin. If concentration is above the integrative critical level, K_I, the level of the price-cost margin will be π_I, which we will view as being close to the joint profit maximizing level; if concentration is below the disintegrative critical level, K_D, the level of the price-cost margin will be π_D, which we will view as being close to the competitive level. For levels of concentration between K_I and K_D, the level of the price-cost margin will depend on whether the industry has arrived at its current position from the direction of a cooperative or price-rivalrous equilibrium.

Our discussion to this point has been purely descriptive. We now attempt to provide a simple model consistent with our hypothesis. In doing so, we draw heavily upon ideas developed by Mancur Olson in *The Logic of Collective Action* (1965).

Let us think of the monopoly price as a collective good that the firms in the industry would like to have provided. The difficulty in providing the good is that it requires organization where the term implies, at the very least, a willingness of member firms not to engage in self-interested behavior to the extent that the collective good will cease to be provided.[8]

The need for organization exists because, while all group members benefit from the provision of the collective good, each individual member would benefit most by being a free rider.

Assuming that an industry desires to be organized, how can it implement its desire? It is useful to divide the costs of organization into those costs that are incurred in the formation of an organization and those that are incurred in maintaining it. The costs that must be incurred in forming an organization arise from the necessity of determining how the costs and benefits of providing the collective good are to be apportioned, and from the necessity of establishing channels of communication and ground rules of behavior. Because organization tends to be a lumpy good, these initial costs of organization may be quite substantial; and the greater the number of members in the group, the greater will be the costs of establishing the organization, and the higher hurdle that must be overcome before any of the collective good can be attained (Olson 1965, pp.47–48).

There are also costs involved in maintaining the organization to provide the monopoly price — that is, of ensuring adherence to the price and output policies agreed to when the organization was formed. These maintenance costs would encompass the expense of communication between firms, of policing agreements, or simply of maintaining a marketing department that must compete vigorously without ruining the market. Maintenance costs would also be expected to increase with the number of firms. We will assume that the costs of both forming and maintaining the organization to provide the monopoly price increase at an increasing rate with the number of firms.[9]

To relate these notions of organizational formation and maintenance costs to our theory of separate integrative and disintegrative critical levels of concentration, we must also assume that the formation costs of admitting one new member to an existing industry organization with N members are lower than the costs of forming an $(N + 1)$-member organization *de novo*. This appears to be a relatively mild assumption: the organization rules are already established, and presumably all that is required is the accommodation of the new member. An industry with a very high level of organization might even have existing rules to handle such a contingency. For the sake of simplicity, we will assume in our analysis below that the formation costs of admitting a new member to an existing organization are not just lower, but are zero. This does not alter the qualitative results of the model.

Finally, let us assume that industries are composed of identical representative firms, and that each shares equally in the benefits and costs of providing the collective good, monopoly price. Together the assumptions made above imply that the level of market concentration that must exist before a currently unorganized industry can establish and maintain a monopoly price will be greater than the level to which market concentration can fall in a currently organized industry before the organization will disintegrate and price rivalry resume; in effect, that we have sticky equilibria.[10]

Let B_1 equal the net benefit that a representative industry member would receive, during the relevant decision period, from the establishment and maintenance of an industry organization to provide the monopoly price. Then

$$B_1 = \Pi^*/N - [O(N) + M(N)]/N, \tag{6.1}$$

where Π^* = the difference between total industry profits under a cooperative equilibrium and under a rivalrous equilibrium;

N = the number of equal-sized firms in the industry;

$O(N)$ = the costs of establishing an organization, assumed to be a function of N, with $O(N) = O$ for $N = 1$, $O'(N)$ and $O''(N) > 0$ and continuous;

$M(N)$ = the costs of maintaining an existing organization, with $M(N) = 0$ for $N = 1$, $M'(N)$ and $M''(N) > 0$ and continuous;

and all variables are defined over the decision period.

Let B_2 equal the net benefit that a representative industry member would receive from the maintenance of an existing organization; then

$$B_2 = \Pi^*/N - M(N)/N. \tag{6.2}$$

If we assume that each firm acts in its own rational self-interest, then a currently organized industry will continue to provide its collectively desired good, the monopoly price, as long as it is in the interest of each firm to do so; that is, so long as B_2 is positive. Similarly, a currently unorganized industry will be able to provide the collective good if and only if B_1 is positive for each firm.

Figure 6-2 displays the relationships between B_1, B_2, $M(N)$, $O(N)$, and Π^*. Our assumptions ensure that a firm that constitutes an entire industry will receive the entire excess profits resulting from establishing the monopoly price in that industry, Π^*. As N increases, both $O(N)$ and $M(N)$ increase until first their sum and then $M(N)$ alone attain a magnitude sufficient to outweigh any gains from organization. These events are indicated in the upper panel of figure 6-2 by the intersections first of $O(N)$ +

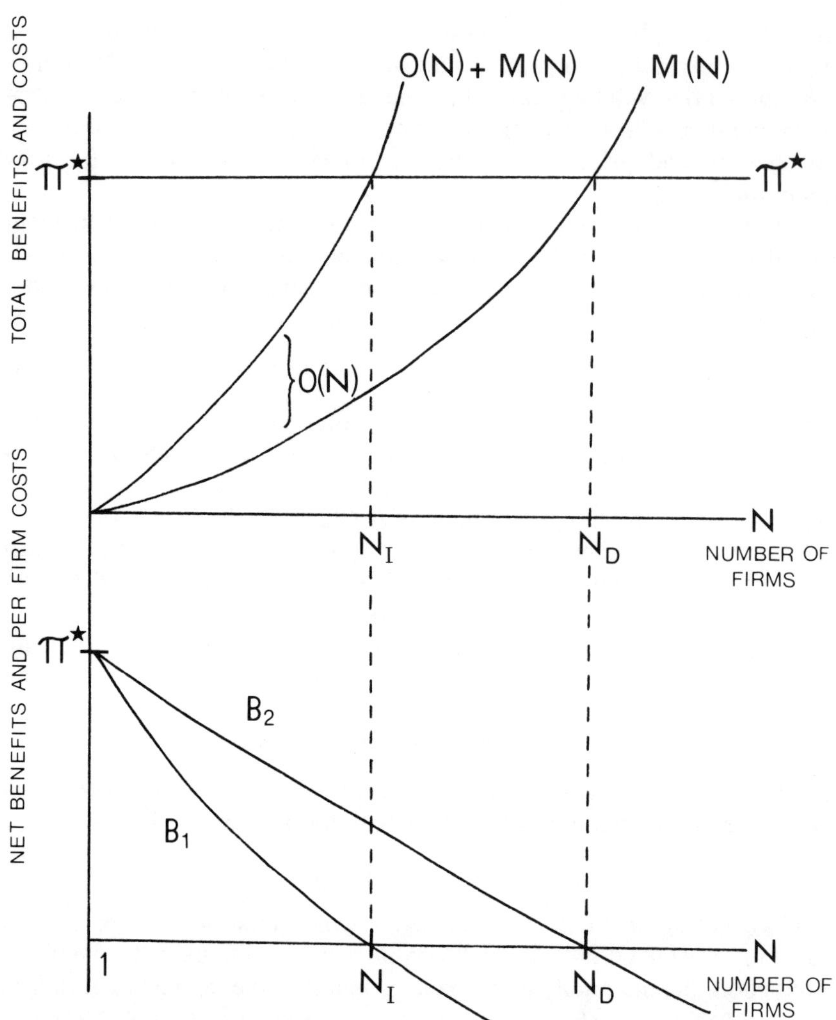

Figure 6-2 Derivation of the Functions B_1 and B_2, Representing Net Average Benefits Per Firm

$M(N)$, with the horizontal line representing Π^* at $N = N_I$, and then of $M(N)$, with the same horizontal line at $N = N_D$. The lower panel depicts the functions B_1 and B_2, which by equations (6.1) and (6.2) must cross the horizontal axis at the same values N_I and N_D defined by the intersections in the upper panel. Our assumptions are sufficient to ensure that the domain of N can be subdivided into three segments, as follows:

Segment 1: $N < N_I$ for $B_1, B_2 > 0$;
Segment 2: $N_I \leqslant N \leqslant N_D$ for $B_1 \leqslant 0 \leqslant B_2$;
Segment 3: $N > N_D$ for $B_1, B_2 < 0$.

Consider the behavior of an industry composed of N identical firms as N increases indefinitely beginning at $N = 1$. For initial small values within segment 1 of N's domain, both B_1 and B_2 are positive, so the industry finds that it is in its interest to organize and to maintain its organization. When N increases to the point that it surpasses N_I but has not yet exceeded N_D (in segment 2), the industry will continue to maintain an existing organization because the profits it obtains from doing so exceed the costs, as indicated by the fact that the B_2 remains positive. But as soon as the number of firms in the industry surpasses N_D (and passes into segment 3), the industry organization will begin to distintegrate because the advantages for each firm of remaining organized are less than the costs of maintaining that organization.

Conversely, suppose an industry which has a great many firms ($N > N_D$) begins to concentrate. As N decreases, it eventually drops below the value N_D at which B_2 becomes positive for the first time. However, the industry does not yet organize because in segment 2 the costs of so doing are still less than the expected benefits. Not until N decreases below N_I and B_1 becomes positive does the industry find that the benefits are worth the costs; at this point it organizes and begins to share any excess profits so gained.

Thus our model predicts that there will be, in general, two separate critical numbers of firms, N_I and N_D, at each of which a discontinuity can occur in the relationship between N and the degree of industry organization. An industry crossing one of the critical numbers is predicted to change its behavior only if it is moving in the appropriate direction.

To convert these predictions about the impact of the number of firms in an industry to predictions about the impact of the four-firm-concentration ratio, note that our assumption of equal-sized representative firms allows us to transform values of N into values of the four-firm concentration ratio according to $K = 4/N$. Thus, corresponding to N_I and N_D we can define two critical levels of the concentration ratio $K_I = 4/N_I$ and $K_D = 4/N_D$.

It follows that, for values of the concentration ratio in the interval $K_D < K < K_I$, B_1 will be negative and B_2 positive, and thus an existing organization to provide monopoly pricing will be maintained, while at the same time it would be impossible to form a new organization to provide that same collective good. This is precisely the story that is depicted in figure 6-1, and the hypothesis to be tested.

Specification of a Model with Two Critical Levels

Let Y_i represent the price-cost margin of industry i. The theory presented in the previous section suggests that Y_i is a function of a set of independent variables including a dichotomous variable that we call D_i which determines whether industry i is on the upper or lower level of the price-cost margin relationship depicted in figure 6-1. In order to focus on the role of D_i, we write the hypothesized structural equation with D_i broken out from the other independent variables as follows:

$$Y_i = \alpha D_i + \beta X_i + \varepsilon_i, \qquad (6.3)$$

where we have assumed the functional form to be linear. In this equation α is a parameter, β is a five-element row vector of parameters, ε_i is a random disturbance term, and X_i is a five-element column vector containing the values of the four independent variables other than D_i, which we suppose to contribute to the explanation of the observed variation of Y_i across a sample of industries.[11]

Our theory and previous theories are alike in positing that the value of the dichotomous variable D_i is a function of the degree of concentration of industry i. To capture the concepts of the integrative and disintegrative critical concentration ratios unique to our model, we specify the dependence of D_i on the concentration ratio CR_i as follows:

$$D_i = \begin{cases} 1 & \text{if } CR_i^t \geqslant K_I \\ 0 & \text{if } CR_i^t < K_D \\ 1 & \text{if } K_D \leqslant CR_i^t < K_I \quad \text{and} \quad CR_i^{t-k} > CR_i^t \\ 0 & \text{if } K_D \leqslant CR_i^t < K_I \quad \text{and} \quad CR_i^{t-k} < CR_i^t, \end{cases} \qquad (6.4)$$

where CR_i^t denotes the concentration of industry i in year t, the period for which the industry's price-cost margin is measured, and CR_i^{t-k} denotes the industry's concentration ratio k years previously, where $(t - k)$ is the date of the earliest available concentration ratio for that industry. We constrain $K_D \leqslant K_I$ and note that when the two critical levels are equal, specification (6.4) reduces to the standard theory of a single critical level of concentration as discussed in the literature reviewed earlier.

The first two lines on the right-hand side of equation (6.4) relate the value of D_i to the values of the two parameters K_D and K_I in an obvious way, reflecting the fact that our theory predicts that an industry, the concentration of which is above the integrative critical level K_I, is likely to be at the higher price-cost margin, and that the industry the concentration ratio of which is below the distintegrative level, K_D, is likely to be at the lower price-cost margin, other things equal.

For industries whose concentration ratios lie in the critical region, we predict the value of D_i by examining the direction of change of the industry's concentration ratio. If that direction is negative, we assume that the industry's concentration ratio is declining from a value that may have been above K_I and we therefore assign D_i the value one to reflect the prediction of our theory that this industry would be expected to retain the high margin that characterizes industries with concentration ratios above K_I. On the other hand, if the direction of change is positive or zero, we assign D_i the value zero according to a parallel argument.

Expression (6.4) is a rather simple and parsimonious specification of the dependency of D_i on the parameters K_D and K_I and on the history of the ith industry's concentration ratio. However, this simplification is achieved at the expense of two minor misrepresentations of our theory of the behavior of industries in the critical region.

First, note that expression (6.4) ignores the history of industry i's concentration ratio in the intervening years between year $t–k$ and year t. Thus expression (6.4) could assign a one to D_i for an industry that should receive a zero according to its more recent history. Fortunately, the sample used to estimate our model contains very few industries whose current concentration ratios are within any reasonable critical region, but whose prior histories include concentration ratios both smaller and larger than the current one to a sufficient degree to generate this problem. Therefore, we ignore this problem in the estimation procedure.

Second, expression (6.4) assigns a value of the dummy to an industry even if its concentration ratio has never been observed outside a given critical region. This practice is in contrast to our model's agnosticism regarding these industries. Rather than discard these observations, we have generalized our model by inferring from an observed decline (rise) in a concentration ratio that prior concentration ratios were even higher (lower) than the earliest observed value of CR_i^{t-k}. Thus we implicitly backcast from the observed change in concentration ratios to prior unobserved values. This leads us to keep the observations in the sample and apply expression (6.4) to them on the assumption that the best guess for the value of D_i for an industry whose concentration ratio is falling (rising) but has never been observed outside the critical region is one (zero).[12]

By substituting specification (6.4) into equation (6.3), we obtain a structural equation that expresses the price-cost margin of industry i as a nonlinear function of the data and the eight parameters, K_D, K_I, α, and β_1 through β_5. Because the function is linear in the remaining parameters once K_D and K_I have been chosen, it is possible to obtain least-squares estimates of all eight parameters by regressing Y_i on D_i and X_i for a large number of possible values of the two critical levels of concentration. The regression that has the smallest sum of squared residuals will provide the least-squares estimates of all eight parameters. Further, if we make the additional assumption that the disturbance term ε_i is normally distributed and that pairs of disturbances are independent, the simple search procedure described above becomes a maximum-likelihood estimation, with all of its desirable asymptotic properties. In the next section we present the results of this estimation procedure.

Test of the Hypothesis of One Critical Level

To estimate our model of the determination of the level of industry price-cost margins, we use data on 310 SIC four-digit industries drawn from the 1972 Census of Manufactures. For our dependent variable, we use the industry price-cost margin (PCM) calculated in the standard fashion as value-added-minus-payroll, divided by the value of shipments.[13] The concentration ratios CR_i^t and CR_i^{t-k}, which are used to define D_i according to specification (6.4), are the four-firm-concentration ratios from the Census of Manufactures from 1947 to 1972.

To control for factors other than the concentration ratio that may influence industry price-cost margins, we include four additional independent variables that have traditionally been thought to be important in this role. These are the capital-output ratio (KO), the Collins and Preston index of geographic dispersion of the industry (GEOG), the growth rate of the industry in the 1967–1972 period (GROW), and the proportion of industry sales going to consumer demand (CONSO).[14]

Since previous studies have never yielded an estimate of a four-firm critical level of concentration outside the interval (0.30, 0.70), we have searched for the minimum sum of squared residuals for pairs of the parameters (K_D, K_I) such that neither of the pair is outside this interval. By allowing the parameter values to vary by 0.02, this decision defines a grid containing 231 individual cells.[15]

Under the assumption that the disturbances are independent normal variables, the log-likelihood of the sample is given by:

$$L = A - (N/2) \log \sum_{i=1}^{N} e_i^2 \tag{6.5}$$

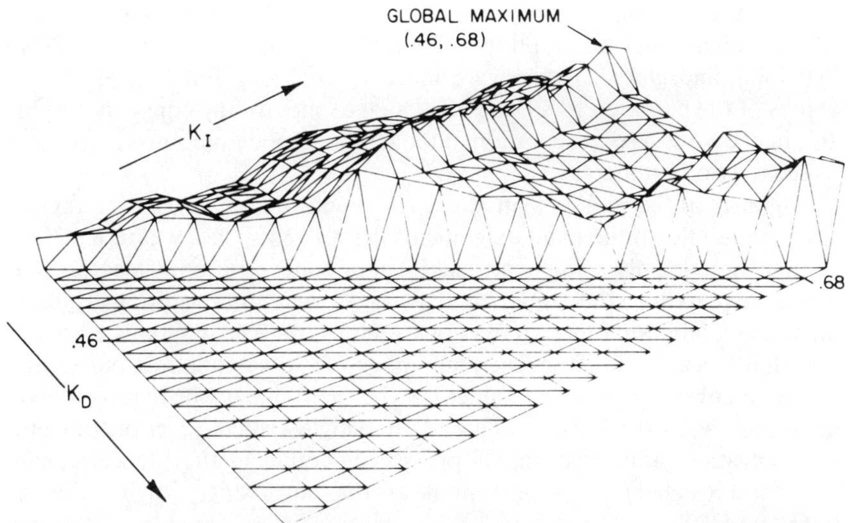

Figure 6-3 The Log-Likelihood Function. Graphics produced with the ASPEX package of the Laboratory for Computer Graphics and Spatial Analysis, Graduate School of Design, Harvard University

where A is a constant for any given sample and e_i is the residual associated with the ith industry and computed using least-squares parameter estimates for given values of K_D and K_I.

In our application the value of the constant A is 449.3 and the second term in equation (6.3) is of the order of magnitude of -100.0. Since it is inconvenient to graph either the large positive numbers corresponding to L or the large negative numbers corresponding to values of the second term of equation (6.5), we substitute for the sum of squared residuals in terms of the coefficient of determination (R^2) to obtain the alternative expression for the log-likelihood:

$$L = A' - (N/2) \log (1 - R^2). \tag{6.6}$$

The constant A' is defined as:

$$A' = -(N/2)\left[1 + \log(2\Pi/N) + \log \sum_{i=1}^{N} (Y_i - \bar{Y})^2 \right], \tag{6.7}$$

and in our sample equals 314.035.

The second term of equation (6.6) assumes values between 21.72 and 32.66. In figure 6-3 we graph this second term (minus a constant = 20 so that local and global maxima are more visible) as a function of chosen values of the parameters K_D and K_I. Thus, except for the constant A' (plus 20), figure 6-3 is a representation of the loglikelihood function with respect to these two parameters.

A glance at figure 6-3 is sufficient to reveal that the best-fitting regressions do not lie on the main diagonal of the K_D, K_I space, where $K_D = K_I$ so that there is only a single critical level of concentration. Closer examination reveals that the values of K_D and K_I which unconditionally maximize the likelihood function over our sample are (0.46, 0.68), a cell of our grid that lies quite far from the main diagonal. If we constrain our search of the likelihood surface to values on the main diagonal, there is a local maximum at (0.46, 0.46), a value of the single critical level of four-firm concentration similar to values previously found in the literature, and a second (higher) local maximum at the surprisingly high value of (0.68, 0.68).

This initial examination supports our more general model against the traditional model of the single critical level of concentration, but any model that allows the data an additional degree of freedom can be expected to fit the data better than a more constrained model. To determine whether the improvement in fit of the general model over the standard model is statistically significant, we compute the value of the generalized likelihood ratio, equal to twice the negative of the logarithm of the ratio of the constrained to the unconstrained likelihood, which is asymptotically distributed as a chi-squared statistic with one degree of freedom (Goldfeld and Quandt 1972, pp. 72–74; Mood, Graybill, and Boes 1974, pp. 440–442). The value of the statistic in the present case is 7.63. Since any value in excess of 6.63 is evidence that the difference between the models is significant at the 99.0 percent-confidence level, this value of the statistic provides strong evidence for rejection of the constraint $K_D = K_I$ in favor of our more general version of the model.

The graphical portrayal in figure 6-3 of the likelihood function conditional on values of K_D and K_I is interesting in itself. Note the pronounced ridge at $K_D = 0.46$, which rises to a peak at (0.46, 0.68). The existence of this ridge lends some confidence to our estimate of the disintegrative critical level. Although it is more difficult to discern from figure 6-3, there is also a ridge at $K_I = 0.68$ that is perpendicular to the first ridge. However, the ridge at $K_I = 0.68$ is highly irregular, with five separate local maxima. The intersection of these two ridges determines the *maximum maximorum*.

Presentation and Interpretation of the Regression Results

The regression equation estimated may be written as:

$$\text{PCM} = \beta_1 + \alpha D + \beta_2\text{KO} + \beta_3\text{GEOG} + \beta_4\text{GROW} + \beta_5\text{CONSO} + \varepsilon, \quad (6.8)$$

where ε is the stochastic error and the independent variables are as described earlier. Theory predicts that β_3 will be negative, and α, β_2, β_4, and β_5 positive.

Because we have estimated regression equations for 231 pairs of K_D and K_I, we will not attempt to provide the complete regression result for each pair. Instead, we will only present the regression results for that K_D, K_I pair (0.46, 0.68) with the highest R^2. We also present a second regression equation that compares the explanatory power of a variable representing our discontinuous model with that of one representing a continuous relation between concentration and price-cost margins. These regression results appear in table 6-1.

Looking first at equation (6.1), we see in table 6-1 that all of the coefficients[16] are significant at the .01 level (one-tailed test) and all have the expected sign. The coefficient of D estimates the impact on the price-cost margin (PCM) of attaining the higher of our two "sticky" equilibria. The magnitude of this estimate is 0.06, which is substantial in relation to the average of 0.27 for the PCM in our sample.[17]

The proportion of sales to consumer demand (CONSO) has a significant positive impact on price-cost margins. This variable does not have an obvious interpretation. It is possible that the positive coefficient reflects higher barriers to entry in consumer-goods industries, or lower elasticities of demand, but it may also reflect the greater advertising to sales ratios in consumer goods industries (Bradburd, 1980) which are not accounted for in calculating the price-cost margin, or a greater degree of oligopsony in producer-goods markets.

In equation (6.2), which attempts to compare the relative explanatory power of our discontinuous variable D and a continuous measure of concentration CR, we see that the coefficient of CR is insignificant at the .01 level. This provides further support for models predicting a discontinuous relation between market concentration and price-cost margins.

It is obviously of interest to know if the price-cost margin is affected by increases in concentration above and below our critical levels of concentration. We attempted to test for the existence of both intercept and slope effects of D assuming a value of one. Unfortunately, the correlation be-

Table 6-1.

Equation	*Dependent Variable*	*Constant*	*D*	*CR*	KO	GEOG	GROW	CONSO	R^2
6.1	PCM	.23	.06		.08	−.04	.05	.05	.19
			(5.33)[a]		(4.35)[a]	(−2.72)[a]	(2.47)[a]	(3.67)[a]	
6.2	PCM	.22	.05	.03	.08	−.04	.05	.05	.19
			(3.09)[a]	(.89)	(4.11)[a]	(−2.81)[a]	(2.45)[a]	(3.56)[a]	

[a]*t*-statistics significant at .01 level, one-tailed test (*t*-statistics are given in parentheses below estimated coefficients)

tween the intercept dummy and the slope dummy is over 0.97, and the multicollinearity is too great to get meaningful results. Not surprisingly, in light of the above, testing a slope dummy in place of *D* yielded results almost identical to those observed with *D* in the equation. Tests for heteroskedasticity were negative for all variables, and we conclude that it is not a significant problem in our study.

Conclusions and Policy Implications

Our empirical results appear to support our hypothesis of separate integrative and disintegrative critical levels of concentration. At the very least, they cast strong doubt on the validity of previous studies that searched for a single critical-concentration ratio. The proposition that industry equilibria are sticky, that patterns of industry behavior at any moment tend to be determined not only by present market structural conditions, but also by previous patterns of behavior and structure, is certainly an appealing one and it seems to be supported by the evidence.

Further work is clearly needed in this area. John Kwoka's recent (1979) paper casts some doubt on the validity of the four-firm concentration ratio as a measure of monopoly power, and instead points to the two-firm concentration ratio — or a discontinuous variant thereof — as a superior measure. Unfortunately, there are no data for us to test our hypothesis of separate critical-concentration levels for two-firm data. Nonetheless, because our results are appealing theoretically, and because they point in essentially the same direction as Kwoka's, we are satisfied that ours are indeed significant results.

The policy implications of our findings may be profound. If our hypothesis is correct, then it provides a rather strong argument for attacking monopoly early. Once industry concentration has been allowed to increase above the integrative critical level, and an industry cooperative equilibrium is allowed to form, it will tend to persist even if concentration subsequently declines substantially, and our results indicate that the impact on price-cost margins is not insignificant.

At the same time, our hypothesis implies that, in order for it to be effective, any dissolution effort would have to be very severe indeed.[18] Depending upon ones' viewpoint, this can be interpreted to mean either that very powerful dissolution efforts are required to eliminate the effects of monopoly; or that the cost of the disruption inherent in such large-scale dissolution activity would outweigh any possible benefits.

Notes

1. Weiss (1974) reviews more than fifty studies in his survey article.

2. The switching regression techniques used by White (1976) and Sant (1978) have the potential advantage over the dummy-variable methods used by Meehan and Duchesneau (1973) and the other cited authors of permitting the analyst to estimate a standard error for the critical level of concentration, as well as estimating the critical level itself. However, this advantage is achieved at the cost of additional computational expense and complexity. For the purpose of this preliminary study, we judged the costs of these more elaborate techniques to be greater than the benefits.

3. However, Kwoka's interpretation of his results is questioned by Scherer (1980, p. 281) who points out that the confounding of price-raising and scale-economies effects in cross-section studies may lead to higher observed correlations for two-firm than four-firm concentration ratios.

4. A common feature of the empirical work reviewed above is the assumption that the degree of concentration of an industry can be treated as an exogenous variable that affects profitability without being, in turn, affected by profitability. We also maintain this assumption in order to generalize the standard model in another direction. However, the possibility of simultaneity between these two variables should be examined more closely.

5. According to Chamberlin (1956) the monopoly equilibrium actually collapses to a Cournot-like equilibrium, which approaches the perfectly competitive equilibrium as the number of firms increases indefinitely.

6. It is worth noting that if we deny the admissibility of the temporal interpretation of the model, the relevance of any findings to public policy seems to be substantially reduced if not entirely eliminated. It is also worth noting that the temporal interpretation is not an idle exercise. Mueller and Hamm (1974) show that there is substantial movement in industry concentration ratios over time.

7. It may be an interesting footnote to intellectual history to guess why this possibility was not considered. It appears that empirical studies of the critical level of concentration are either not based on any formal model at all, as Bain (1951), simply letting the data decide, or they make reference to the Chamberlin model (White 1976, Weiss 1974). Chamberlin's discussion (1956, 48–49) only deals with the conditions leading to the abrupt collapse of a monopoly price-equilibrium, never those leading to an abrupt shift from a competitive to a monopolistic equilibrium.

8. Note that the collective good has at least some properties of nonexcludability but very clearly not the property of nondiminishability; the attempt by any member to increase his share of the monopoly profit deriving from the provision of the collective good must harm other group members when the collective good has already been provided at the group optimal level.

9. Some support for this assumption is provided by the fact that the number of two way communication flows that must occur in an N-firm industry where each firm must communicate with every other firm is $N(N - 1)/2$, and thus, communication costs increase geometrically with the number of firms. (Scherer 1970, pp. 183–84; Phillips 1962, pp. 29–30; Williamson 1965, p. 600).

10. Dropping the assumptions of equal size and equal sharing complicates the analysis, but does not seem to alter the qualitative results.

11. The first element of X_i is the integer 1.0, so that β_1 is the intercept parameter.

12. Work is currently in progress to relax this rather strong assumption without discard-

ing these observations. Our approach is to allow D_i to assume values in the open-unit interval for all industries whose concentration ratios have never been observed to lie outside the critical region, where the exact value of D_i would be determined by the magnitude as well as the direction of the observed change within that region. While this work is methodologically intriguing, we do not expect it to alter appreciably the reported results.

13. Previous studies of the relation between profitability and concentration have often used the price-cost margin as their measure of profitability. See Weiss (1974) for details.

14. Sources and more complete descriptions of these variables may be found in a data appendix available from the authors.

15. A table summarizing the result of the search procedure over these 231 pairs of values for the two critical levels of concentration may be obtained from either of the authors.

16. The statistics presented below the coefficients have the t-distribution conditional on $K_D = .46$ and $K_I = .68$. The conditional t-statistic presented for the coefficient of D_i is larger than the unconditional t-statistic to an unknown degree because our search procedure has in effect chosen the values of D_i which maximize this statistic. However, for the other coefficients the differences between the conditional t-statistics presented and the unconditional ones, could the latter be computed, are unlikely to be important.

17. Descriptive statistics are provided in a data appendix available from the authors.

18. Interestingly, our empirical results seem to indicate that dissolution efforts along the lines suggested by Kaysen and Turner (1959, pp. 98–99, 112–119, 266–270) would be insufficient to have a noticeable effect on industry price-cost margins. Kaysen and Turner proposed a policy of limiting the four-firm concentration ratio from surpassing the level 0.80.

References

Bain, Joe S., "Relation of Profit Rate to Industry Concentration, American Manufacturing, 1936–40," *Quarterly Journal of Economics*, 65 (August 1951): 293–324.

Bradburd, Ralph M., "Advertising and Market Concentration: A Re-examination of Ornstein's Spurious Correlation Hypothesis," *Southern Economic Journal* (October 1980).

Chamberlin, Edward H., *The Theory of Monopolistic Competition*, 7th ed. (Cambridge: Harvard University Press, 1956.)

Collins, Norman and Lee Preston, *Concentration and Price-Cost Margins in Manufacturing Industries*. (Berkeley, Cal.: University of California Press, 1968.)

Dalton, James E. and David W. Penn, "The Concentration-Profitability Relationship: Is There a Critical Concentration Ratio?" *Journal of Industrial Economics* 25 (December 1976): 133–42.

Goldfeld, Stephen M. and Richard E. Quandt. *Nonlinear Methods in Econometrics*. (Amsterdam: North Holland, 1972.)

Kamerschen, David. "The Determination of Profit Rates in 'Oligopolistic' Industries," *Journal of Business*, 42 (July 1969): 293–301.

Kaysen, C. and Donald F. Turner, *Antitrust Policy*. (Cambridge: Harvard University Press, 1959.)

Kilpatrick, Robert W., "The Choice Among Alternative Measures of Industrial Concentration," *Review of Economics and Statistics*, 49 (May 1967): 258–260.

Kwoka, John. "The Effect of Market Share Distribution of Industry Performances," *Review of Economics and Statistics* 61 (February 1979): 101–109.

Mann, H. Michael, "Seller Concentration, Barriers to Entry, and Rates of Return in 30 Industries, 1950–1960," *Review of Economics and Statistics* 43 (August 1966): 296–307.

Meehan, James W. and Thomas D. Duchesneau, "The Critical Level of Concentration: An Empirical Analysis," *Journal of Industrial Economics* 22 (1973): 21–35.

Mood, A. M., F. A. Graybill, and D. C. Boes, *Introduction to the Theory of Statistics*. (New York: McGraw-Hill, 1974.)

Mueller, Willard F. and Larry G. Hamm. "Trends in Industrial Market Concentration, 1947 to 1970." *Review of Economics and Statistics* 56 (November 1974): 511–520.

Olson, Mancur, *The Logic of Collective Action*. (Cambridge: Harvard University Press, 1965.)

Phillips, Almarin, *Market Structure, Organization and Performance*. (Cambridge: Harvard University Press, 1962.)

Sant, Donald T. "A Polynomial Approximation for Switching Regressions with Applications to Market Structure-Performance Studies," Federal Trade Commission staff working paper. (Washington, D. C.: U. S. Federal Trade Commission, February, 1978.)

Scherer, F. M. *Industrial Market Structure and Economic Performance*. 2nd ed. (Chicago: Rand McNally College Publishing Company, 1980.)

Schwartzman, David. "Effect of Monopoly on Price," *Journal of Political Economy* 67 (August 1959): 352–362.

U. S. Bureau of the Census. *1972 Census of Manufactures*. (Washington, D. C.: Government Printing Office 1975.)

Weiss, Leonard W. "The Concentration-Profits Relationship and Antitrust," in Harvey Goldschmid et al., eds., *Industrial Concentration: The New Learning*. (Boston: Little, Brown, & Co., 1974.)

White, Lawrence J., "Searching for the Critical Industrial Concentration Ratio," in Stephen Goldfeld and Richard E. Quandt, eds., *Studies in Non-Linear Estimation* (Cambridge: Ballinger, 1976): 61–75.

Williamson, Oliver F., "A Dynamic Theory of Interfirm Behavior," *Quarterly Journal of Economics* 79 (November 1965): 600.

7 INDUSTRIAL ORGANIZATION AND TECHNOLOGICAL CHANGE: RECENT ECONOMETRIC FINDINGS

Edwin Mansfield

Although economists have long recognized that an industry's market structure influences its rate of technological change, there has been considerable disagreement over the nature of this influence. Some, such as Joseph Schumpeter (1947) and John Kenneth Galbraith (1952), have argued that the rate of technological change will tend to be higher under imperfect competition than under perfect competition. Others, such as John Stuart Mill (1852, IV, p. 351) and J. B. Clark (1907, p. 374), have argued that the opposite is true. In recent years, there have been empirical studies to try to understand better the ways in which the size of a firm and industrial concentration are related to various measures of technological performance, such as research and development (R&D) expenditures, major innovations, and the rate of diffusion of innovations. In the opening sections of this chapter, I shall summarize the principal results of some recent econometric investigations of this sort.

For many years, economists also have recognized that technological change influences market structure, as well as being influenced by it.

The findings presented here are based on research supported by the National Science Foundation. Of course, the foundation is not responsible for the views expressed here.

Clearly, the nature and extent of this influence depends, in part, on how cheaply and quickly firms can imitate an innovation. Yet no information whatsoever is available concerning the costs of imitation and their effects on entry and concentration. I then present a number of findings on this score. Another important topic that has received surprisingly little attention from economists is the patent system. Despite its venerability, its effects continue to be a subject of debate. Some new results pertaining to this topic are also presented.

Size of Firm and R&D Expenditure

There have been many studies of the relationship between a firm's size and its R&D expenditures. In most industries, there is little evidence that the percentage of sales devoted to R&D increases with firm size throughout the full range of firm sizes. Instead, the percentage of sales devoted to R&D generally increases with firm size up to some point, but then decreases with further increases in firm size. Good reviews of the literature on this topic are provided by Kamien and Schwartz (1975) and by Scherer (1980). Based on his summary of about ten recent studies, Scherer concludes as follows:

> By far the most common finding for U. S. industries has been that research and development employment or spending rose either just proportionately or less than proportionately (i.e., exhibiting diminishing returns) with firm size, especially after some size threshold near the bottom range of *Fortune's* 500 industrials listing was reached. This means that the largest firms in any given industry group did not support R and D more intensively relative to their size than did smaller counterparts, and in many instances they provided less intensive support. Chemicals may have been an exception, with the largest companies, and duPont in particular, spending more in relation to sales than medium sized chemical producers.[1] However, this difference appears to have faded over time, for in 1975 there was no indication of a positive correlation between R and D/sales ratios and firm size among the 54 industrial and specialty chemicals producers. . . . (Scherer 1980, p.420)

Although studies of this sort are of considerable interest and use, they focus attention solely on the total amount spent on R&D, not on its composition. This is a very important limitation. As is well known, R&D includes fundamental investigations as well as superficial ones, work directed at major new products and processes, as well as projects aimed at minor modifications of existing processes and products; and long-term and risky projects as well as short-term and safe ones. It is widely recognized that attempts should be made to disaggregate R&D expenditures in studies of this type, but no attempts along this line have been carried out. To make a start in this direction, I obtained data recently from 108 firms (all of which spent over $10 million on R&D in 1976) regarding the composition of their company-financed R&D expenditures in 1977. This sample, which includes firms in twelve industries (metals, chemicals, aerospace, automobiles, petroleum, drugs, food, instruments, soap and cosmetics, machinery, electronics and electrical equipment, and office equipment and computers), accounted for about one-half of all industrial R&D expenditures in the United States in 1976.[2]

An examination of these data shows that, in most industries, increases in size of firm are associated with more than proportional increases in the amount spent on basic research. (The difference from proportionality is statistically significant.) Also, in most industries, increases in size of firm are associated with more than proportional increases in the amount spent on R&D projects lasting five or more years. (However, this tendency does not seem to be statistically significant.) In most industries, increases in size of firm tend to be associated with less than proportional increases in the amount spent on R&D projects aimed at entirely new products and processes. (This difference from proportionality is statistically significant.) There is little consistent tendency for increases in size of firm to be associated with more or less than proportional increases in the amount spent on R&D projects with less than a fifty-fifty estimated chance of success.[3]

Consequently, whereas the biggest firms seem to carry out a disproportionately large share of the basic research (and perhaps the long-term R&D) in most industries, there is no consistent tendency for them to carry out a disproportionately large share of the relatively risky R&D or of the R&D aimed at entirely new products and processes. Instead, they generally seem to carry out a disproportionately small share of the R&D aimed at entirely new products and processes. These results are not contradictory. Basic research is by no means the same thing as R&D aimed at entirely new products and processes. Neither is long-term R&D the same as R&D aimed at entirely new products and processes. Also, since both basic research and applied R&D can be relatively risky, the riskiness of a firm's R&D need not be closely correlated with the percentage of its R&D devoted to basic research.

When industry is held constant, the coefficients of determination between a firm's sales and these characteristics of its R&D expenditures are only about 0.4. Thus, one cannot predict the composition of a firm's R&D expenditures very well on the basis of its size alone. While a firm's size does seem to have an effect on the composition of its R&D expenditures, it is, of course, only one of many relevant variables. With a firm's size held constant, there is still considerable variation among firms in the same industry regarding the composition of their R&D expenditures. Some of the factors responsible for this variation are discussed in Mansfield (1981).

Concentration and R&D Expenditure

Some leading economists argue that industries composed of a few big firms will tend to have rapid rates of technological change (Galbraith 1952, p. 91). One reason why a relatively high level of industrial concentration might promote technological change is that it might lead to relatively large amounts of R&D spending. In fact, although the results of empirical studies of this topic have not been entirely consistent, some of the best-known studies have concluded that, while there is a relationship between an industry's concentration level and its R&D spending, this relationship is not linear.

According to Scherer,

> the available empirical evidence suggests a very crude generalization. In the study of 56 manufacturing industries, tests were conducted to determine whether there was a nonlinear pattern in the ratio of scientific and engineering effort to total employment in the low (traditional) and intermediate (general and mechanical) technological opportunity fields. Each revealed that below a four-firm concentration ratio of 10 to 14, virtually no scientific and engineering effort takes place. The maximum intensity of scientific and engineering employment occurred between concentration levels of 50 and 55, implying that a modest degree of oligopoly is beneficial in fields of limited technological opportunity. Concentration in excess of this magnitude appears on average to be unnecessary for, and perhaps detrimental to, the vigorous exploitation of opportunities for technical advance. (1980, p. 437)

Another reason why a relatively high level of industrial concentration might promote technological change is that it might lead to a larger share of R&D spending going for relatively basic, long-term, technically ambitious, and risky projects. At present, nothing is known about whether or not this is true. To help fill this major gap, I correlated an industry's four-firm-concentration level with four characteristics of its R&D portfolio: (1) the percentage of its R&D expenditures going for basic research, (2) the percentage of its R&D projects lasting five or more years, (3) the percentage of its R&D expenditures aimed at entirely new products and processes, and (4) the percentage of its R&D expenditures going for projects with less than a fifty-fifty estimated chance of success. The results provide little or no indication that more concentrated industries tend to devote a larger percentage of R&D expenditures to basic research and to relatively long-term, ambitious and risky projects.

Instead, the results show that more concentrated industries devote a smaller, not larger, percentage of R&D expenditures to basic research. Moreover, the difference in this regard between more and less concentrated industries is statistically significant and quantitatively quite large. More concentrated industries also tend to devote a relatively small, not large, proportion of their R&D expenditures to long-term projects and to projects aimed at entirely new products and processes, but these relationships are far from statistically significant. While there is a positive correlation between an industry's concentration level and the proportion of its R&D expenditures going for relatively risky projects, this correlation too is far from statistically significant.

Size of Firm and Innovation

A classic issue of public policy has centered on the size of innovating firms. Schumpeter argued many years ago that the largest firms tend to carry out a disproportionately large share of the major innovations. Some evidence bearing on this issue was presented in the 1960s regarding the iron and steel, bituminous coal, and petroleum industries. The results indicated that, in two of the three industries (coal and petroleum), the four largest firms introduced a disproportionately large share of the innovations, while in the third (steel) the largest four firms introduced a disproportionately small share of the innovations. In this context, a disproportionately large (small) share was defined to be one that was bigger (smaller) than the market share of these firms. However, when the full range of firm sizes was studied, it was found that in all three industries the biggest few firms did not do the most innovating relative to their size. Instead, the sixth-largest firm seemed to do the most innovating (relative to its size) in petroleum and coal, and relatively small firms seemed to do the most innovating (relative to their size) in steel (Mansfield 1968).

In 1971, a similar study of the ethical drug industry was presented in Mansfield, et al. (1971). This study concluded that, if innovations are not weighted by importance, the four largest firms do a relatively small share of the innovating, but if innovations are weighted by their economic importance, the share of the innovations introduced by the largest four firms was equal to their share of the market. However, when the full range of firm sizes was studied, it was found, as it was in the previous three industries, that the largest few firms did not do the most innovating (relative to their size). Instead, the twelfth largest firm seemed to do the most innovating relative to its size in the pharmaceutical industry. However, in the late 1960s and early 1970s, the largest few drug firms may have increased their share of the industry's innovations. According to Grabowski and Vernon, there has been a noteworthy shift of this kind (Grabowski 1976).

In 1977, Mansfield et al. (1977) made a detailed study of the chemical industry. In the case of process innovations (and developments), there is no evidence that the biggest chemical firms did any more innovating (or developing), relative to their size, than somewhat smaller firms. But with regard to product innovations (and developments), the biggest firm, duPont, turned in a very impressive performance. For its size, it was responsible for the most product innovations (and developments).

Thus, duPont seems to be the only case encountered thus far where the biggest firm in an industry has done the most innovating (relative to its size) — and even in the case of duPont, this is true only for products, not processes. This result is in close accord with previous findings concerning the chemical industry, which indicate that this is the one major industry where the biggest firm has spent more, relative to its size, on R&D, than somewhat smaller firms. It is also in accord with our previous findings that duPont has been regarded by other firms in the industry, and knowledgeable observers outside the industry, as having had the industry's most productive R&D establishment.[4]

An important reason why the chemical industry is the single case where the biggest firm has done the most innovating (relative to its size) is that innovations, and particularly new products, have tended to be particularly expensive in this field, relative to the distribution of firm sizes. For example, the costs of the major synthetic fiber innovations were not too different from the costs of the major cracking innovations in oil, even though the chemical firms tended to be much smaller than the oil firms. The largest firms would be expected to account for a disproportionately large share of the innovations if the advances in technology are such that innovations are very costly relative to the average size of the relevant firms.

However, duPont's innovative performance cannot be attributed to its size alone. In many respects, its size may have been a hindrance rather than a help. Other chemical firms that were close to duPont's size at the beginning of the earlier period that we studied produced few major innovations, while some relatively small firms — like Dow, which was very small in pre-World War II days — did a great deal of innovating (and developing) relative to their size. If duPont is omitted, the other firms among the biggest four in the industry generally accounted for no larger share of the innovations than they did of the industry's assets. It seems likely that much of duPont's success during the period we studied was due to the attitudes of its management and to the quality of its personnel, not to its size.

Clearly, one cannot conclude from these results that the biggest firms — or high levels of concentration — are needed in most parts of the economy to promote rapid technological change. Instead, what they seem to indicate is that, in those industries where the development and introduction of new products and processes require great resources, the largest firms are likely to do a disproportionately large share of the innovating. (Also, they indicate that, just as some small and medium-sized firms have been fortunate and adept in their choice of people and their styles of management, so too have some very large firms, like duPont.) But it is by no means clear that the costs of innovating are so high in most other industries that very large firms are needed. On the contrary, as noted above, the available data seem to indicate that the chemical industry has been the exception, not the rule.[5]

Size of Firm, Concentration, and Diffusion

Neither successful R&D nor successful innovation can insure that a new technology will have its full social and economic effects. Unless the technology is accepted and adopted, it can have little impact. A number of studies have been made of the relationship between an industry's market structure and the rate at which it accepts a major process innovation. Many of these studies have been based on the following simple model (Mansfield 1968): Letting $\lambda_{ij}(t)$ be the proportion of firms in the ith industry not using the jth innovation at time t that introduce it by time $t + 1$, it is assumed that

$$\lambda_{ij}(t) = f_i(P_{ij}(t), \pi_{ij}, S_{ij}, \ldots),$$

where $P_{ij}(t)$ is the proportion of firms in this industry that have introduced it at time t, π_{ij} is the profitability of installing this innovation (compared to the profitability of alternative investments), and S_{ij} is the investment required to install this innovation as a percentage of the average total assets of the firms. In other words, the model assumes that the probability that a nonuser will use the innovation between times t and $(t + 1)$ depends on the proportion of firms already using the innovation, the profitability of using the innovation, and the investment required to install the innovation.

There are good reasons for believing that this probability will increase with increases in $P_{ij}(t)$, the proportion of firms already using the innovation. The larger the proportion of the firms already using the innovation, the less risky it is for a nonuser to begin using it, and the more competitive pressure there may be on a nonuser to begin using it. Also, there tends to be a band wagon effect. Turning to the effects of π_{ij}, it seems eminently reasonable that more profitable innovations will tend to be accepted more rapidly. Also, one would expect that increases in S_{ij}, the investment required to introduce the innovation (as a percent of the average total assets of the firms), would result in a slower rate of diffusion.

If $\lambda_{ij}(t)$ can be approximated adequately by a Taylor's expansion that drops third and higher-order terms, and if the coefficient of $P_{ij}^2(t)$ in the expansion is zero, it can be shown that the growth over time in the number of firms having introduced the innovation should conform to a logistic function. Specifically,

$$P_{ij}(t) = [1 + e^{-(L_{ij} + \phi_{ij}t)}]^{-1}.$$

It can also be shown that the rate of imitation depends only on ϕ_{ij}, and on the basis of our assumptions,

$$\phi_{ij} = b_i + a_1\pi_{ij} + a_2S_{ij} + z_{ij},$$

where the a's and b's are parameters and z_{ij} is a random error term.

This model has been tested against data for dozens of innovations in many industries, the results usually being quite favorable (if the assumptions are reasonably close to being valid). In general, the growth in the number of users of an innovation (or the percent of output or other such indexes, depending on the sort of diffusion measure used) can be approximated by a logistic curve. And there is definite evidence that more profitable innovations and ones requiring smaller investments had higher rates of imitation, the relationship being similar to that predicted in the above equations (Mansfield 1968, Griliches 1957). Moreover, Hsia (1973) has found that this model provides a good fit to data regarding 26 innovations in the plastics, textiles, and electronics industries in Hong Kong, and this model has proved useful in studies of machine tools and of the U. S. aircraft-engine industry (Blackman 1971; Mansfield et al. 1977; Romeo 1975).

One of the factors that seems to affect b_i is the ith industry's concentration level. Based on the results concerning the bituminous coal, iron and steel, brewing, and railroad industries, it appeared that the interindustry differences in b_i were roughly consistent with the hypothesis that rates of diffusion are higher in less concentrated industries. However, there was too little data to warrant a conclusive statement. More recently, a rich body of data has been obtained concerning the diffusion of numerically controlled machine tools in ten industries. These data should help to shed additional light on this important, but rather murky, topic. There has been considerable speculation about the effects of industrial concentration on the rate of diffusion, but little or no agreement has been reached on *a priori* grounds.

Our results seem to indicate that the rate of diffusion is definitely higher in less concentrated industries, at least in the case of numerically controlled machine tools. Both the number of firms in the industry and the inequality of firm sizes have a statistically significant effect on the rate of diffusion, when other factors are held constant. Of course, these results only apply to a single innovation, numerically controlled machine tools, but they are quite consistent with previous results pertaining to other innovations. The fact that innovations tend to spread more rapidly in less concentrated industries is particularly noteworthy, given the common impression that industries composed of a few giant firms tend to be the most technologically progressive.

Turning from the effects of an industry's concentration level to the effects of a firm's size, big firms often tend to introduce an innovation before small firms, holding constant the profitability of the innovation. In some industries, this may be due to the fact that larger firms — although not necessarily the largest ones — tend to be more progressive than smaller firms. But even if the larger firms are not more progressive and do not introduce more than their share of the innovations, one might expect them to be quicker, on the average, to begin using a new technique than smaller firms, for reasons discussed elsewhere (Mansfield, 1968). Thus, there is no contradiction between this finding and the conclusion in the previous section that, in most industries, the largest firms do not seem to introduce more innovations, relative to their size, than somewhat smaller firms. Also, there is no contradiction between this finding and the hypothesis that the rate of diffusion of innovations does not tend to be higher in more highly concentrated industries.

For innovations where the costs of introduction are relatively low compared with the assets of the firms in the industry, this effect of firm size is less likely to show up, since (for one thing) this effect arises partly because bigger firms are better able to finance the large investments required for some innovations, and to take the risks involved. In accordance with this proposition, there is a significant inverse relationship between firm size and the rapidity with which a chemical firm adopts relatively costly innovations, but little or no such relationship for less costly innovations (see Mansfield et al. 1977).

Imitation Costs and Market Structure

In some fields, reverse engineering — which, crudely speaking, involves analyzing and tearing a product apart to see what it consists of and how it is made — is a well developed art. Even if a new product or process is not subject to reverse engineering, it may be possible to invent around the patents on which it is based (if it is patented). Because much of the relevant technology frequently is transferred (more or less involuntarily) to potential imitators, the costs of imitating an innovation frequently are substantially lower than the cost of developing and introducing the innovation itself.

Imitation costs are a very important, if neglected, topic. If imitation costs are substantially below the cost to the innovator of developing and introducing the innovation, there may be little or no incentive for the innovator to carry out the innovation. Also, as pointed out above, imitation costs may affect concentration, since an industry's concentration level may tend to be relatively low if its members' products and processes can be imitated cheaply. But despite the major roles played by imitation costs, little or no attempt has been made to measure these costs or to estimate their effects.

To carry out such a study, we obtained data from firms in the chemical, drug, electronics, and machinery industries concerning the cost and time of imitating (legally) 48 product innovations. Imitation cost is defined to include all costs of developing and introducing the imitative product, including applied research, product specification, pilot-plant or prototype construction, investment in plant and equipment, and manufacturing and marketing startup. (If there was a patent on the innovation, the cost of inventing around it is included.) Imitation time is defined as the length of time elapsing from the beginning of the imitator's applied research (if there was any) on the imitative product to the date of its commercial introduction. Also, in each case, data were obtained from the innovating firm concerning the costs of the innovation, as well as the time it took to bring the innovation to market (from the beginning of applied research to the data of its commercial introduction).

The ratio of the imitation cost to the innovation cost averaged about 0.65, and the ratio of the imitation time to the innovation time averaged about 0.70. As would be expected, there is considerable variation about these averages. In about half of the cases, the ratio of imitation cost to innovation cost was either less than 0.40 or more than 0.90. In about half of the cases, the ratio of imitation time to innovation time was either less than 0.40 or more than 1.00. Products with a relatively high (low) ratio of imitation cost to innovation cost tended to have a relatively high (low) ratio of imitation time to innovation time.[6]

For reasons cited above, we would expect an industry's concentration level to be relatively low if its members' products and processes can be imitated easily and cheaply. For each of the 16 detailed industries included in the sample, we calculated the mean value of the ratio of imitation cost to innovation cost, the mean for the jth industry being denoted by $\bar{C}_j$. Then to estimate the relationship between the mean-imitation cost and the concentration level, we regressed each industry's four-firm-concentration ratio, K_j on $\bar{C}_j$, the result being

$$K_j = \underset{(8.80)}{6.22} + \underset{(12.8)}{61.5}\bar{C}_j.$$

This finding, which seems to be the first empirical evidence regarding the relationship between the ease of imitation and the level of concentration, is entirely consistent with the above hypothesis. Given the large number of factors influencing an industry's concentration level, it is interesting that this relationship is relatively close ($\bar{r}^2 = .60$). Differences among industries in the technology transfer process (including transfers that are both voluntary and involuntary from the innovator's point of view) may be able to explain much more of the interindustry variation in concentration levels than is generally recognized.

The Effects of Patents on Imitation Costs and Innovation

One factor that affects the ratio of imitation cost to innovation cost is whether or not the innovator has patents on the new product. Contrary to popular opinion, patent protection does not make entry impossible, or even unlikely. Within four years of their introduction, 60 percent of the patented successful innovations in our sample were imitated. Nonetheless, patent protection generally increases imitation costs. To obtain information concerning the size of this increase, the firms in our sample were asked to estimate how much the imitation cost for each patented product increased because it was patented. The median-estimated-increase was 11 percent.

Each innovating firm was also asked whether it would have introduced each of its patented innovations in our sample if patent protection had not been available. Although answers to such questions have obvious limitations and must be treated with caution, they should shed some light on this topic, about which so little is known (see Taylor and Silberston 1973). According to the firms, about one-half of the patented innovations in our sample would not have been introduced without patent protection. The bulk of these innovations occurred in the drug industry. Excluding drug innovations, the lack of patent protection would have affected less than one-fourth of the patented innovations in our sample.

To understand why patents frequently are not regarded as crucial, it is important to recognize that they often have only a limited effect on the rate of entry. For about half of the innovations, the firms felt that patents had delayed the entry of imitators by less than a few months. While patents generally increased the imitation costs, they did not increase the costs in these cases enough to have an appreciable effect on the rate of entry. Although patent protection seems to have only a limited effect on entry in about half of the cases, it seems, however, to have a very significant effect in a minority of them. For about 15 percent of the innovations, patent protection was estimated to have delayed by four or more years the time when the first imitator entered the market.

Conclusion

The purpose of this chapter has been to summarize very briefly some of the principal results of several econometric studies that we have been conducting. More detailed reports, which describe the methods, findings, and limitations, appear elsewhere (see Mansfield 1981; Mansfield, Schwartz, and Wagner 1981; Mansfield et al. 1982). At least four general conclusions seem to follow from these studies. First, the role of the largest firms in the innovative process seems to vary enormously from industry to industry. In some industries, like steel, the biggest firms have carried out relatively few major innovations; in other industries, like chemicals, the biggest firm seems to have performed very well (at least up to about 1970). Moreover, the results vary, depending on the type of innovation. For example, the biggest chemical firm seems to have played a much more important role in product innovation than in pure process innovation. The results also can vary substantially, depending on whether one looks at innovations, developments, or the basic concepts underlying innovations, and as stressed earlier, the results vary, depending on whether one looks at basic research, long-term R&D, or R&D aimed at entirely new products and processes. This diversity is strikingly at odds with some of the simple generalizations found frequently in the literature.

Second, our findings do not lend much comfort to those who believe that very high levels of concentration promote rapid technological change. Highly concentrated industries seem to devote a relatively low percentage of their R&D to basic research, long-term R&D, and R&D aimed at entirely new products and processes. (With regard to long-term R&D and R&D aimed at entirely new products and processes, this relationship is not statistically significant.) Highly concentrated industries seem to have lower rates of diffusion than other industries, at least in the case of numerically controlled machine tools. Without question, much more research on this general topic is needed. But bearing in mind the obvious limitations of these findings, it is noteworthy that they point so consistently in the same direction.

Third, innovators routinely seem to introduce new products despite the fact that other firms can imitate these products at about two-thirds (often less) of the cost and time expended by the innovator. In some cases, this is because, although other firms could imitate these products in this way, there are other barriers to entry (for example, lack of a well-known brand name) that discourage potential imitators. But to a greater extent (at least in this sample), it seems to be due to a feeling on the part of the innovators that, even if imitators do begin to appear in a relatively few years, the innovation still will be profitable. As stressed previously, an industry's concentration level seems to be directly related to how costly and time-consuming the imitation of its products is. Much more attention should be devoted to imitation costs, which, despite their importance, have been neglected totally in empirical work.

Fourth, our results also shed new light on the effects of the patent system, which (despite the system's age) are very imperfectly understood. Contrary to the assumption of some economic models, patented innovations are frequently imitated within a few years of their initial introduction. It is by no means true that a patent results in a 17-year monopoly over the relevant innovation. But patents do tend to increase imitation costs, particularly in the drug industry. (As pointed out above, the median-estimated-increase in imitation cost due to patents was 11 percent.) According to the relevant firms, about one-half of the patented innovations in our sample would not have been introduced without patent protection. Excluding drugs, patent protection did not seem essential for the development of at least three-fourths of the patented innovations, according to the firms themselves.

Notes

1. For some evidence that this was the case, see Mansfield (1968). For an interesting early study of the origins of the inventions underlying duPont's innovations, see Mueller (1962).

2. These data were also used in Mansfield (1980a). Albert Link at Auburn University has also begun some work focusing on the composition of R and D expenditures. Based on its title, I assume that his paper at this conference will present some of his findings.

3. For further discussion of these results, see Mansfield (1981).

4. Of course, these results pertain to the past. The data pertaining to innovations relate to the period from 1930 to about 1970. Some observers believe that duPont's lead over its rivals is much smaller now.

5. Kamien and Schwartz (1975), in their review of the literature, stress too that the chemical industry is atypical in this regard.

6. For further discussion of these results, see Mansfield, Schwartz, and Wagner (1981).

References

Blackman, A. W., "The Rate of Innovation in the Commercial Aircraft Jet Engine Market," *Technological Forecasting and Social Change,* 1971.

Clark, J. B., *Essentials of Economic Theory* (New York: 1907).

Galbraith, J. K., *American Capitalism* (Boston: Houghton Mifflin Co., 1952).

Grabowski, H., *Drug Regulation and Innovation* (Washington, D. C.: American Enterprise Institute, 1976).

Griliches, Z., "Hybrid Corn: An Exploration in the Economics of Technological Change," *Econometrica* (October 1957).

Hsia, R., "Technological Change in the Industrial Growth of Hong Kong," in B. Williams (ed.), *Science and Technology in Economic Growth* (New York: Macmillan Co., 1973).

Kamien, M., and N. Schwartz, "Market Structure and Innovation: A Survey," *Journal of Economic Literature* (March, 1975).

Mansfield, E., "Basic Research and Productivity Increase in Manufacturing," *American Economic Review* (December 1980a).

———, "Composition of R and D Expenditures: Relationship to Size of Firm, Concentration, and Innovative Output," *Review of Economics and Statistics* (November 1981).

———, *Industrial Research and Technological Innovation* (New York: W. W.

Norton for the Cowles Foundation for Research in Economics at Yale University, 1968).

Mansfield, E., et al., *Research and Innovation in the Modern Corporation* (New York: W. W. Norton, 1971).

Mansfield, E., et al., *The Production and Application of New Industrial Technology* (New York: W. W. Norton, 1977).

Mansfield, E., et al., *Technology Transfer, Productivity, and Economic Policy* (New York: W. W. Norton, 1982).

Mansfield, E., M. Schwartz, and S. Wagner, ''Imitation Costs and Patents: An Empirical Study,'' *Economic Journal* (December 1981).

Mill, J. S., *Principles of Political Economy* (London: 1852)

Mueller, W., ''The Origin of the Basic Inventions Underlying duPont's Major Product Innovations, 1920 to 1950,'' in *The Rate and Direction of Inventive Activity* (Princeton, N. J.: National Bureau of Economic Research, 1962).

Romeo, A., ''Interindustry and Interfirm Differences in the Rate of Diffusion of an Innovation,'' *Review of Economics and Statistics* (August, 1975).

Scherer, F. M., *Industrial Market Structure and Economic Performance,* Second Edition (Chicago: Rand McNally, 1980).

Schumpeter, J., *Capitalism, Socialism, and Democracy* (New York: Harper & Row, 1947).

Taylor C., and Z. Silberston, *The Economic Impact of the Patent System* (Cambridge: Cambridge University Press, 1973).

8 CONCENTRATION AND PERFORMANCE IN LOCAL RETAIL MARKETS

Peter J. Meyer,
with the assistance of
Katherine M. Garber,
and Barbara A. Pino

Everything you want in a store and a little bit more.

— Safeway advertisement

Since we're neighbors let's be friends.

— Safeway advertisement

Pricing of identical items will be uniform among and within COOP centers.

— COOP sign in monopoly store

The authors acknowledge the assistance of the University of California Santa Cruz Task Force on Instructional Improvement and Committee on Research. We would also like to thank the University of California computer center and William R. Bush for providing computer resources. Daniel Ginsberg and Ray Rabel of the United States Bureau of Labor Statistics were generous in providing us information from the CPI that enabled us to construct our market basket. Thanks also to George Evans and Pauline Andrews of the University of Stirling for their help with the statistical methodology. Jonathan Harris was also very kind to consult on the leasing practices of shopping centers.

Our prices bring you in, our people bring you back.

— Albertson advertisement

If you can find a lower total on [any 25] items at any other supermarket that week, Alpha Beta will refund 10% of the total price of your order in cash.

— Alpha Beta advertisement

If the total amount for the same or comparable items is less at [any] other supermarket, we'll refund you double the difference.

— Lucky advertisement

The connection between market structure and pricing is well established in the industrial organization literature (for a review see Weiss 1974). Relatively little work has been done in downstream industries such as retailing, for reasons that will be discussed below.

There are persuasive reasons to study downstream markets, especially food retailing. A number of authors have pointed to rapidly increasing concentration in the last decade and a half and there has been some discussion of the effects on prices and profits. The losses to consumers from oligopolization may be at least as high in downstream markets as in the markets made by manufacturers. Discrimination is much more severe among local markets that contain different classes of consumers.

This paper will examine the extent to which a high degree of local concentration raises prices and lowers quality. We will present a new geographic definition of the retailing market. Along the way, we will help explain why "the poor pay more."

Literature Review and History

As early as the 1920s and 1930s authors such as Mullen (1924), Faville (1936), and Phillips (1936, 1939) pointed to increasing concentration as chains replaced independents. By and large, those authors praised that development, arguing that economies of scale and better management led to lower prices.

The major political disagreement was over whether these same chains used their oligopsony position to secure pecuniary advantages from suppliers (Phillips 1936). At least at this early stage, there was no fear expressed of higher prices, only of harm to the petit-bourgeois independent operators, who were to be protected by the Robinson-Patman Act.

Thirty years later there was growing concern over the concentration of retail-supermarket chains. The Federal Trade Commission's investigation into the National Tea Company reflected this concern and led to a ten-year ban on mergers by that company. Mori and Gorman (1966) pointed to increased concentration in particular Middle Western markets.

These authors tested the hypothesis that higher concentration caused higher prices by an intercity comparison of prices and concentrations. Their regression of city price-level on the market share held by the largest one, two, three, or four firms, showed the coefficient on concentration to be insignificant. Their hypothesis that higher concentration caused higher prices was rejected (Mori and Gorman 1966, p. 167).

Other authors used the National Food Marketing Commission data to support the observation of a trend to concentration in supermarket retailing. Parker (1976, p. 857), apparently using his own data, points to growing four-firm, eight-firm and twenty-firm concentration ratios in over 200 SMSAs. He also points to substantial growth in the national concentration ratio for marketing (Parker 1976, p. 857). The same author also warns

> . . . significant barriers to entry and significant pecuniary advantages of size to the largest established food chains in local markets. Pecuniary advantages of large size are especially important in newspaper advertising and in procurement. The largest established chains in cities and regions also have advantages in the selection of store sites and, when their market share are high, they have neighborhood pricing strategies available to them that can discourage new entrants. (p. 857)

Parker goes on to an empirical test. He correlates food-chain gross margins and profit rates with market share. He finds a significant relationship, with large food chains losing money in areas where their market shares are very low (p. 857). But, on average, food retailers make long-run-profit rates that are one-and-a-half times the retail-industry average.

Marion, et al. (1979) second Parker's concern over the increasing concentration in food retailing. They point to an average four-firm-concentration ratio of 0.52 in the 194 largest SMSAs. They also use firm-supplied data to confirm a correlation between profit and market share and between price level and four-firm-concentration ratio on an SMSA-by-SMSA basis (Marion, et al. 1979, p. 421).

In summary, there is widespread agreement that concentration is increasing in the food retailing industry and has been doing so for decades. There is debate, however, over whether higher concentration, at least in the ranges observed, leads to higher prices, when markets are defined on an SMSA basis.

The courts have also been paying attention to the issue of the trends in the concentration of food retailing markets. In the often discussed *Von's Grocery Company-Shopping Bag Food Stores* merger case, Justice Black drew the following conclusions:

> The market involved here is the retail grocery market in the Los Angeles area. . . . [T]he number of owners operating single stores in the Los Angeles retail grocery market decreased from 5,365 in 1950 to 3,818 in 1961. By 1963, three years after the merger, the number of single-store owners had dropped still further to 3,590. During roughly the same period from 1953 to 1962, the number of chains with two or more grocery stores increased from 96 to 150. While the grocery business was being concentrated into the hands of fewer and fewer owners, the small companies were continually being absorbed by the larger firms through mergers. *United States* v. *Von's Grocery Company,* 348 U. S. 270 (1966), 272–73

The Court's decision, in one paragraph, expresses a number of themes. The Court sees the metropolitan area as the relevant geographic extent of the market. It is concerned with the disappearance of small firms. A trend to concentration of ownership in larger hands is another concern. Finally, the court concludes:

> It is enough for us that Congress feared that a market marked at the same time by both a continuous decline in the number of small businesses and a large number of mergers would slowly but inevitably gravitate from a market of many small competitors to one dominated by one or a few giants, and competition would thereby be destroyed. *United States* v. *Von's Grocery Company,* 348 U. S. 270 (1966), 278

Compare this view with the dissenting opinion of Justice Stewart:

> The Court makes no effort to appraise the competitive effects of this acquisition in terms of the contemporary economy of the retail food industry in the Los Angeles area. Instead, through a simple exercise in sums, it finds that the number of individual competitors in the market has decreased over the years, and, apparently on the theory that the degree of competition is invariably proportional to the number of competitors, it holds that this historic reduction in the number of competing units is enough under [section] 7 to invalidate a merger within the market . . . . *United States* v. *Von's Grocery Company,* 348 U. S. 270 (1966), 282–83

The purpose of this study is to address the question of concentration, the conduct of food retailers, and price. Our results include a strong positive connection between concentration on the one hand and price and other performance variables on the other, with considerable variation in conduct from store to store. We find the neighborhood, rather than the SMSA used by the court, to be the relevant geographic market in which concentration exerts an influence on the conduct and performance of stores.

Hypotheses

The formal hypotheses include:

1. Price levels are higher in concentrated markets than in unconcentrated ones.
2. Service is poorer in concentrated markets.
3. Prices are identical among competing stores in a market.

In fact, we expected this last hypothesis might be rejected for two reasons. There is some pseudo-random variation from store to store on an item by item basis. (Naden and Johnson [1967] provide an explanation. Consumers compare stores, they argue, not on the basis of the prices of individual items, but on the basis of the total price of a market basket.) But a chain may also have a different overall price level from a chain with which it competes.

Various explanations are suggested. At least some consumers possess imperfect information regarding price and quality. Stores can take advantage of this by using market-segmentation techniques. Some stores cater to price-conscious customers, others to customers with loyalty to an established store, perhaps still others get only those customers who are least aware of price.

These phenomena must be contrasted with another: various chains seem to enter different sorts of markets. Safeway, according to our casual observations, most often seeks out monopoly locations, while Lucky is more often in competitive ones.

Another alternative to the third hypothesis is that some stores respond to local market conditions while others do not. This may be the result of blind central control or perhaps of some segmentation strategy described above.

Methods

We began by collecting very low-level-price data on an item by item, store by store, and neighborhood by neighborhood basis. Our purpose here is twofold.

First, by collecting store-by-store data, we can avoid doing our analysis on an SMSA-by-SMSA basis. Especially in large SMSA's, the relevant geographical area is most often much smaller than an SMSA. The important question is how many stores are accessible at what cost, not how many stores exist in a census metropolitan-statistical area.

Also, we need not rely on management-supplied data, which may be as unreliable as their other claims reported in the introduction. (For example, the prices in monopoly and competitive COOP's were far from equal.) Of course, this method of data collection is more costly, so we were able to survey fewer stores.

Our first task was to construct a survey instrument. In order to construct an unbiased list of product items, we began with the Bureau of Labor Statistic's (BLS) list of survey items for the Consumer Price Index (BLS 1980).

Unfortunately, the BLS's item descriptions were very broad. Therefore, for each four-digit-BLS category, we constructed descriptions of from one to six particular items. An example would be

BLS four-digit category:

1701 nondiet colas

Our five-digit items:

1701.1 cola, returnable bottle, 32 fluid ounces

Coca-Cola brand

1701.2 cola, returnable bottle, 26 fluid ounces

Pepsi-Cola brand

The result was a list of 183 item descriptions. Careful specification of items, sizes, brand, and quality was made to insure precise matching from store to store.

The second step was the collection of price data. Prices were surveyed directly from the items in the store that met the description. Prices were collected within as short a time as possible in various markets to avoid the problems of inflation and changing market conditions. Often, items were priced within a few hours in the stores.

Occasionally, a few days separated price-data collections. But the surveyors were careful to avoid spanning time periods when sales began or ended, or new advertisements were placed in the newspapers.

In addition, prices were surveyed for the least-expensive item that a consumer might accept as a substitute. Our purpose here was to see if competition, where it occurred, was more intense in the name-brand or the generic items.

The survey was replicated in two areas in California: the Santa Cruz-Capitola area and the Berkeley city-Oakland hills area. Within each area, costs faced by managements (such as labor or land and buildings) are very similar. Price differences across stores within each survey area are not due to cost differences, but to differences in market structure and conduct.

However, prices cannot fairly be compared across the two areas, both because of different operating costs and for reasons peculiar to this survey. The two areas were surveyed at different times (but both in the summer of 1980). The weighting system described below was applied separately to each area. Thus, price differences in the two surveys may be due to factors other than market-structure differences.

The second stage, after data collection, was processing. The BLS-relative-importance scheme (BLS 1972) was used to establish weights for the various items. First, the BLS-relative importances for four-digit categories were distributed equally across each of our five-digit items in that category. Then weights were constructed as follows:

$$W5(i,j) = \frac{RI4\ (i)/N4\ (i)}{N5}$$
$$\text{SUM}\ (P5(i,j,k)|P5(i,j,k)\ \text{is known})/N5\ (i,j)$$
$$k=1,$$

where: W5 (i,j) is the weight for item j and i,

RI4 (i) is the BLS relative importance of category i,

N4 (i) is the number of items in category i,

P5 (i,j,k) is the price in store k of item j in category i, where that price is known, that is, where that item is available in store k,

N5 (i,j) is the number of places it is available.

In other words, the weight was arrived at by dividing the share of the relative importance attributed to that item by the average price of the item in all the stores where it was available.

The unavailability of an item in a particular store was noted. Obviously, any test along the lines of a paired t-test of the hypothesis that one store is less expensive than another would have to exclude any item that was not available in both stores. But counts of the number of missing items are useful in evaluating stores.

The relevant statistical tests were paired t-tests. That is, to test if the price was significantly lower in one market than another, a test was performed on the difference in price between the stores. This difference was calculated for each of the 183 items, and then the hypothesis that this difference had a (weighted) mean significantly different from zero was tested.

This paired t-test can be performed on two supermarkets and on the average price prevailing in two market areas (a concentrated and an unconcentrated one, for instance).

The second hypothesis can be tested only informally. The surveyors noted such factors as the cleanliness of the stores, and the helpfulness of the staff.

Results

Concentration and Price

The most important result is a strong, significant price difference between concentrated and unconcentrated markets. The relevant geographical extent of the market is the neighborhood in food retailing. Neighborhoods with a high concentration, with only one or two supermarkets, had significantly higher prices.

We define a neighborhood as an area in which residents are likely to confine their shopping. Neighborhoods were well defined and discrete; there were no stores straddling neighborhood boundaries. Supermarkets were not located every 5, 10, or 20 blocks. Rather, there might be one, two, or three stores on a street, then none for miles.

In the first area studied (Santa Cruz and Capitola, California), there were three different market structures in various neighborhoods. Some neighborhoods had only one supermarket. This structure we label monopoly.

These neighborhoods include the downtown area and the neighborhood closest to the university. These are also the neighborhoods with the highest percentages of the population without automobiles and hence dependent on the local store, strengthening the monopoly power of that store. Both a Safeway and an Albertson were in this position.

The second sort of structure was a concentrated oligopoly. These neighborhoods had either two supermarkets or else one supermarket that was less isolated from nearby markets. For example, one neighborhood in this category had only a Safeway, but immediately across a freeway (a short drive, but not an easy walk) were other supermarkets. In another neighborhood, a Safeway and an Alpha Beta shared the market.

The third sort of structure was an unconcentrated oligopoly. One neighborhood had three supermarkets (an Albertson, an Alpha Beta, and a Lucky) on one long block. On the other side of the freeway was the Safeway mentioned above.

The results of the paired *t*-test (explained previously) were

	Market Structure		
	monopoly	oligopoly: concentrated	oligopoly: unconcentrated
compared to:			
monopoly	—	1.15 (0.25)	4.06 (0.000)
concentrated	1.15 (0.25)	—	3.47 (0.001)
unconcentrated	4.06 (0.000)	3.47 (0.001)	—

(The numbers in parentheses are significances.)

Remember that the above table refers to a typical urban-family market-basket and contains mostly brand name products with some generics. Substituting generic items for the brand names:

monopoly	—	−.71 (0.48)	2.29 (0.023)
concentrated	−.71 (0.48)	—	2.75 (0.007)
unconcentrated	2.29 (0.023)	2.75 (0.007)	—

(The numbers in parentheses are significances.)

In the second area studied, Berkeley and part of the Oakland hills in California, there are two sorts of neighborhood-market structures, monopoly and unconcentrated. Again, an unconcentrated neighborhood was one with three competing supermarkets. For example, a Safeway, a Lucky, and a Consumers' Cooperative are located within two blocks of each other. There were also many monopoly markets, neighborhoods with just one store. For example, a COOP is the only supermarket serving the western half of this city of 100,000.

The results in this city, for the typical market-basket:

	unconcentrated
monopoly	2.44
	(0.016)
for the generic equivalents:	
monopoly	2.14
	(0.034)

The results so far can be summarized easily: prices are higher in monopoly markets than in unconcentrated ones. The price differences between concentrated and unconcentrated oligopoly markets are also significant, while there is no significant difference between monopoly and concentrated oligopoly markets. Thus, prices are higher not just in monopoly markets, but also in concentrated oligopolies.

These results were roughly the same for a typical market basket and for one that contains almost exclusively generic items. Price differences may not be quite so severe for generics; when monopoly and concentrated markets are compared, price differences are totally insignificant.

Another useful source of information is an examination of the prices themselves as shown in table 8-1.

The entries in this table represent the total cost of purchasing one of each item from our market basket available in every store. No weights were applied.

The interpretation of this table is consistent with the results of the weighted t-tests above. In the first region studied, monopoly prices are more than 5 percent higher than prices in unconcentrated markets. On average, brand name items are 5 percent more expensive in a monopoly store than in one of a number of stores in an unconcentrated neighborhood. The differences are less severe, although still substantial, for generic items. In the second city, the price differences are almost 5 percent for the typical market basket, and about 6 percent for the generics.

Of course, these results may be biased by the inclusion of only those

Table 8-1 Price Differences, by Area

	1		2	
	Branded	*Generic*	*Branded*	*Generic*
Monopoly	$202.12	$187.27	$188.09	$177.28
Concentrated oligopoly	198.34	186.03	NA	NA
Unconcentrated oligopoly	192.10	179.83	179.24	167.46

products that are available in all the stores (in order to make the comparison) and the absence of weighting. Another comparison can be made by summing, for each store, weighted, available prices and then dividing the total by the sum of the weights of the available items, regardless of their availability in the other stores:

$$\text{Index}(k) = \frac{\sum_{j=1}^{183} \left[(P5(j,k) \mid P5(j,k) \text{ is known}) * W5(j)\right]}{\sum_{j=1}^{183} \left[W5(j) \mid P5(j,k) \text{ is known}\right]}$$

where Index (k) is the price index for store k,

P5 (j,k) is the price of item j in store k,
W5 (j) is the weight of item j.

For the first city studied, this procedure yields results that indicate basically the same price differences. In the second city, the results are quite different. The use of weighted prices yields quite lower price differences. This indicates that the price differences between monopolists and oligopolists is greatest for the items with the lower weights, that is, the less frequently bought items that are less in the minds of the consumer.

Neighborhood Income and Price

Economists have written about price differences faced by poor and middle-income shoppers. Alexis and Simon (1967), for example, noted the dependence of poor shoppers on independent stores, whose higher prices they attributed to a lack of private-brand merchandise. They also discovered that high-income shoppers paid high prices. Finally, they noted a range of prices faced by each group, but the explanation was not within the scope of their paper.

Kunreuther (1973) also asks "Why the Poor Pay More for Food." His major finding is the dependence of the poor on local stores that victimize immobile consumers. The House Committee on Government Operations published a report with similar conclusions (Committee on Government Operations 1968).

The chains deny the charge: "We do not distinguish between proverty (sic) neighborhood and other stores within the pricing area." (Committee on Government Operations 1968, p. 21)

A study of many more stores is necessary for a definitive test. We observed the highest prices in the most concentrated markets. In our study, these concentrated markets are the lowest- and the highest-income neighborhoods; various chains did business in each. The unconcentrated markets were the middle-income neighborhoods.

It would not be surprising to find poor neighborhoods to be the most concentrated markets. The reluctance of chains to locate in poor neighborhoods is well documented. This reluctance leaves the residents of poor neighborhoods in the grip of the local monopolist: "A result . . . is that many poverty area residents are denied the benefits of meaningful competition; that is, lower prices. . . ." (Committee on Government Operations 1968, p. 48) "Where a semblance of competition does exist in the low-income area, it is frequently intrachain competition."

Variation in Store Location and Response

Our third hypothesis concerned differences in the conduct of the various stores when faced with different local market structures. Two distinct questions are raised: where do stores locate, and how do they respond to neighborhood market-structure.

Because most chains are found in a variety of structures, we can compare the prices charged by the stores of any given chain in a variety of structures. This comparison yields some interesting results: Some chains respond and others do not to different neighborhood market-structures.

The largest chain, Safeway, does respond, with a weighted price index of 99.70 in its monopoly store in the first city and 97.65 and 96.43 in two stores, both in less-concentrated, but far from competitive, areas. The same result was found in the second city.

Other chains respond even more strongly. Alpha Beta had an index of 93.86 for its concentrated oligopoly store and 89.09 for its store in an unconcentrated oligopoly structure. The COOP, had an unweighted total market-basket cost of $184.84 in its store in a competitive market, and $188.82 in its monopoly store. Their claim is false: "Pricing of identical items will be uniform among and within COOP centers," (COOP sign in monopoly store).

But not all chains respond. Albertson showed the least response. This chain had weighted indexes, within 0.2 percent for the typical basket in its monopoly store and its store in the unconcentrated market. The weighted generic index and total-basket costs were also very close. In their own words; "Our prices bring you in, our people bring you back." (Albertson advertisement).

Most chains locate in a variety of structures. For example, Safeway was found in the monopoly and concentrated oligopoly sectors of the first city, and in the monopoly and unconcentrated sectors of the second. Similarly, Albertson was found in both the monopoly and unconcentrated sectors in the first city, as was COOP in the second. Alpha Beta was in concentrated and unconcentrated sectors, and so on.

One store was only in competitivc locations in both cities. This store (Lucky) often seemed to precipitate the competitive conduct among neighboring stores. The same chain also had the lowest prices, brands and generics, of all the chains, with one exception. That exception was the store (an Alpha Beta) across the street in the competitive neighborhood in the first city. Elsewhere, Alpha Beta was more expensive.

Ironically, both chains claim to be the cheapest in all their locations:

> If the total amount for the same or comparable item is less at [any] other supermarket, we'll refund you double the difference. Lucky advertisement.

> If you can find a lower total on [any 25] items at any other supermarket that week, Alpha Beta will refund 10% of the total price of your order in cash. Alpha Beta advertisement

Another store, Safeway, seems to seek out monopolistic locations for its newer stores, with at least one monopoly store in each city studied. In the words of their own advertisement:

> Since we're neighbors let's be friends. Safeway advertisement.

A more geographically wide-ranging study is called for to establish statistically the location patterns of the various chains.

Nonprice Performance

The second hypothesis dealt with aspects of conduct other than pricing. An economist might expect a trade-off offered the sovereign consumer between low price and high levels of service. We observed that the (expensive) stores in monopoly locations also offered the lowest level of service. These stores were able to use their market power both to charge higher prices and to offer lower-quality merchandise, smaller selections, and less pleasant conditions. These quality measures are the most difficult to quantify. We must rely on the observations of the surveyors.

The monopoly stores surveyed were inevitably the dirtiest, the most crowded, the most difficult to shop in (especially a monopoly Safeway). The lowest-quality produce and meats were found at the monopoly COOP. The managers of the competitive stores were friendlier to the surveyors, perhaps because, they were least embarrassed by their prices.

Remember that these are not comparisons across chains, but across stores in the same chains in different market structures. One might expect some chains to appear cheaper by selective stocking of merchandise. In fact, the cheapest store in each city carried the highest percentage of the items in our market basket, because of competitive pressures.

Conclusion

In summary, unconcentrated retail markets do have prices lower than monopoly ones, on the order of 5 percent lower for supermarkets. Most chains do respond to local market structures. One chain seems to seek out competitive locations and charge low prices consistent with its discount image. The one store that did not respond to local market structure is the best established chain locally, one that is seeking to promote a high-quality image and capitalize on the loyalty of its customers.

The implications for antitrust policy are clear when neighborhood concentrations do make a difference. Consider the restrictive agreements commonly found between shopping-center developers and stores. They disallow leases to potentially competitive stores within the same center (in exchange for which the chains agree not to open stores in any nearby centers). The result is higher prices, some of which may be captured by the center owners.

The implications for merger policy are also self-evident. Market power must be considered on a very local level. A merger between two chains with competing stores in a neighborhood (but small national or even SMSA market shares) will lead to higher prices.

In short, neighborhood-market concentration is one determinant of the conduct of chain stores. This conclusion, in the face of the recent trends towards concentrations, can only lead to higher grocery prices.

Postscript

Of course, this relationship between concentration and performance of retail stores can be observed in other product markets. Our results from supermarket retailing can be compared to stereo retailing.

The two product markets are quite different. While groceries are perishable, quickly consumed, small-ticket items, stereos are durable, large-ticket items. They are purchased infrequently by consumers. The equipment is sold on a commission basis by salespeople who negotiate prices and credit. The purchasers have far from perfect information about stereo products and prices.

The markets in this industry are somewhat larger geographically than in grocery retailing. Because of the amount of money involved, purchasers are likely to travel farther for price comparison. As a result, there are no monopolists, but there is differentiation among the chains through the brands they carry.

There are also some similarities in the two markets. For example, both rely heavily on advertised brand names.

We were able to obtain data on the gross margins of a number of stores in a large stereo chain. We can calculate the average gross margin of stores in concentrated and unconcentrated markets for part of 1980.

The results are as follows:

	Jan.	Feb.	Mar.	Apr.	May	June	Aug.
unconcentrated	25.5	30.9	33.1	26.1	28.9	31.2	28.4
concentrated	29.4	33.5	35.5	30.0	31.5	33.5	31.5

The results are as clear as in grocery retailing. While markups may vary from month to month, prices are higher in locally concentrated markets. The price differences are lower than in grocery retailing, but the markets are less distinct. It is more difficult for stores in a locally concentrated market to raise their prices more than a small percent, since purchasers of these large-ticket items will travel to the next market. This industry is also experiencing a trend to concentration as marginal stores go bankrupt. Our prediction for this industry is the same: higher prices.

References

Alexis, Marcus and Leonard S. Simon, "The Food Marketing Commission and Food Prices by Income Groups," *Journal of Farm Economics*, 49 (February 1967): 436–446.

Ambrose, David M., "Retail Grocery Pricing: Inner City, Suburban, and Rural Comparisons," *Journal of Business*, 52 (January 1979): 95–102.

Baumol, William J., Richard E. Quandt, and Harold T. Shapiro, "Oligopoly Theory and Retail Food Pricing," *Journal of Business*, 37 (October 1964): 346–363.

Dipman, C. W., "Merchandising Trends in the Food Trade, with Special Reference to Supermarkets," *Journal of Marketing*, 3 (January 1939): 269–273.

Faville, D. E., "Comparison of Chain and Independent Grocery Stores in the San Francisco Area," *Journal of Marketing*, 1 (1936): 87–90.

Goodman, Charles S., "Do the Poor Pay More?" *Journal of Marketing*, 32 (January 1968).

Gray, Roger W. and Roice Anderson, "Advertised Specials and Local Competitions among Supermarkets," in *Empirical Foundations of Marketing*, Alexis, Holloway, and Hancock, eds. (Chicago: Markham Pub. Co., 1969).

Holdren, Bob R., "The Nature of Competition Among Food Retailers in Local Markets," *Journal of Farm Economics*, 46 (December 1964): 1306–1315.

Holdren, Bob R., "Competition and Concentration in Food Retailing," *Journal of Farm Economics*, 47 (December 1965): 1323–1351.

Kunreuther, Howard, "Why the Poor Pay More for Food: Theoretical and Empirical Evidence," *Journal of Business*, 46 (July 1973): 368–383.

Marion, Bruce W., et al., "The Price and Profit Performance of Leading Food Chains," *American Journal of Agricultural Economics*, 61(August 1979): 420–433.

Mihichiello, Robert J., "The Real Challenge of Food Discounters," *Journal of Marketing*, 31(April, 1967): 37–42.

Moore, John R., "The Effect of Financial Arrangements of Shopping Centers on Concentration in Food Retailing," *Journal of Farm Economics*, 178 (February 1962): 178–183.

Morgan, Howard E., "Concentration in Food Retailing: Criteria and Causes," *Journal of Farm Economics*, 48 (August 1966): 122–136.

Mori, Hiroshi and William D. Gorman, "An Empirical Investigation into the Relationship between Market Structure and Performance as Measured by Prices," *Journal of Farm Economics*, 48 (August 1966): 162–171.

Mueller, Willard F. and Leon Garoian, *Changes in the Market Structure of Grocery Retailing* (Madison, Wisc.: University of Wisconsin Press, 1961).

Mullen, Wadsworth H., "Some Aspects of Chain-Store Development," *Harvard Business Review*, 3(October 1924): 69–80.

Naden, Kenneth D. and George A. Jackson, Jr., "Price as Indicative of Competition Among Retail Food Stores," *Journal of Farm Economics*, 35 (May 1953): 236–248.

Parker, Russell C., "Antitrust Issues in the Food Industries," *American Journal of Agricultural Economics*, 58 (December 1976): 854–860.

Peies, Y., "On the Uses of Private Brands," *Journal of Industrial Organization*, 20 (April 1972): 173–178.

Phillips, C. F., "The Robinson Patman Anti-Price Discrimination Law and the Chain Store," *Harvard Business Review*, 15(1936): 62–75.

Phillips, C. F., "The FTC's Chain Store Investigation: A Note," *Journal of Marketing*, 2 (January 1938): 190.

Phillips, C. F., "Supermarket and Chain-Store Food Prices," *Journal of Business*, 12(October 1939): 323.

United States Department of Labor, Bureau of Labor Statistics, *BLS Handbook of Methods*, (Washington, D. C.: Government Printing Office, 1976).

United States Department of Labor, Bureau of Labor Statistics. "Relative Importance of CPI Items." Washington, D. C., February 12, 1980, unpublished printout.

United States Federal Trade Commission, *Economic Report on the Structure and Competitive Behavior of Food Retailing, (Washington, D. C.: Government Printing Office, 1966).*

United States Federal Trade Commission Bureau of Economics and United States Department of Agriculture Economics, Statistics, and Cooperative Service, *Grocery Retailing Concentration in Metropolitan Areas, Economic Census Years 1954–72. (Washington, D. C.: Government Printing Office, 1979).*

United States House of Representatives Committee on Government Operations, *Consumer Problems of the Poor: Supermarket Operations in Low Income Areas and the Federal Response*. Thirty-Eighth Report, 1968.

Walters, F.E., "The Impact of Changing Structure of the Food Industries on Food Supply and Price," *American Journal of Agricultural Economics*, 57 (May 1975): 188–195.

Weiss, Leonard W., "The Concentration-Profits Relationship and Antitrust," in *Industrial Concentration: The New Learning*, Harvey J. Goldschmid, J. Michael Mann, and J. Fred Weston, eds., (Boston: Little Brown & Company, 1974).

III TOWARD A MINIMUM SOCIALLY OPTIMAL SCALE

9 ECONOMIES OF SCALE AND MONOPOLY PROFITS

William G. Shepherd

Among the large unresolved issues in industrial organization is the question: do monopoly positions and their profits arise from the economies of scale, or from the pursuit and exercise of market power? In 1895–1910, the newly formed industrial trusts were defended as embodiments of modern technology. New methods of large-scale production, it was said, made the large market shares for trusts inevitable. The issue was intensely controversial then, and it still is.

The issue lies at the core of the field of industrial organization, and its answer can be crucial in setting antitrust policy toward dominant firms. If economies of scale were large, they would pose an antitrust dilemma. Seeking to reduce monopoly power would entail a sacrifice of economies of scale.

Despite its importance, the issue has never been tested directly. Bain, Scherer, Weiss and others have shown that actual concentration exceeds

I am grateful to William J Adams, Peter A. Asch, Kenneth D. Boyer, Lee E. Preston, Ralph Bradburd and David Sappington for advice on the contents and to David D. Smith, Edward G. Cavin, Theodora B. Shepherd, and Douglas Woodham for research assistance.

the levels required by minimum-efficient scale in a number of important industries, though not in others. Yet that comparison does not indicate the *degree* of trade-off between scale economies and monopoly power. Therefore the critical comparison — between the relative strength of scale economies and market power — has not been made.

Recently two new bodies of data, plus a renewed focus on individual dominant firms, have made it possible to evaluate those gradients directly. This chapter presents an effort to appraise their relative importance. It focuses on single leading-firm market shares, not on oligopoly concentration. Therefore it does not address the question of whether the whole array of industrial concentration arises from economies of scale.

One body of data is composed of recent estimates of economies of scale in a range of major industries, made by Scherer et al. (1975), Pratten (1971), Weiss (1976), and others. The second body of data is the detailed structural analysis of large-firm profit rates, by Shepherd (1972a, 1975), Mueller (1977), Buzzell, Gale, and Sullivan (1975), and others. Working from those findings, I will try to estimate the role of scale economies.

The issue will be posed in this form: how much of the monopoly profits (that is, the extra rate of return) arising from high market shares can be credited to economies of scale? Is that share the whole of the profits, as some observers say; or none, as others say; or some ratio in the middle? The results I reach are only provisional, but they do indicate that scale economies' role is minor.

The format of the chapter is as follows. First I will define precisely the gains from technical economies of scale. Although those gains have seemed to be intuitively obvious, this defines the minimum-socially-optimal market share of the firm. It is determined by the cost curve and by the social impacts of monopoly power. Next I will analyze the alternative sources of extra profits. Then I will define the cost gains provided by economies of scale. Empirical estimates of the cost effect are given next, and then there is a concluding summary of the findings.

Cost Conditions and Socially Optimal Scale

Our focus is on the average cost curve of the firm, with the standard shape illustrated in figure 9–1. There is a range of economies of scale, ending at point *A*, the minimum efficient scale (MES) of the firm. At higher outputs there may be diseconomies of scale as shown by curve 1, or constant costs as shown by curve 2.

Our interest centers on two conditions: (1) the size of MES compared

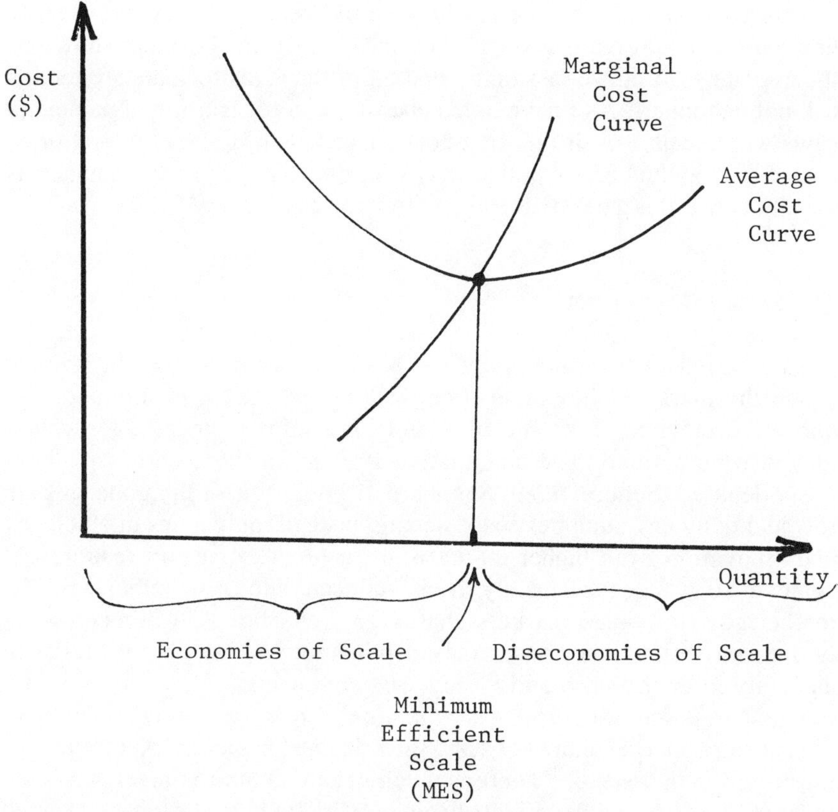

Figure 9-1 Scale Economies in the Typical Cost Curve.

to the size of the entire market, and (2) the slope of the average cost curve as it declines down to the MES point. If MES is large relative to the market, it may require firms to have large market shares in order to be efficient. But MES alone does not set a rigid floor under the firm's market share. The cost gradient also matters.

The Minimum-Socially-Optimal Market Share

I will define a minimum-socially-optimal market share (SOMS). To do that, one first recognizes that the social objective is to minimize not just the private cost of production but the total cost. Total cost includes (1) private cost, and (2) social costs created by whatever market power the firm exerts. The private costs are internal to the firm. They are shown by the average cost curve, assuming that all of the gains to scale are technical, not pecuniary. As I have noted elsewhere, a recognition of pecuniary gains will usually result in a true cost curve which is above the reported cost curve at higher output levels. Filtering out pecuniary gains may usually cause the true MES to lie below the apparent MES.

The Social Cost Function

The net social costs of monopoly are those that occur outside the firm but inside the market. They arise from well-known effects of monopoly on allocative efficiency, X-efficiency and innovation. Other larger values may also be harmed. The quantitative strength of these effects is vigorously debated (Scherer 1980, Shepherd 1979). A few of my colleagues in the field deny any such net costs, seeing, instead, only gains in efficiency and innovation from higher market shares. Most experts instead expect some costs to occur, mainly from reduced allocative efficiency, X-inefficiency and — as markets shares go well above 30 percent — retarded innovation. The social costs also include less tangible values such as equity in distribution and various social impacts.

One can define the *social cost function* of monopoly power as beginning at some market share (M_1) and then rising at higher market shares, as illustrated in figure 9–2.[1] There is much debate about the level of M_1: do monopoly's negative net effects begin at market shares as low as 15 or 30 percent, or perhaps as high as 50 or even 60 percent? The slope of the social cost function is also controversial. It reflects several elements, and it may depend on entry barriers as well as market share. The curve may be steep or virtually horizontal. It probably has an upward curvature as shown, but that too is unsure.

I must save an analysis of the cost function and its role for another paper, but one can immediately see that *it can cause the minimum-socially-optimal market share (SOMS) to be below the MES level.* The higher MES is, and the lower the cost gradient is, then the further SOMS will diverge below MES. The conditions are shown in figure 9–3. *The social optimum is reached where the absolute values of the average cost curve and the social cost function have identical slopes.* There the added social cost from increased output (and market share) just offsets the private scale economies.

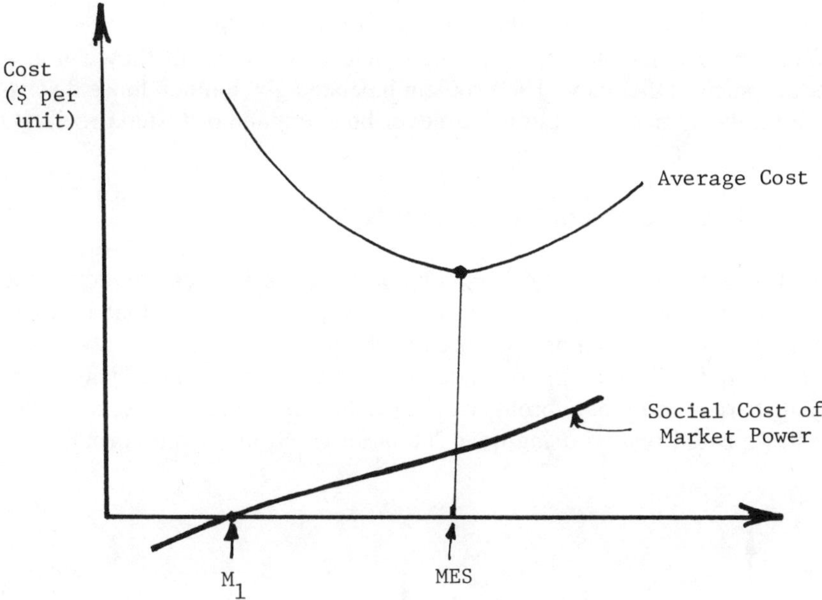

Figure 9-2 Private Costs of Production and the Social Cost of Market Power

Surplus Market Share

Meanwhile the firm's profit-maximizing output depends on its costs (including pecuniary gains) and demand. Often that output will be much larger than the SOMS level. I define this gap between SOMS and actual market share as *surplus market share*. It provides private gain, in the form of extra profit, but it provides no social gain in efficiency. To the contrary, it causes social inefficiency because of the social costs of monopoly.

I am not asserting here that the social cost function necessarily starts at low market shares nor that it is steeply sloped. The point is merely if the cost function exists, it can cause SOMS to be below MES. If SOMS is horizontal at a zero level, then SOMS equals MES. Even in that case, market shares above MES are still functionless and therefore surplus.

All of this helps us to understand that the antitrust dilemma need not be a simple intuitive matter. How acute that dilemma is will depend on both the cost conditions and the strength of market power's effects on efficiency. Higher market shares can yield efficiency, but they can also reduce social efficiency. The problem has been given much loose discussion for many decades, but it has never been defined or tested precisely.

Alternative Sources of Excess Profits

I will be able to make only a first step in this chapter, trying to define the cost savings that economies of scale may provide. Once that is done, those cost savings can be compared to the firms' extra profits, above the cost of capital. That comparison deals directly with the standard question: what share of monopoly profits can be credited to the economies of scale?

In repeated testing using over 200 large U. S. industrial corporations

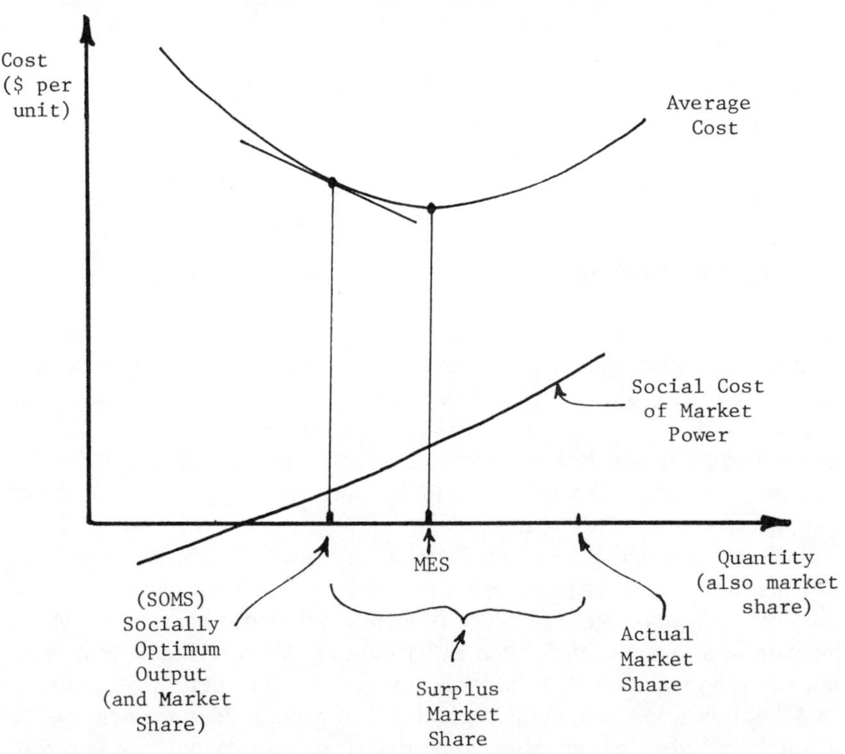

Figure 9-3 Socially Optimum Market Share and Surplus Market Share.

(Shepherd 1972a, 1975), I have found the coefficient of market share on the firm's profit rate on equity to be about 0.25.[2] Each added ten points of market share adds about 2.5 points to the profit rate on equity. That is shown in figure 9-4. Research on the "PIMS" data set has shown similar patterns (Buzzell et al.).

What causes the shaded area of excess profits in figure 9-4? It might be scale economics, or X-efficiency, or innovation, or a learning process, or random luck, as some have suggested.[3] Or it could be monopoly power. I will now show briefly that monopoly power could be the sole cause. This discussion may be needed because of some recent claims that monopoly power is bound to be weak, insufficient to generate much excess profits.[4]

Market Power as a Source of Excess Profits

The classic economic effects of monopoly are familiar. As its market share rises, a firm gains increasing control over prices, profits, output, and the process of innovation. The market power is a matter of degree, varying from nil to high. From any given market position, monopoly

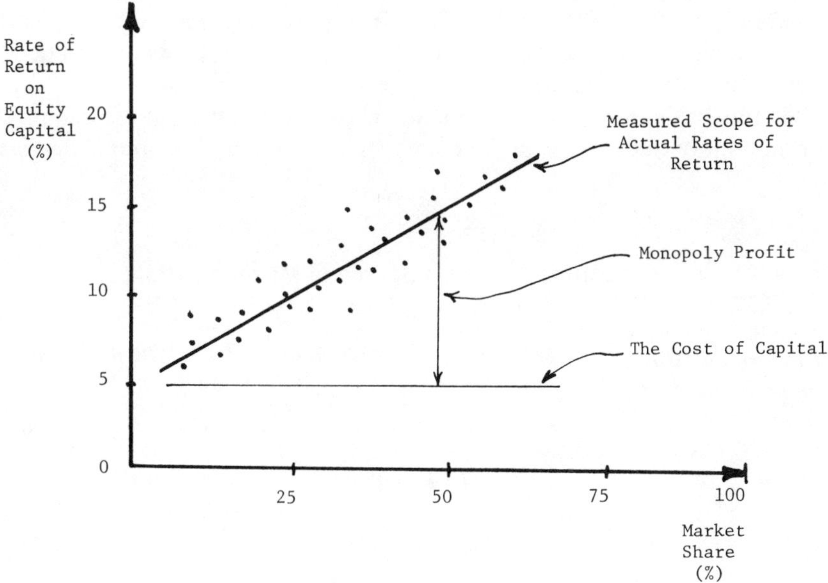

Figure 9-4 The Relationship Between Market Share and the Rate of Return

profits may be extracted, via three types of separate monopoly actions: (a) a simple rise in price, (b) price discrimination, and (c) pecuniary gains from using monopsony power to get lower input prices.

In recent decades, the rates of return for dominant firms in U. S. industry have been mainly in the range of 12 to 20 percent, probably about five-to-ten percentage points above the cost of capital. From now on, the discussion is about such extra rates of return above the cost of capital. Could the three sources of monopoly profits — price discrimination, simple price-raising, and pecuniary gains — account for such extra profit rates? I consider that now as a matter of logical possibility, reserving actual tests of the cost share to the next section.

Price Discrimination. Could price discrimination alone account for the extra returns? Yes, it could, as will now be shown. Consider the demand elasticities that would be required for firms to reach high rates of return, even though they can set high price-cost margins on only part of their output. We focus on net profit, above the cost of capital. In large U. S. firms, sales revenue has been about 2.75 times the volume of equity capital, on average, while taxes have run about 42 percent of gross profit. Therefore, a 10 percent net return on equity (after taxes) translates to a price-cost margin of 5.1 percent. One uses the familiar elasticity formula (where elasticity $= P/P - MC$). To a first approximation, average cost is a reasonable estimate of marginal cost where constant costs prevail (as is seen later to be common).

On this basis, table 9–1 presents the elasticities that would be required for monopoly rates of return on equity (that is, the margin above the cost

Table 9-1. Price Discrimination as a Source of Monopoly Profit

Company-wide Rates of Return on Equity (above the Cost of Equity): Monopoly Profit (percent)	*Percentage of Company Sales from Which Monopoly Profit Is Extracted:*			
	100%	*50%*	*25%*	*20%*
	Required Demand Elasticity on that Portion of Sales:			
(1)	(2)	(3)	(4)	(5)
5	40.0	19.6	9.8	7.8
10	19.6	9.8	4.9	3.9
15	13.3	6.7	3.3	2.7

of capital) of between 5 and 15 percent, for varying portions of the firm's sales. The extra profit is assumed to be gained only on 20 or 50 percent of sales: the rest of the firm's sales are conservatively assumed to be made at zero extra profit (above the cost of capital).

The lesson of table 9–1 is clear: *price discrimination can be a powerful source of extra profits*. The elasticities in table 9–1 are equal or above those observed in the common run of firms with high market shares.[5] Elasticities of two to five would be the usual range for the entire output of such firms. Evidently, price discrimination alone can generate substantial rates of true profit, even if the monopolized sales are below 50 percent of the firm's sales and the elasticities on those sales are at five and above. For example, the 4.9 in line 2, column 3 shows that a 10 percent extra rate of return for the entire firm would result even if demand elasticity is as high as 4.9 on one-quarter of the firm's output (and infinite on the other 75 percent). High elasticities reflect strong actual or potential competition. The elasticities noted here — infinite on at least half of sales and at three or more on the rest — do not embody implausibly high degrees of monopoly.

Therefore, price discrimination alone could be a sufficient condition to explain much or all of the observed pure profit in large U. S. firms. It is not a necessary condition, for the other factors may also operate to give monopoly profits, as I will shortly note.

From deduction and averages, we turn now to pricing in some actual cases. Price discrimination is known to have been sharp in a variety of dominant firms, though not, of course, in all. Antitrust and regulatory cases, and various hearings, have shown the pricing patterns in some of these firms. Other cases are familiar in the trade and professional literature. Table 9–2 presents a small selection of such instances. Evidently, price discrimination is often deep. In fact, virtually all sizable firms with diverse customers groups do practice discrimination, by setting differing price-cost ratios in line with the differing demand elasticities. By contrast, in strict homogeneous-good oligopolies there is likely to be little discrimination. The uniformity of output, and the firms' limited market shares, do not permit it. By focusing on such oligopolies, much of the recent literature — such as on limit pricing, entry barriers and concentration — has missed the important problem of market dominance and price discrimination.

Price discrimination is the missing link between the firm's market share and its monopoly profit. *Even if simple price-raising effects and pecuniary gains were absent, discrimination could cause most or all of the observed profits*. Yet in fact, simple price-raising and pecuniary gains are not absent, as I will now note.

Table 9-2. Practical Instances of Extensive Price Discrimination

Industry and firms	*Type of Price Discrimination*	*Extent of Discrimination*
Pharmaceuticals	Between bulk buyers and the retail trade.	Deep. Price-cost ratios range from 1.5 to 8
Copiers (Xerox)	Among machine types. Among users by size. Complex volume discounts.	Deep. Price-cost ratios vary by up to multiples of 4.
Computers (IBM)	Among system types, from small to large. Among equipment types. Among users of standard equipment types.	Deep. Price-cost ratios vary by up to multiples of 2.5.
Shoe machinery (United Shoe Machinery Corp.)	Among machine types and between machines and supplies. Among users by size and needs.	Deep. Price-cost ratios varied between 1.5 and 5.
Automobiles	Among car models. Between cars and parts.	Extensive. Price-cost margins range up to 2 on luxury cars and certain parts.

Sources:

Automobiles: Lawrence J. White, *The Automobile Industry Since 1945* (Cambridge: Harvard University Press, 1971), and various trade sources.

Copiers: *FTC: In the Matter of Xerox Corporation* (Docket 8909), 1973–75; and *SMC Corp.* v *Xerox Corp.*, 1978–79.

Computers: Gerald W. Brock, *The U. S. Computer Industry* (Cambridge: Ballinger, 1975); W. G. Shepherd, *Market Power and Economic Welfare* (New York: Random House, 1970); *U. S.* v *IBM Corp.*

Pharmaceuticals: Subcommittee on Monopoly, *Report on Competitive Problems in the Drug Industry,* U. S. Senate Select Committee on Small Business (Washington, D. C.: U. S. Government Printing Office, 1971), Part 20.

Shoe Machinery: Carl Kaysen, *U. S.* v *United Shoe Machinery Corp* (Cambridge: Harvard University Press, 1956).

The Simple Raising of Price. Entry is not free in many important industrial markets, and potential competition is often slight or nil. This gives established firms the scope to exercise the market power that arises from their market shares, by simply holding price above cost. The simple raising of price on all of the firm's business (with no discrimination) can yield high returns (as the second column in table 9–1 shows), even if demand elasticities are high. A demand elasticity as high as 13 can still yield a net profit rate as high as 15 percent on equity.

The firm is, of course, primarily limited by its actual competitors. Despite a large volume of recent commentary about potential competition, that external kind of possible pressure is likely to be less direct and relevant than actual competition. Some recent observers have even seemed willing to sacrifice all actual competition, as long as there is some prospect of potential competition. But that is an extreme view, suggesting a misconception about the nature of competition. Actual competition will almost always be more important than potential competition.

The narrow focus on potential competition also misconstrues Bain's (1956) seminal work on entry barriers. He noted correctly that barriers can reinforce the ability of firms to exploit their markets. Some newer writers have tried to reverse that logic. They assert instead that no market power can occur without barriers, and that barriers are the sole source of market power. That view goes much too far, and it has little empirical support. It also is at odds with the common focus of practical business managers and investors upon market share as the key part of a firm's market position.

Pecuniary Gains. If firms exercise monopsony power in buying inputs, they can raise their pure profits without achieving technical economies. In short, suppliers may price discriminate under pressure from large buyers. Though such pecuniary gains have long been recognized, they have rarely been documented and have been increasingly neglected. Such price discounts are probably common, and often sizable.

Yet their impact is probably moderate, compared to the two price effects just discussed. The pecuniary gains would arise mainly in (1) materials inputs and (2) the supply of capital. Large firms commonly do get volume discounts on both of these categories, discounts ranging as high as 10 percent or more. Yet such items comprise less than 50 percent of total cost for most firms, so the impact on average total cost is diluted. Also, the price discounts often reflect technical economies for the supplier, and so they are social economies in a partial sense.

An Alternative Model

For lack of evidence, views about the sources of monopoly profits have varied, often to extremes. Some colleagues have urged recently that the high profit rates of dominant firms must reflect economies of scale. That possibility deserves a careful analysis here.

The essential point is as follows. Assume that there is a well-defined market for one homogeneous good, with one price ruling throughout. Then any firm earning higher profits must be attaining scale economies or superior X-efficiency or innovation, not market power. Figure 9-5 illustrates this simple case. If scale economies are lacking, the dominant firm may choose to hold the price very high, often called an umbrella price.[6] But such a high price can last (in the absence of scale economies) only if there are entry barriers. Otherwise, entry will occur and eliminate the monopoly profits — and the dominant firm's position, too.

In this simple model, a correlation between market shares and profit rates will only (or primarily) reflect economies of scale. Such an interpretation is often presented as definitive, not just as a probable tendency or as a matter of balance. Thus, my own finding of a close partial correlation between market share and rate of return (Shepherd 1972a) has been said to show merely that scale economies are at work.

But that one-sided conclusion is far too simple. It leaves out at least three basic conditions in industrial markets, which need to be included in the premises.

1. Most significant markets have a variety of segments and submarkets: differing products and customer groups that have varying demand elasticities. Dominant firms can and do practice price discrimination among

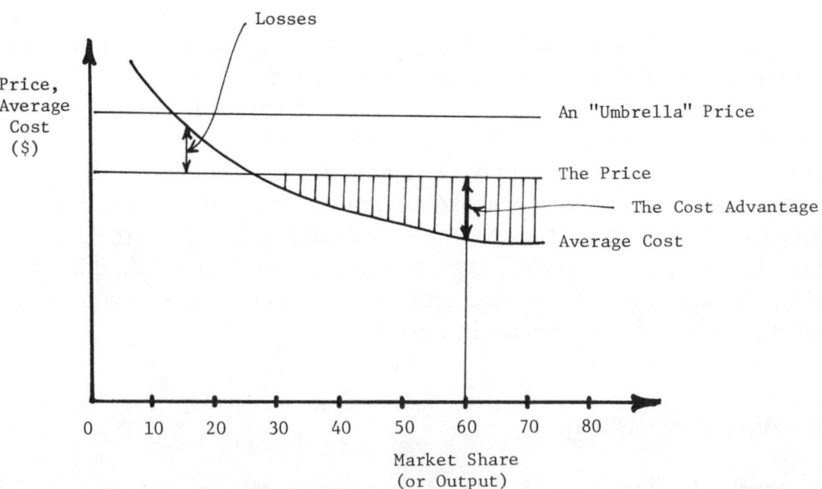

Figure 9-5 The Simple Model with All Profits Reflecting Economies of Scale

these parts, often extensively, as I have noted. The simple single-price premise would be incorrect. The price discrimination can yield ample monopoly profits not related to scale economies.

2. Entry does not uniformly affect all parts of the market when there are submarkets. Dominant firms can often protect some submarkets from new competition, even when scale economies and entry barriers are absent.[7]

3. Some gains to scale are pecuniary, not technical, as I have also noted. A prime source of pecuniary gains is the cheaper input prices that may be gained by applying monopsony power.

As a matter of logic, therefore, a firm can gain market dominance and monopoly profits, even if technical economies of scale and entry barriers are small or absent. The matter is eminently one for empirical tests. Now we need to define the role of economies of scale precisely, as a basis for testing it empirically.

Defining the Cost Effect

In the analysis here, I will use a simple cost curve with no diseconomies of scale, as in figure 9–6. I will also ignore any possible pecuniary element in the cost curves. The simple comparison is as follows. The MES in this case is at 16 percent of the market, at an average cost of AC_M. This firm's profit-maximizing output happens to be at Q_M (which is 34 percent of the market), with price at P_M. The flow of monopoly profits is $(P_M - AC_M)$ Q_M, the shaded rectangle in figure 9–6. Some share of this flow probably reflects scale economies; but how much? The literature provides no precise criterion for measuring that share, so I define one as follows.

The possible trade-off — the dilemma — is between (1) monopoly power, with its several negative social effects, and (2) technical economies of scale, which save resources. Only if MES is large enough to yield a market share that gives market power is there a trade-off. At the lower end, an MES at 2 percent of the market is too small to matter; an MES at 60-percent market share obviously does create market power. The threshold value of market share lies somewhere in between.

A Maximum-Competitive-Market-Share Benchmark

The key is to specify a maximum-competitive market share which, if held equally by all firms, is still consistent with fully effective competition in

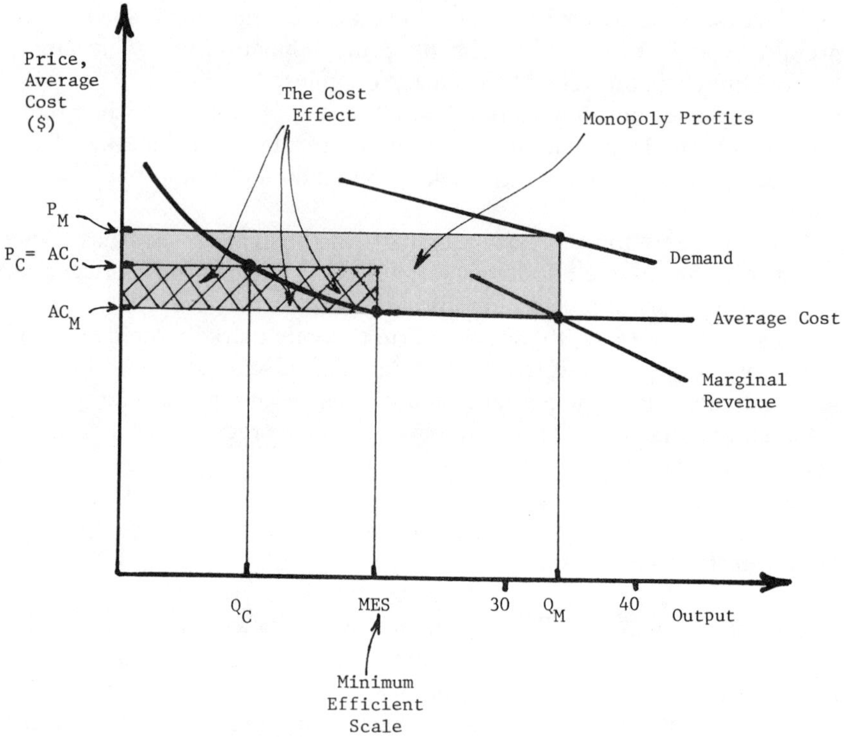

Figure 9-6 Scale Economies, Monopoly Profit and the Cost Effect

the market. (Fully effective means that price is forced down to average cost.) If all firms could be reduced to that market share, full competition would ensue. But scale economies might be sacrificed at that market share, with average costs higher than their MES level. That increment to average cost would be the objective measure of the role of scale economies.

In figure 9–6, let Q_C be that maximum-competitive market share. Then AC_C is the average cost incurred by that competitive firm, and $AC_C - AC_M$ is the cost sacrifice. It is the degree of penalty — of higher costs — which would have to be incurred in order to obtain full competition. Conversely, an output level (and market share) exceeding Q_C will involve a degree of market power, but it may also provide cost reductions from AC_C down to AC_M. The range between Q_C and MES is where the welfare trade-off — the antitrust dilemma — may occur.

Notice that the specifying the Q_C inevitably influences the level of AC_C. That is inherent in the problem. The cost curve itself gives no specific benchmark for measuring the cost effect. One must specify that benchmark as accurately as possible, in light of the competitive objective. Only with such a specific benchmark can the role of economies of scale be objectively measured.

Specifying Q_C

Fortunately, Q_C can be estimated by objective criteria. The literature offers several guides. There is first the basic distinction between loose oligopoly and tight oligopoly. Tight oligopoly commonly involves a degree of price coordination, either implicit or tangible. Loose oligopoly usually does not. The margin between loose and tight oligopoly is widely agreed to be at about a four-firm concentration of 50 percent of the market. Some analysts give 40-percent concentration as the upper limit for fully effective competition under loose oligopoly. If the limit is indeed in the range of 40 to 50 percent, then Q_C for each of the four firms would be 10 or 12 percent. There would be, respectively, at least ten or eight equal-sized firms in such a fully competitive market.

The literature on strategic pricing suggests that a Q_C of 10 percent might be a little too high (Scherer 1980). With only ten firms, all holding 10-percent market shares, collusion might emerge. Equal shares as low as 5 or 8 percent (with twenty or twelve equal-sized firms, respectively) might usually be necessary to insure that competition holds price firmly down to average cost. Yet views vary, and some neo-Chicago School specialists say that market shares well above 12 or 15 percent — even 40 or 50 percent — may be fully consistent with effective competition. Q_C may therefore be 15 or 20 percent or even higher.

Of course, the higher Q_C is, the lower will be the resulting value for AC_C. That is because the shift to the right of Q_C moves AC_C down the cost curve. Therefore an overestimate of Q_C will reduce the apparent role of economies of scale.

The true Q_C probably lies in the range between 5 and 15 percent of the market. For the purpose of generating concrete estimates, three benchmark values for market share — 6, 8, and 10 percent — will be used alternatively in the present study. I will indicate how sensitive the results are to the various Q_C benchmarks.

In short, the choice of the Q_C benchmark is not arbitrary. The range of reasonable estimates for it derives from the basic literature on industrial organization. The values can be imputed from the literature about the fundamental conditions for competition. By using alternatives and showing how sensitively they affect the results, I am trying to limit the element of arbitrariness.

The Cost Effect

The cost effect is the degree of cost penalty that full competition would incur ($AC_C - AC_M$) multiplied by the amount of output over which it would need to be spread. That output is MES in figure 9-6: under full competition, output up to MES would be converted into Q_C-sized firms, at the cost level labeled AC_C. The cross-hatched area therefore is a measure of the cost effect.

The firm's extra market share above MES (the interval from MES to Q_M in figure 9-6) gives no added cost reductions. It is functionless for economic efficiency, but it does increase market power and its effects. Therefore, it is logical to omit that functionless range of market share — the *surplus market share* — from the cost effect. To illustrate with an extreme case, if the firm had somehow gained a market share (Q_A) of 90 percent in figure 9-6, it would be absurd to say that the upper 70 percent of its market share (above MES) has provided any cost saving at all. There is no antitrust dilemma between MES and Q_A. Therefore Q-MES is a rough estimate of surplus market share. (The study of the added range of surplus market share between SOMS and MES (figure 9-3) is beyond the present research.)

The cost effect is to be compared with the shaded area representing the firm's extra profits, which are permitted by the firm's degree of monopoly. As figure 9-6 illustrates, the cost effect is about one-third of the extra profits. Contrasting cases are shown in figures 9–7 and 9–8. The cost effect is zero in figure 9-7, because all scale economies are exhausted at an output level below Q_C. By contrast, the large scale economies in figure 9–8 provide a cost share of about 90 percent.

Possible Overstatement of Efficiency Gains

The cost effect, as just defined, probably overstates the degree of efficiency gains for two reasons other than the fact that it ignores the possibility that SOMS may be below MES, as noted earlier.

Another reason concerns the misallocation burden. By setting price

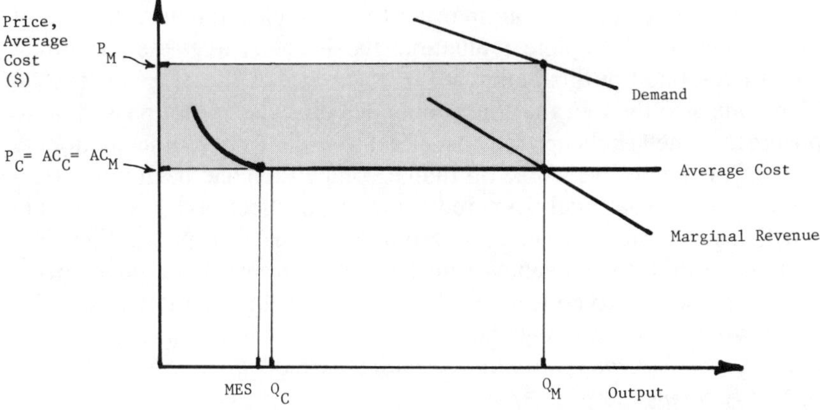

Figure 9-7 Scale Economies are Slight, and the Cost Share is Zero

above cost at Q_M, the firm will also cause a misallocation burden, as shown by the conventional welfare triangle. (Second-best conditions may reduce the triangle to some degree.) This additional welfare loss should be included as an offset to the cost effect, in appraising the net gain in efficiency. The size of misallocation burden will depend on demand elasticity, marginal cost, and other well-known conditions.[8] I have omitted

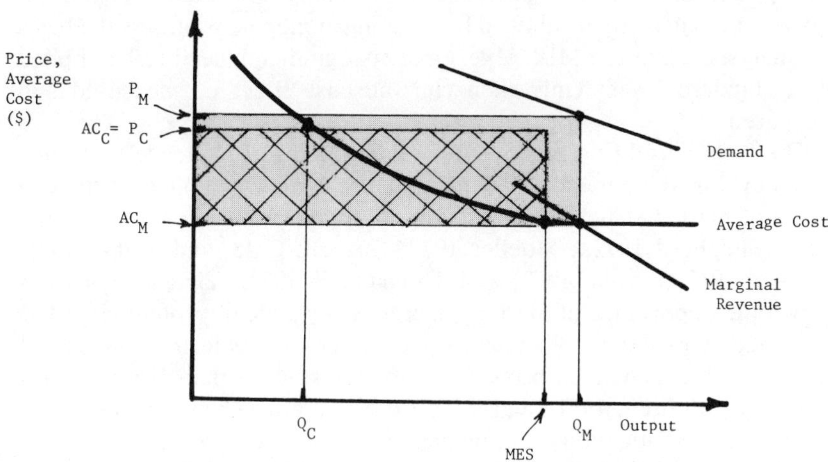

Figure 9-8 Scale Economies are Large, and so is the Cost Share

that burden in this discussion, in order to accomplish the first step, but it would belong in a complete evaluation. Its absence leaves the cost effect further overstated in this paper.

There is also the fact that the economies of scale are not passed on to consumers. The firm keeps the cost effect to itself, as part of its monopoly profits. Consumers are worse off than if competition had been fully effective at Q_C. Some analysts credit the cost effect as a social gain nonetheless, because fewer real resources are used in production. Yet others have said the efficiency gains have a clear normative value only if they are passed on to consumers. Only if price is brought down to AC_M, in their view, can economies be said to justify a market share above Q_C. In short, *scale economies might explain part of monopoly profits but not justify them.*

In any event, the cost effect does not alter the basic existence and nature of the profits: they still reflect monopoly pricing and have the usual negative effects. That fact is often ignored, but it is basic. Just because there may be some justification for a monopoly, that does not make the monopoly cease to exist. It still continues to have monopoly effects.

Empirical Analysis

The quantitative estimates present several technical problems. First one needs to identify firms with substantial market shares, say above 25 percent. Next those firms' differences in relative X-efficiency and innovativeness need to be allowed for, leaving monopoly profits as the basis for analysis. Then the MES levels and cost gradients need to be applied on a standard basis. Only then can the cost effect be measured and compared.

The tests here bring together two main bodies of evidence that have been developed independently, mainly since 1965. One concerns the elements of market structure, as they relate to the profit rates of industrial firms (Shepherd 1972a; Mueller 1977; Buzzell, Gale, and Sultan 1975; Sullivan 1977; Kwoka 1977; and Thomadakis 1977). That analysis has shown the importance of market share as a correlate of profitability. The other set of evidence is about the economies of scale in a variety of industries. It is contained primarily in several studies (Bain 1956; Scherer et al. 1975; Pratten, 1971; Weiss, 1976), plus a number of antitrust cases and official investigations. Supplementing these two parts is a wide variety of published evidence and evaluation about industrial conditions.

Methods

Taken together, these bodies of evidence permit a provisional weighing of the role of cost effect in high profits. Ideally there would be five research steps to take if complete information were available: (1) One would identify firms that have had high market shares during a recent long, relatively stable, period. One would also determine the firms' net rates of profit during the period — their rates of return on equity, as margins above their costs of equity capital. (2) Next, one would estimate deviations of their relative X-efficiency and innovativeness from the norm. Profit rates would be then adjusted for those deviations. The remaining residual monopoly profit rates would then reflect only higher monopoly power or scale economies. (3) One then would apply measures of the actual scale economies, to (4) determine the cost effect as a share of the extra profits. (5) Finally, one would analyze that cost effect, in light of the other structural determinants of profitability.

I have attempted all five steps in this study. Yet the data have various defects, some more than others. To let the reader judge, I will present alternative findings. For convenience and consistency with earlier studies, I focus the tests here on profit rates in relation to market share. This is a simple conversion from the output and price-cost–margin analysis in figures 9-5 to 9-8. The scale economies are incorporated by calculating them as differences among the profit rates that would be realized at suboptimal sizes. This provides for a clear comparison, without changing the underlying nature of the cost measures.

The coverage in this study is all large U. S. industrial firms during 1960–1969 whose average market shares were clearly above 20 percent. There were eighty-five such firms, after highly diversified firms and other unclear cases were sifted out. The 1960–1969 period is the most stable recent ten-year period, because the 1970s were turbulent and marred by inflation.[9] The 1960s decade is long enough to give a meaningful average among short-run variations. The rate of return on equity is used, as in many previous studies, as a valid indicator of the degree of profitability on the voting owners' stake in the firm. The accounting profits have certain known defects, but some of the measurement errors may average out during the ten-year period. At any rate, the accounting biases are likely to understate the profitability of firms with high market shares, rather than to overstate them. Therefore such a bias would tend to overstate the relative cost effect compared to its true level.

The cost of equity capital was about 10 percent during the 1960–1969 period, for the normal run of firms in competitive markets.[10] Most of the 85 large firms in the present panel were more secure (better risks) than that — because of their large size or high market shares, entry barriers, and so forth — and so their cost of equity capital was estimated to be 8 percent.[11] The results are not sensitive to the cost of capital, in any event.

Next, estimates of relative X-efficiency and innovativeness were made, based on a comprehensive search of the official, expert, and other business literature about company performance.[12] Most of the firms were of normal X-efficiency and innovativeness, but for each criterion about two-fifths of the panel were regarded as clearly above or below the norm. The effects on profits rates were estimated conservatively, within the range of ±3 percent return on equity. The estimates were made only when there was a clear consensus among alternative sources in the literature. Many of the firms were prominent and thoroughly evaluated by many independent sources. Some estimates may be in error, but the error is probably not large or systematic. Despite the possible error, the estimates are included because they are logically appropriate. Otherwise the profit differences could be attributed solely to X-inefficiency and innovation. They do not, in fact, affect the estimated cost effects strongly, nor do they affect the coefficients in the regression analysis.

Then the measures of scale economies were introduced. The minimum efficient scale for plants was drawn from Scherer et al. (1975), Weiss (1976), and related sources, often compared with evaluations from other evidence. The minimum efficient scale for the firm was also introduced, though the evidence on that is usually less firm. I drew mainly on Scherer et al. (1975), Weiss (1976), and a variety of other academic research on individual industries. A range of other expert, official and industrial literature was also used. Then the cost gradient below the firm's MES was estimated from the same sources, using the standard concept of the percentage increase in cost when the unit is one-third the size of MES. Both MES and the cost gradients were estimated liberally, perhaps at levels that are above the true values.

Estimates of the Cost Effect

I now turn to the findings. Table 9–3 presents the main variables, with their average values and standard deviations.

The 85 firms had market shares averaging 34 percent and monopoly rates of return (with the cost of capital and other factors netted out) of 8.6

Table 9-3. Mean Values and Standard Deviations for Variables, 85 Large U. S. Industrial Firms, 1960–1969

	Mean value	*Standard deviation*
Average Market Share	34.4%	11.4%
Average 4-firm concentration	76.3%	13.3%
Sales revenue, 1964 ($ million)	$805	$2139*
Assets, 1964 ($ million)	$640	$1524*
Equity, 1964 ($ million)	$427	$1016*
Rate of return on equity	16.4%	5.7%
Net rate of return (above the cost of capital)	8.4%	5.6%
Monopoly rate of return	8.6%	4.4%
Minimum efficient scale of the firm as a % of the market	11.6%	2.7%
Cost gradient (added cost at ⅓ of MES)	6.6%	2.2%
Surplus market share (average market share minus MES)	22.8%	
Added rate of return from scale economies-market-share benchmark		
10%	1.1%	1.4%
8%	2.6%	1.7%
6%	4.1%	1.9%
The cost share in the firms monopoly profits-market-share benchmark		
10%	3.9%	
8%	9.4%	
6%	13.6%	

*Distributions of these variables are skewed.

percent during 1960–1969. The average MES was 11.6 percent of the market.

The cost effect can be calculated immediately: various alternative estimates of it are included at the bottom of table 9–3. The estimates cover a range from 4 to 14 percent. Using a 10-percent market-share benchmark for Q_C, the cost effect is only 4 percent of monopoly profits. The effect might be as high as 14 percent of monopoly profits, using the strictest 6 percent market-share basis for Q_C.

The cost effect is fairly sensitive to the assumptions about the competitive market share and the nature of the cost effect. It is also sensitive to different values of MES and the cost gradient, as table 9–4 indicates. If MES is raised by half to an average market share of 17.5 percent, the cost effect ranges from 20 to 39 percent of monopoly profits.

Table 9-4. Sensitivity of the Cost Effect to Rises in MES and Cost Gradients

The Maximum-Competitive Share (Q_C)	*The Cost Effect as a Percent of Monopoly Profits, if:*		
Basis for Measuring the Cost Effect (market-share benchmark)	*(1) Cost gradients are raised by 50% to an average 10.0% effect on rate of return*	*(2) MES is raised by 50% to a 17.5 market share*	*(3) Both MES and cost gradients are raised by 50% as in columns (1) & (2)*
10%	35.5%	19.5%	32.5%
8%	13.3%	29.6%	44.9%
6%	23.5%	39.0%	59.1%

If both MES and cost gradients are raised by 50 percent, then the cost effect ranges from 33 to 59 percent. Such a sharp double rise is implausible: both MES and the cost gradients were already estimated liberally. Yet even this large double rise would probably leave the cost effects at half or less of monopoly profits.

After working in great detail with these issues and facts, I think *the true cost effect is almost certainly below 30 percent of monopoly profits*. The most reliable estimate would be in the range of 10–20 percent.

The scale economies do correlate significantly with profit rates, as follows:

$$\text{Net rate of return} = \underset{(4.38)}{0.39} \text{ minimum efficient scale (firm)} + \underset{(4.05)}{0.64} \text{ cost gradient}$$

$$R^2 = 0.19$$

(with *t*-ratios in parentheses). Yet the regression explains only 19 percent of the variation in profit rates. A fuller analysis is needed in order to distinguish the role of cost effect in the presence of market structure.

Economies of Scale within the Structural Analysis

In table 9-5, line 1 shows that the eighty-five firms accord closely with the general model of structure and profitability, which has been fitted earlier for panels of 231 and 245 large U. S. industrial firms (Shepherd 1972a, 1975). The analysis includes market share, a modified concentration ratio, absolute size, advertising intensity, and growth. Line 2 shows that the consistency also holds for monopoly profit rates (profit rates after filtering out the cost of capital and the relative X-efficiency and innovativeness of firms). Since the main patterns hold when the estimates for X-efficiency and innovation are omitted, in line 1, or present, in lines 2–4, the accuracy of those two performance estimates is evidently not important after all.

When the effects of scale economies are added (in line 3), the role of structure stays almost unchanged. Market share's role, especially, is steady, its coefficient moving only from .24 to .22. The steadiness holds even when the extreme assumption about scale economies (the 6-percent benchmark) is used (in line 4). Indeed, the scale-economies variable is scarcely statistically significant in the presence of structural variables. Throughout, the coefficient of the market-share variable stays in a narrow range between .21 and .25.

Yet perhaps the causation is different. Economies of scale might be a joint cause of both high market shares and high profitability. To disentangle this pattern, one could compare (1) the market-share coefficients with monopoly profit rates, against (2) the market-share coefficients with monopoly profit rates minus the cost share. This is done in table 9-6, for the alternate cases of a 10-percent benchmark (line 5), and a 6-percent benchmark (line 6) for the competitive market share. Comparing line 2 with lines 5 and 6, one finds again that the market-share coefficient scarcely changes at all, even when scale economies are explicitly introduced. Evidently, scale economies explain only a small part of the correlation between market share and profit rates.

The same pattern holds under a variety of other tests involving various subgroups of the 85 firms. Several tests are given in table 9-6. In lines 1-3, the constant term is omitted. That does not change the outcome, although market share's coefficient rises a little. The 49-firm panel focuses on firms in these industries for which the measures of scale economies are especially strong, drawn exclusively from monographs by Bain, Pratten, Scherer et al., or Weiss, or from detailed official sources. For these firms, the market share coefficient on monopoly profits is even higher than in the full panel (about .34). Scale economies still only reduce the market share coefficient by .02 at the most, or about 6 percent of its value.

Table 9-5. Analysis of Profitability, Market Structure and Scale Economies: U. S. Firms, 1960–1969

Dependent Variable	*Constant Term*	*Independent Variables:* *Market Share*	*Group (concentration minus market share)*	*Size (log of assets)*	*Advertising Sales Ratio*	*Growth*	*Scale Economies*[a]	R^2
1. Profit rate on equity; 1960–1969	**14.9** (3.94)	**.220** (3.91)	.04 (.88)	**−1.74** (4.10)	.46 (2.35)	.38 (1.02)	——	.43
2. "Monopoly" profit rate on equity; 1960–1969	3.3 (1.20)	**.238** (5.75)	.06 (2.05)	**−1.17** (3.74)	.23 (1.62)	.11 (.39)	——	.49

3. "Monopoly" profit rate on equity; 1960–1969	3.5 (1.25)	**.225** (5.07)	.06 (2.05)	**−1.17** (3.71)	.25 (1.72)	.07 (.23)	.24SE_{10} (.78)	.49
4. "Monopoly" profit rate on equity; 1960–1969	.8 (.27)	**.215** (5.08)	.07 (2.34)	**−.97** (3.03)	.27 (1.88)	.01 (.03)	.45SE_6 (2.02)	.51
5. Pure monopoly profit rate (10% benchmark)	3.2 (1.15)	**.228** (5.51)	.06 (1.97)	**−1.16** (3.69)	.28 (1.95)	.08 (.28)	———	.47
6. Pure monopoly profit rate (6% benchmark)	.6 (.23)	**.245** (5.98)	.07 (2.15)	**−1.04** (3.34)	.30 (2.11)	.04 (.15)		.49

t-ratios are in parentheses.
Coefficients in **boldface** are significant at the 1% level.
[a]SE_{10} is scale economics based on a 10% market-share benchmark; SE_6 is based on a 6% market-share benchmark.

Table 9-6. Further Analysis of Profitability, Market Structure and Scale Economies, U. S. Firms, 1960–1969

Dependent Variable	*Independent Variables*							
	Constant Term	*Market Share*	*Group (concentration minus market share)*	*Size (log of assets)*	*Advertising Sales Ratio*	*Growth*	*Scale Economies*	R^2
1. "Monopoly" profit rate on equity; 1960–69	———	**.265** (7.63)	**.09** (3.68)	−**.94** (3.81)	.24 (1.71)	.10 (.37)	———	.48
2. Same	———	**.255** (6.78)	**.09** (3.71)	−**.92** (3.73)	.26 (1.80)	.07 (.23)	$.21SE_{10}$ (.68)	.48
3. Same	———	**.219** (5.59)	**.08** (3.28)	−**.92** (3.84)	.27 (1.94)	.00 (.01)	$.48SE_6$ (2.36)	.51
49 Firms with Monograph Estimates of Scale Economies								
4. Profit rate on equity; 1960–69	**12.2** (3.28)	**.393** (5.75)	.11 (2.58)	−**2.08** (5.19)	.14 (.72)	−.63 (1.77)	———	.60

5. "Monopoly" profit rate on equity; 1960–69	2.7	**.344**	**.10**	**−1.38**	−.07	−.52		.61
	(.90)	(6.24)	(2.94)	(4.29)	(.44)	(1.82)		
6. Same	1.2	**.322**	**.11**	**−1.24**	−.07	−.54	$.24SE_6$	.62
	(.34)	(5.45)	(3.11)	(3.49)	(.44)	(1.86)	(1.00)	
7. Same	———	**.368**	**.12**	**−1.21**	−.04	−.55	———	.60
		(7.70)	(4.61)	(4.67)	(.25)	(1.94)		
8. Same	———	**.327**	**.11**	**−1.16**	−1.0	−.55	$.28SE_6$	.61
		(5.77)	(4.57)	(4.43)	(.39)	(1.93)	(1.32)	
53 Consumer-goods Firms								
9. Same	.7	**.241**	.09	**−1.37**	.16	1.42	———	.55
	(.19)	(4.92)	(2.32)	(3.16)	(.77)	(2.15)		
10. Same	−2.43	**.223**	**.10**	−1.17	.21	1.22	$.50SE_6$	.58
	(.60)	(4.56)	(2.70)	(2.64)	(1.20)	(1.87)	(1.75)	

t-ratios are in parentheses
Coefficients in **boldface** are significant at the 1% level.

In still another subgroup — of 53 consumer-goods firms — the coefficients are virtually the same as for the entire panel of eighty-five firms (compare lines 2 and 4 of table 9-5 with lines 9 and 10, respectively, of table 9-6). The role of scale economies is as before: minor.

Entry Barriers. It appears that high market share does generate true monopoly profits. Yet might this really reflect, instead, the power of entry barriers? The answer is: only to a small extent.

The main economic sources of barriers are scale economies, high capital requirements arising from large size, and product differentiation. I consider them now in order. Scale economies have now been shown to have only a minor role in explaining the profitability of dominant firms, in the presence of market share. The size variation is consistently negative in tables 9-5 and 9-6, in conformity with earlier studies (see Shepherd, 1972a, and references there). Apparently, any extra profits arising from size (and capital-market) barriers are more than offset by added X-inefficiency from large size. Therefore, one could not regard absolute size as a barrier favoring firms' market power.

The third barrier element — shown here by advertising-intensity — also has little role in the full analysis, as shown in tables 9-5 and 9-6. The advertising variable is usually not statistically significant, and often it is extremely low. This raises doubt that the effect of advertising on profit is, in fact, significant (compare with Comanor and Wilson 1975). In any event, the coefficients of advertising in tables 9-5 and 9-6 indicate, as in earlier studies, that the average effect on profitability could be only several rate-of-return points, even when advertising intensity is high. So even in the rather few industries where advertising is most intensive, it does not substitute for the main role of market share or concentration as a source of monopoly profits.

To give a more complete test, I replaced these three estimators of barrier elements with a single estimate of barrier height. It is based mainly on measures made by Bain (1956) and Mann (1966). The outcome in table 9-7 suggests that barriers do affect the role of concentration strongly. Concentration's coefficient drops by one-third (from .11 to .074) when the single estimate of barriers height is used. This sharp effect fits theory: collusion by oligopolists may be fragile, vulnerable to strong influence by potential entry.

In contrast, market share's role is affected only a little. Its coefficient drops only from .238 (table 9-5, line 2) to .204 (table 9.7, line 6), or some 14 percent. This fits earlier findings that market share's role is relatively robust and independent of entry conditions (Shepherd 1972a, 1975). Market share appears to be the main element in the formation of monopoly profits by dominant firms.

In short, several sets of regression analyses attest that scale economies have a minor role in monopoly profits. The findings are consistent with the indication in tables 9-3 and 9-4 that the cost effect is between 10 and 20 percent of monopoly profits, and surely less than 30 percent.

Two Contrary Views. My analysis has rested on conventional static assumptions about causation: certain conditions (of cost and demand) may cause certain outcomes (monopoly profits and cost effects). This is a valid approach, and it is in the mainstream of research in this field. The results are subject to further testing and perhaps revision. Yet some other analysts may prefer a more time-related analysis, based on changes and advantages that evolve over time.

A Learning Curve? The market share-profitability relationship may reflect the learning process, as Buzzell, Gale, and Sultan (1975) and others have suggested. They note that the first firm to gain a high share in the market will move down the learning curve first, thereby gaining higher profits, and perhaps securing a lasting position.

The point is internally consistent, but it affects only the first stage in the existence of a leading market position. The second stage is the retention of high market share after the learning process has occurred and all needed knowledge is generally available. Learning is not a meaningful explanation or justification for long-held high market shares. Most of the market shares in this study were indeed of long standing. To that degree, the learning process is not germane to them.

A Dynamic Process? Demsetz, McGee, Peltzman, and other Chicagoans have offered a different system of belief about the problem.[14] They reject the long-established mainstream analysis, looking instead at what they call dynamic processes. They posit that the first firm to gain dominance earns merely a rent for its lower costs from realizing the latent scale economy. This, they say, justifies the firm's initial dominance and any later enlargement of it, since all firms had an equal opportunity at the start.

My analysis may not satisfy such observers, but it does put the burden of proof against their approach. Especially where high market shares are stable and long established, as in this study, it strains logic to assert that the analysis must be exclusively dynamic. Perhaps dynamic factors could be added as a refinement in further testing.

Table 9-7. The Role of Entry Barriers in the Analysis of Profitability, Concentration, and Scale Economies, U. S. Firms, 1960–1969

Dependent Variables	*Independent Variables*										
						Barrier					
	Constant Term	*Concen-tration*	*Market Share*	*Group*	*Size*	*High*	*Medium*	*Adver-tising Sales Ratio*	*Growth*	*Scale Eco-nomies*	R^2
1. Monopoly profit rate on equity; 1960–1969	.41 (1.33)	**.111** (3.43)	——	——	**−1.14** (3.29)	——	——	.30 (1.90)	.69 (2.60)	——	.36
2. Same	4.4 (1.47)	**.102** (3.19)	——	——	**−1.14** (3.35)	——	——	.34 (2.20)	.46 (1.63)	$.67SE_{10}$ (2.17)	.40
3. Same	−.2 (.06)	**.110** (3.62)	——	——	−.84 (2.45)	——	——	.33 (2.25)	.36 (1.33)	$.73SE_6$ (3.29)	.44
4. Same	−.6 (.21)	.074 (2.06)	——	——	——	3.42 (2.31)	1.42 (1.05)		.62 (2.20)	——	.29

5. Pure monopoly profit rate, based on SE_6; 1960–1969	−2.1 (.78)	.081 (2.26)	——	——	——	2.96 (1.99)	.87 (.65)	.55 (1.96)	——	.29
6. Monopoly profit rate on equity; 1960–1969	−2.1 (8.2)	——	**.204** (4.17)	.04 (1.24)	——	2.41 (0.71)	1.12 (.89)	.12 (.42)	——	.40
7. Pure monopoly profit rate, based on SE_6; 1960–1969	−3.7 (1.48)	——	**.219** (4.50)	.05 (1.42)	——	1.89 (1.35)	.56 (.45)	.03 (.10)	——	.40

t-ratios are in parentheses
Coefficients in **boldface** are significant at the 1% level.

Conclusions

I have defined several attributes of the role of scale economies. They include the concepts of minimum-socially-optimal market share, a social cost function, surplus market share, the maximum competitive market share, and the cost effect. These concepts make it possible to define the role of scale economies compared to monopoly effects. I have then tried to estimate the role of scale economies for leading firms in major U. S. industrial markets. The method used here seems much more likely to overstate that role than to understate it.

It emerges that economies of scale provided little efficiency basis for market shares above 20 percent, in a variety of major U. S. industrial markets in the 1960s. There were substantial surplus market shares. For the firms included here, the cost effect appears to be in the range of 10 to 20 percent of monopoly profits, and surely no higher than 30 percent.[15]

Now imagine that, by some magic, the market shares of the 85 firms had all been put back to 10 percent, restoring full competition in all of the markets. If the cost effect had been 10 percent of monopoly profits, then the resulting loss of economies of scale would have been small. It would have been about 1.2 percent of the firms' equity capital, or about 0.6 percent of their costs. Such small lossses might easily be outweighed by improved allocation and equity effects, plus the probable gains in innovation and X-efficiency, under increased competition. The cost effect may not have passed on to consumers in any event. In short, there was, in the 1960s, little antitrust dilemma for most dominant firms in large-scale U. S. industry.

Market share remains the central element of market structure. The flow of pure monopoly profits it yields is sizable. In the 1960s, the flow was about $4.3 billion yearly for the 85 firms in this study. That flow might have had a capitalized market value of $25 to $40 billion at that time.

The problem of market dominance is a focused one. Only 16 of our 85 firms had market shares that were above 40 percent and rates of return that were more than 9 percent above the cost of capital.

Accordingly, there does appear to be an economic basis for actions to reduce or set restraints on some dominant market positions. The problem is identifiable and limited, much less common than the tight oligopoly problem. The social aim is to eliminate the monopoly effect on price, while gaining any scale economies that may actually be present. Structural changes might not be necessary. There may be many ways to press prices down toward cost while also retaining market shares high enough to provide all true scale economies.

Further study may improve the measures of scale economies and the other concepts tested in this study. In the meantime, we are wise to give scale economies little weight in interpreting the profitability of most dominant firms in leading industries.

Appendix

Inclusion of Firms

The eighty-five firms are those among the largest industrial corporations in the 1960's whose market shares could be estimated with some confidence (see Shepherd, *The Treatment of Market Power,* 1975, and "The Elements of Market Structure," *Review of Economics and Statistics,* 1972) and estimated average market shares were clearly above 20 percent. (Eight such firms from just below the top 500 are also included.) Exclusions are primarily: (1) highly diversified firms, (2) firms in highly fluid or unstable markets, (3) firms under special conditions, from regulation (for example, Western Electric), military purchases, or other agencies, (4) firms with major mergers, (5) firms with market shares below the 20–25 percent range, (6) firms in industries presenting special difficulties in estimating economies of scale. Therefore, the panel of 85 firms represents an attempt at a complete coverage of the known dominant positions among the large U. S. industrial firms. It is not a sample.

Market Share

Estimates were done in the same way as they were done for the previous panels of large firms (Shepherd 1972a, 1975). The firm's primary markets were identified, including product types and geographic boundaries. Then the firm's weighted average share in these relevant markets was estimated. Data were drawn from many sources, including monographs, industry reports and data, market surveys, Form 10–K from the firms, antitrust case records, the *Fortune Plant and Product Directory,* and others. The estimates are believed to be accurate within 3-to-5-percentage points either way.

Concentration

These estimates also followed the approach taken in the earlier studies. In the firm's primary markets, the degree of concentration was drawn from the measures in official census reports, as adjusted in Shepherd (1970 and 1972b). The estimates were checked for consistency with concentration estimates by Hall and Weiss (1967).

Advertising-Sales Ratios

These were computed from data about advertising by firms, as reported in *Advertising Age, Printers' Ink,* company information, and other varied sources. The percentages are averages for the years 1961, 1964, and 1968. They are probably correct within 1 percentage point either way.

Barriers to Entry

Barriers are estimated as high, medium, or low. Sources are primarily Bain (1956), Mann (1966), various monographs, and other industrial sources.

Accounting Adjustments to Profit Rates

Four firms presented the likelihood that special accounting aspects cause a downward bias in their reported profit rates. Two (IBM and Xerox) had large stocks of rental equipment in the 1960s. Two (U. S. Steel and Alcoa) had large accelerated depreciation, which understated true profit levels. The accounting adjustments attempted to show how much higher the true profit rates would have been.

Cost of Capital

During the 1960s, the cost of capital for competitive firms with a standard degree of risk was probably in the range of 9 to 11 percent. It is discussed in standard finance textbooks and in many utility rate cases. As a reasonable benchmark, a 10 percent return on equity is taken as the level for such firms. For larger, more secure firms with dominant positions, especially in rapidly growing markets, the cost of capital is assumed to be as much as two points lower (that is, 8 percent in equity). Such a disparity is within the range indicated in studies of the cost of capital for firms under varying conditions.

Relative X-Efficiency

Monographs, articles, and the business press were combed for judgments about the performance of management in using the firm's resources. Material published in the 1970s was often the best source in judging conditions in the 1960s. There is no strictly technical method for estimating the degree of X-efficiency. An attempt was made to fit the consensus of well-informed observers. Only significant departures from average performance were included. Estimates of the effect on the average rate of return were made for 32 firms. The estimates ranged from +3 to −3 percentage points on equity. This would correspond to +1.5 to −1.5 percent of costs (because total equity is typically about one-half of total costs and/or revenues). Therefore the estimates of X-efficiency are probably conservative.

Relative Innovation

There is no technical method for measuring the relative innovativeness of firms, compared to their technological opportunities for innovation. One must rely on a careful search of monographs, articles, the business press, and other sources in attempting a rounded judgment. The normative comparison (of performance with opportunities) is especially difficult, requiring one to go beyond simply considering the rate of change. I attempted only to isolate the clear cases of divergence from the average performance of innovation.

Estimates of the effect on profitability are given for 28 firms. As with X-efficiency, the best evaluations of performance in the 1960s often were found in the literature of the 1970s, reflecting a longer view. A reasonable amount of objective discussion was available for every firm in the panel. The estimated effect ranged from +3 to −3 percentage points on equity (equivalent to +1.5 to −1.5 percent of costs). Therefore these too are conservative estimates of the probable effects.

Minimum Efficient Scale of Plant and Firm and of Cost Gradients

The method began with estimating the MES of plants in the firm's main markets. Then any important multiplant economies of scale were estimated in identifying the probable MES of firms. This also provided estimates of the cost gradient: the increment to average cost per unit from being only one-third as large as MES for the firm (see Scherer et al. 1975).

Three types of sources were available. One is the monographs of engineering estimates of economies of plant and multiplant scale, by Bain (1956), Pratten (1971), Scherer et al. (1975), and Weiss (1976). These four major sources are supplemented by survivor estimates of the MES for plants, by Stigler (1968), Weiss (1964), and Shepherd (1967). Also, the *Fortune Plant and Product Directories* for 1963–1964 and 1965–1966 list the plants (by size classes) for the large U. S. industrial firms, by industry. This class of evidence — monographs giving direct estimates — covered 29 firms in the panel (though the *Plant and Product Directory* was valuable for every firm).

The second set of sources is the numerous monographs, articles, official reports, antitrust-case records, and other semi-official sources of evidence about the conditions in specific markets. These are often quite detailed and reliable, though one must evaluate their evidence carefully. This class of evidence covered 34 firms in the panel (including 20 firms not covered by the first type of evidence).

The third category of sources is published reports and evaluations in the business press of all types, ranging from specific industry journals over to general business periodicals. As noted above, these accounts vary in quality, but all firms were the subject of at least a moderate degree and variety of discussion.

The resulting estimates of MES and cost gradients are not definitive, of course, but they are probably an unbiased set of first approximations to the true levels. They represent a marshalling of the core of technical estimates, plus the wide variety of supporting evidence from a range of independent sources and viewpoints.

Effects of Scale Economies on Profits

The effect of profits varies with the benchmark assumed, Estimates are given for benchmarks of 10-percent, 8-percent and 6-percent market shares. The quantities follow directly from the MES of the firm and the estimated cost gradients, as explained in the text.

Notes

1. The social cost function may rise through point M_1 from below the x-axis as shown in figures 9-2 and 9-3. (This was suggested to me by David C. Colander.) This would reflect the penalty of being too small to innovate optimally (as Scherer's 1980 summary of the literature suggests). How strong that effect might be is debatable.

2. The correlation between the firm's market share and its profit rate has been shown by Shepherd (1972a, 1975), Mueller (1977), Kwoka (1977), and Buzzell, Gale and Sultan (1975), and others. As tested in a full structural model, the relationship affirms the primary role of market share, with oligopoly concentration and entry barriers being significant but usually secondary. See also Sullivan (1977), and Thomadakis (1977), for studies confirming these patterns.

3. On X-efficiency, see especially Leibenstein (1976), and Shepherd (1979). On innovation, see Scherer (1967 and 1980). The other factors are usually treated as minor in the literature. If a risk premium were relevant, it would only sharpen the findings reached below. Luck (or random processes) may also be present, but, by definition, it is not a significant factor. Random sequences are probably not a major source of monopoly profits, and so they would not supplant monopoly power and/or scale economies: see Albin and Alcaly (1979), and Shepherd (1975).

4. For the main lines of demand analysis, see Houthakker and Taylor (1970). Data on individual firms' elasticities are not abundant, but the range of like elasticities is relatively clear.

5. See also Stigler (1968) and Worcester (1957).

6. The point is also analyzed in a different way, using a concept of mobility barriers within the industry, by Caves and Porter (1977).

7. See Scherer (1980) and Shepherd (1979), for discussion and references on these factors.

8. The interval between 1969 and the present has seen the emergence of much important evidence about the firms during 1960–1969 in scholarly works, antitrust cases, official studies, and the business press. Therefore the data here can be reasonably complete, even though the 1960s period is some time back. The data here reflect an extensive search of the professional literature, case materials and a variety of industrial sources.

9. This is, of course, an approximation, but it is based on a careful analysis of conditions in financial markets at the time. (The much higher interest rates in the 1970s are, of course, irrelevant to the cost of capital in the 1960s.) The literature and regulatory proceedings provide many thorough estimates of the cost of capital at that time for firms of this sort. The literature on company finance includes Jensen (1972), and Weston and Brigham (1975): see the many cases cited there. On the lower cost of capital for firms with large size and/or market power, see Archer and Faerber (1966) and Sullivan (1977).

10. The differences between 8 and 10 percent as the cost of equity do not significantly affect the analysis. Any bias in the whole set of cost-of-capital estimates could bias the measures of the cost share, but that effect would not be large. Thus if the true cost of capital were a full two points above my estimates, the measures of cost share (below) would only

rise from 4 percent to 8 percent (and comparably for the upper-bound estimates). Also the later regression analysis would be scarcely altered at all, for the slopes would not be changed.

11. Though they are approximations, the estimates are based on the best published judgments. For most firms there were at least several independent sources and a reasonable consensus about managerial and innovative performance. In any event, the estimates do not much affect the research results that follow. It is important to include them in case they were decisive (even though they were not).

12. Conceivably the stable market share could mask a churning among new and old products, in which the firm is continually moving down the learning curve of the new products as they replace the old. Such a Schumpeterian process could dilute the simple monopoly-power interpretation of the stable market share.

The issue is an empirical one, in which the presumption is that a monopoly position is what it seems to be. If, instead, evidence of product churning can overcome the burden of proof for the mass of firms, that could affect the interpretation.

Yet even a full learning-process interpretation is still subject to the same normative limits as scale economies. That is, price should still be pressed down to cost levels, so that the gains are passed on. Retention of the profits by the firm would still reflect, in part, the exertion of monopoly power.

13. See Demsetz (1974), McGee (1971 and 1975), and Peltzman (1977). Peltzman's analysis focuses on a process of change in concentration, giving indirect inferences about cost curves. Yet the concentration data are very faulty, as is well known (Shepherd 1979, Scherer 1980). Moreover, Peltzman's method relies heavily on an inverse relationship between growth rates and changes in concentration ratios. That relationship, in fact, has been shown in repeated testing to be quite weak, and it may well not exist at all (see Shepherd, 1975 and 1979). That is one reason why Peltzman's findings are, in the event, statistically weak. Also, Peltzman's measures of economies do not filter out pecuniary gains. Therefore his measures do not address the real question, which is the possible role of *technical* economies, apart from *pecuniary* elements. That omission is crucial, both in concept and possibly in empirical findings.

From such concepts and data, no strong conclusions can be drawn either way. Scherer (1979 and 1980) shows that other conditions could account for Peltzman's findings. Note, finally, that one needs to focus on the market positions of individual firms, as in this study, in a model which also includes other elements. Concentration is a cruder basis for testing the roles of structure, profits and scale economies.

14. Further, this study has ignored possible diseconomies of scale, at sizes above MES. If any such diseconomies exist (and there is evidence that they do exist, in some cases), then the efficiency basis for market dominance is even smaller than it has been shown to be here.

References

Albin, Peter S., and Roger E. Alcaly, "Stochastic Determinants of Interfirm Profitability Differences," *Review of Economics and Statistics,* 61 (November, 1979): 615–18.

Archer, S. H., and L. G. Faerber, "Firm Size and the Cost of Externally Secured Capital," *Journal of Finance,* 21 (March 1966): 69–83.

Bain, Joe S., *Barrier to New Competition,* (Cambridge: Harvard University Press: 1956).

Bothwell, James L., and Theodore K. Keeler, "Profits, Market Structure and Portfolio Risk," in Robert T. Masson and P. David Qualls, eds., *Essays on Industrial Organization in Honor of Joe S. Bain,* (Cambridge, Mass.: Ballinger, 1976).

Brozen, Yale, "Bain's Concentration and Rates of Return Revisited," *Journal of Law and Economics,* 23, (October 1971): 351–69.

Buzzell, Robert D., Bradley T. Gale and Ralph G. M. Sultan, "Market Share — A Key to Profitability," *Harvard Business Review,* 53 (January–February 1975): 97–106.

Caves, Richard E., and Michael E. Porter, "From Entry Barriers to Mobility Barriers: Conjectural Decisions and Contrived Deterrence to New Competition," *Quarterly Journal of Economics,* 91 (May 1977): 241–61.

Comanor, William S., and Thomas Wilson, *Advertising and Market Power* (Cambridge: Harvard University Press, 1975).

Demsetz, Harold, "Two Systems of Belief About Monopoly," in *Industrial Concentration: The New Learning,* Goldschmidt, Mann, and Weston, eds., (Boston: Little Brown & Company, 1974).

Goldschmid, Harvey J., H. Michael Mann and J. Fred Weston, eds., *Industrial Concentration: The New Learning*. (Boston: Little, Brown, & Company 1974).

Houthakker, Henrik S., and Lester D. Taylor, *Consumer Demand in the United States, 1929–1970* (Cambridge: Harvard University Press, 1970).

Jensen, Michael C., ed., *Studies in the Theory of Capital and Capital Markets*. (New York: Praeger 1972).

Kahn, Alfred E., *The Economics of Regulation,* 2 vols. (New York: John Wiley & Sons 1971).

Kwoka, John E. Jr., "Market Shares, Concentration, and Competition in Manufacturing Industries," Federal Trade Commission Staff Report, Washington, D. C. 1977.

Leibenstein, Harvey J., *Beyond Economic Man* (Cambridge: Harvard University Press, 1976).

MacAvoy, Paul W., James W. McKie and Lee E. Preston, "High and Stable Concentration Levels, Profitability and Public Policy: A Response," *Journal of Law and Economics,* 14 (October 1971): 493–500.

Machlup, Fritz, *The Political Economy of Monopoly*. Baltimore Md.: Johns Hopkins University Press, 1952).

Mann, H. Michael, "Seller Concentration, Barriers to Entry and Rates of Return in Thirty Industries, 1950–1960," *Review of Economics and Statistics,* 48 (August 1966): 296–307.

McGee, John S., *In Defense of Industrial Concentration* (New York: Praeger Publishers, Inc., 1971).

McGee, John S., "Efficiency and Economics of Size," chapter in Goldschmidt Mann, and Weston.

Mueller, Dennis C., "The Persistence of Profits above the Norm," *Economica,* 44 (November 1977): 369–80.

Phillips, Charles F., Jr., *The Economics of Regulation,* rev. ed. (Homewood: Ill.: Irwin Publishers, Inc., 1969).

Peltzman, Sam, "The Gains and Losses From Industrial Concentration," *Journal of Law and Economics,* 22 (October 1977): 229–63.

Pratten, C. F., *Economies of Scale in Manufacturing Industry* (Cambridge: Cambridge University Press, 1971).

Robinson, Joan, *The Economics of Imperfect Competition* (London: Macmillan, 1933).

Scherer, F. M., "Research and Development Resource Allocation Under Rivalry," *Quarterly Journal of Economics,* 81 (August 1967): 359–94.

———, "The Causes and Consequences of Rising Industrial Concentration," *Journal of Law and Economics* (vol. 22 no. 1 April 1979).

———, *Industrial Market Structure and Economic Performance,* rev. ed. (Chicago: Rand McNally, 1980).

Scherer, F. M. et al., *The Economics of Multi-plant Operation: An International Comparisons Study* (Cambridge: Harvard University Press, 1975).

Shepherd, W. G., "What Does the Survivor Technique Show About Economies of Scale?" *Southern Economic Journal,* 34 (July 1967): 113–22.

———, "The Elements of Market Structure," *Review of Economics and Statistics,* 54 (February 1972): 25–37 (1972a).

———, "The Elements of Market Structure: An Inter-industry Analysis, *Southern Economic Journal,* 38 (April 1972): 531–37 (1972b).

———, "Structure and Behavior in British Industries, with U. S. Comparisons," *Journal of Industrial Economics,* 21 (November 1972): 35–54 (1972c).

———, *The Treatment of Market Power* (New York: Columbia University Press, 1975).

———, *The Economics of Industrial Organization* (Englewood Cliffs, N.J.: Prentice-Hall, 1979).

Stigler, George J., *The Organization of Industry* (Homewood Ill.: Irwin, 1968).

Sullivan, Timothy G., "A Note on Market Power and Returns to Stockholders," *Review of Economics and Statistics,* 59 (February 1977): 108–13.

Thomadakis, Stavros B., "A Value-based Test of Profitability and Market Structure," *Review of Economics and Statistics,* 29 (May 1977): 179–85.

Weiss, Leonard W., "Optimal Plant Size and the Extent of Suboptimal Capacity," in Masson and Qualls, 1976.

Weston, J. Fred, and Eugene F. Brigham, *Managerial Finance* (Hinsdale Ill.: Free Press, 1975).

Worcester, Dean A., "Why 'Dominant Firms' Decline," *Journal of Political Economy,* 65 (August 1957): 338–47.

IV EXTENDING THE REACH OF ANTITRUST

10 MICRO DETERMINANTS OF CONGLOMERATE MERGERS

Steven Schwartz

For many years, mergers have represented a troublesome public-policy issue. The passage of the Sherman Act (1890) was prompted by concerns about the impact of horizontal concentration. The Clayton Act (1914) and amendments attached to it (1950) were prompted by similar concerns. The Clayton Act amendments, in fact, were aimed specifically at creating an unattractive climate for corporate acquisitions (horizontal and vertical). To an extent, they have succeeded. Since 1950, the number of large vertical and horizontal mergers has declined sharply, but merger activity has continued. Firms have taken to expansion through conglomerate acquisition.[1] Conglomerate expansion has continued and increased to the point where the overwhelming majority of mergers are conglomerate in nature, though not necessarily purely conglomerate. Such acquisitions present especially vexing policy problems. Conglomerate mergers are difficult to attack on anticompetitive grounds; yet, they may threaten the competitive nature of the economy through their impact on aggregate concentration.

The data clearly show that mergers occur in waves. From the mid-1950s through the 1970s, the number of mergers has fluctuated in a clear wave-like pattern, as shown in figure 10–1. Nelson (1959) has suggested

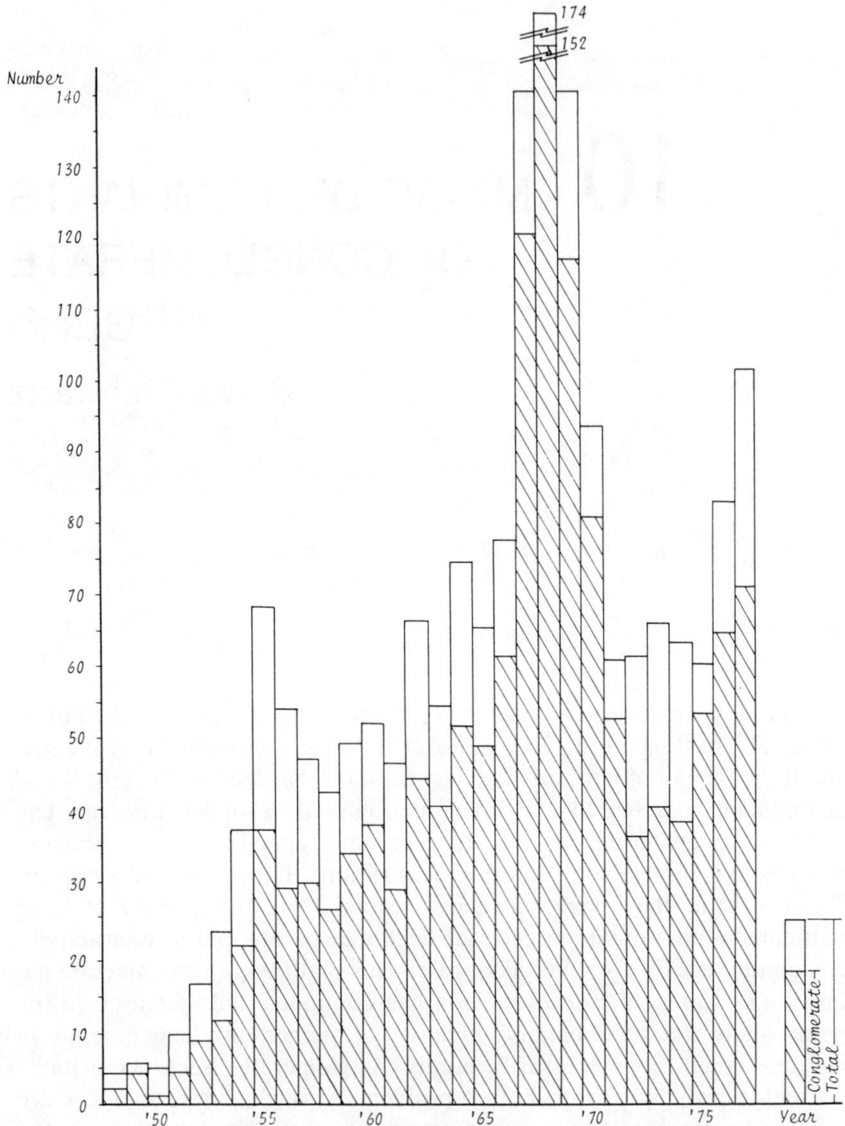

Figure 10-1 Total Number of Large and Large Conglomerate Mergers

that merger waves coincide with fluctuations in the stock market. It is argued here that increases in merger activity and stock-market booms coincide for two reasons: (1) stock market booms imply lower managerial costs of external capital, or (2) cash flows are higher (and the cost of internal capital lower) in the more prosperous periods in which booms occur.

In fact, a major hypothesis of this chapter is that corporate mergers will be more likely as cash flows increase and, consequently, that merger waves will occur in times of prosperity and large internal cash flows (Nelson 1959).

Other Research

The conglomerate merger wave has been described by Steiner (1975, p. 22 as "a post-1950 phenomenon." The Celler-Kefauver amendments to the Clayton Act effectively foreclosed large horizontal or vertical acquisitions; thus, expansion-oriented firms were left with the conglomerate-expansion option. Unfortunately, with conglomerate acquisitions, the simple motive of a desire for market power, which is often invoked to explain horizontal and vertical acquisitions, does not explain merger activity.

A variety of motives have been suggested for conglomerate mergers. One suggested motive is the desire to reap the benefits of synergies.[2] The most obvious synergies occur when a merger confers market power gains on the acquiring firm or results in the acquiring firm being able to exploit economies of scale. With conglomerate acquisitions, however, the potential importance of these synergistic effects is reduced. The nature of conglomerate expansion implies a low probability of (1) meaningful market power gains being realized, and (2) any real economies of scale emerging.[3]

Various synergistic effects consistent with conglomeration have been suggested;[4] however, the empirical support indicates that while synergistic effects may be important for particular mergers, it is clear that they can not be invoked to explain merger activity in general.

Another suggested motive is Michael Gort's disturbance theory which says that the discrepancies in valuation between buyers and sellers necessary for a merger to occur "arise from differences in expectations about future income streams and the risks associated with expected income" (Gort 1969, p. 626). For Gort's argument to hold, there must be asymmetrical responses to economic disturbances by buyers and sellers. Gort's theory has, as a necessary condition, the requirement that outsiders place less reliance on past behavior than do the owners of the target firm's stock.

This creates an awkward situation since the managers of a firm are best able to evaluate the potential impact of an economic disturbance such as a technological advance, for example. They have more information than either the owners of the firm or outsiders seeking to acquire the company. Owners and outsiders have essentially the same information; therefore, there is no reason to expect outsiders to react any differently to an economic disturbance than do stockholders.[5]

Financial motives represent a third class of possible determinants of mergers. The category of financial motives includes the following: favorable tax treatment resulting from certain mergers; gains from increased leverage or lower cost of debt; price/earnings [P/E] magic; and bankruptcy avoidance.

Favorable tax treatment can be dismissed as a general motive behind merger activity over time. Tax provisions may lead firms to have relatively higher retention ratios than they would otherwise have; however, the tax laws do not lead firms to prefer one use of retentions over another. Thus, there is nothing to suggest that tax laws that lead to higher retentions cause mergers. Tax laws may encourage firms to finance acquisitions in a particular way; however, there is no evidence suggesting tax laws motivate merger activity (Steiner 1975, p.106).

In general, the gains-from-increased-leverage motive is a reasonable general motive for expansion through acquisition. There are economies of scale in obtaining credit, especially in terms of transactions costs; however, the leverage motive is unable to explain cyclical-merger behavior, since there is no reason to expect the synergies implied by the leverage hypothesis to vary cyclically. Thus, while leverage synergies may be important in particular cases, cyclical merger activity mitigates against a claim of a desire for a leverage synergy as a general merger motive.

Bankruptcy avoidance results when two firms with independent income streams merge, thereby reducing the probability of bankruptcy and risk to lenders. While not objectionable, *a priori*, this motive is probably not very helpful as a general proposition since neither acquired nor acquiring firms are typically on the verge of bankruptcy.[6]

The P/E-magic motive derives from the automatic increases in shareholder wealth that result when two firms with different price/earnings ratios merge, to the extent that the combined firm is valued by the market at the higher of the two P/E ratios. Steiner (1975, p.106) argues that the P/E-magic motive is relevant for explaining many mergers in the late 60s. Two problems prevent us from claiming P/E magic as a general merger motive. First, if markets are efficient and no real synergies result from the merger, the gains from P/E magic are only transitory. Thus, we can claim P/E magic as a general motive for mergers only if we believe markets adjust with a (long) lag or managers pursue transitory gains for their shareholders. Second, as Steiner notes, the importance of the P/E-magic motive is markedly lower in the early part of the 1960s and in the 1970s.

While any of these motives discussed can be invoked to explain some mergers, none is sufficiently general to explain all mergers. Steiner claims that an eclectic theory is nothing more than a statement that some motive will explain any given merger and no motive will explain all, or even most, mergers. This is not a particularly illuminating theory. Indeed, not all of the alternatives have been tested. One such alternative is outlined below.

The Managerial/Life-Cycle Theory of Mergers

The theories on which the determinants-of-mergers model tested here is based are Robin Marris' growth-maximization theory and Dennis Mueller's life-cycle theory of the firm. The Marris (1964) model argues that the separation of ownership and control enables managers to maximize their own utility subject to a minimum-profitability constraint. Managerial utility is a function of growth and security.[7]

On the surface, the applicability of the managerial model to the merger question is clear. Managers seek to exploit growth opportunities in the process of optimizing their utility function. For the most part, these growth opportunities are internal, requiring only that firms expand their scale of operation. As these internal opportunities begin to dry up, firms become outward looking; that is, they must look for merger opportunities.

According to the life-cycle hypothesis (Mueller 1972), this turn outward (growth through acquisitions) occurs as the industry in which firms operate matures. In the life-cycle model, firms initially exploit their internal growth possibilities because internal growth is preferred. As maturity approaches and internal opportunities disappear, growth by merger becomes the preferred option.

Mueller argues that the discount rate for a growth-maximizing manager will be lower than for a profit-maximizing owner;[8] therefore,

> the stock market value of a firm (even at its maximum) will always be less than the present value . . . to a growth maximizing manager since the latter's discount rate is below that of a marginal shareholder. Thus, even if the managements of all other firms maximized shareholder welfare, these firms would be attractive candidates for a takeover raid by a growth maximizing management.

> (Thus,) a growth maximizing manager will be faced with a seemingly boundless set of merger opportunities, all priced below their present value to the managerial group. (Mueller 1969)

Thus, in this theoretical context, the mature growth-maximizing firm will have no shortage of external-growth opportunities.

A Formal Model

The determinants-of-mergers model derived here is really part of a simultaneous system. The system contains three equations: a mergers equation, a dividends equation, and a capital investment equation. It is argued here that earnings (after tax) can be used for several purposes. They may be distributed as dividends or retained and used for investment or acquisitions. The level of investment, dividends, and the decision to acquire are thus codetermined variables, endogenous to the system (see appendix for a formal derivation of the model).

The dependent variable in the merger equation can be specified as either a 0/1 dummy with value = 1, if the firm made an acquisition; or the dollar value of assets acquired. It might be argued that the proper variable is total expenditure on acquisitions because it includes the premium paid for the shares of the acquired firm. In fact, it is because total expenditures include the premium paid that it is inappropriate. The model we are testing is of determinants of mergers. The questions to be answered are what factors determine whether a company makes an acquisition and what is the size of such acquisitions. These issues are separate from the determination of the price paid for assets acquired.

The exogenous variables of the merger equation fall into three general categories: owner/manager-control variables, life-cycle variables, and an antitrust-related variable.

Since the Marris model requires that there be a separation of ownership and control, the ability of managers to pursue growth-producing mergers, regardless of their profitability (subject, of course, to a security constraint), depends on the extent to which managers are insulated from shareholders.

Note that there are severe problems in measuring the separation of ownership and control. The proxies included in this equation are imperfect; therefore, the empirical importance of the separation of ownership and control may be smaller than is predicted by the theory.

Three proxies for the separation of ownership and control are included. The first is the average number of shares held per stockholder, adjusted for stock splits. This variable measures the dispersion of stock ownership. The rationale behind its inclusion is that the more highly dispersed the stock ownership, the higher the transactions costs of shareholders challenging management. A negative coefficient is expected.[9]

A second variable is the overlap between the officers of a corporation and that corporation's board of directors. This variable measures the extent to which managers are a part of the ultimate decision-making process.

Two assumptions are relevant to this variable. The first is that the goals of individual managers are compatible with each other, though not necessarily uniform. There need not be absolute unanimity among managers, but it is necessary that a general set of goals be internalized by any managers serving as directors.

The second assumption says that managers who also serve as directors should not be influenced by their role as directors. We assume that the managers' growth-maximizing preferences are not altered by a position on the board of directors. If both of these assumptions are correct, the coefficient should be positive. If at least one is not correct, the coefficient could be positive, negative, or zero.

Managerial control is also influenced by shareholder satisfaction. Two different measures of satisfaction will be tested: earnings per share, properly adjusted, and the rate of return on shares of common. The rationale behind including the satisfaction variable is that the more satisfied shareholders are with their position, the less likely they are to challenge managerial actions. A case can be made for either of the two variables; therefore, both variables will be tested.[10]

The life-cycle variables are a particularly important class of variables because the life-cycle model predicts a clear link between a firm's life-cycle position and its merger activity. The difficulty is in determining a firm's position in the life cycle.

Age of the firm is a first approximation of maturity. While old age is neither necessary nor sufficient for maturity, age (measured as years since initial incorporation) is a reasonable proxy.

An alternative measure that will be tested is a variable indicating the age of the firm's technology. A technology-age measure used by Grabowski and Mueller is used here (1972). The variable is specified as a 0/1 dummy, with the value equal to one if the firm has a young technology. Both age variables should have positive coefficients.

Another way to measure position in the life cycle is with some measure of technological advance or innovation. If firms are innovating, there must be some internal-growth opportunities. If there are such internal-growth opportunities, mergers are less likely to occur since growth-maximizing managers prefer internal to external growth.

Patents are used as a proxy for the technological opportunities available to a firm, and, therefore, the growth possibilities that are available to the firm. The patent variable will be specified to include patents by wholly-owned subsidiaries to completely represent the opportunities available to the parent firm. The patent variable's coefficient should be negative. That is, firms with high patents/sales ratios will have opportunities for internal expansion. Given this, *ceteris paribus*, firms are likely to do less acquiring.[11]

Another life-cycle variable is firm diversification (at the two-digit SIC level). Mature growth maximizing firms will diversify in the process of gaining access to growth opportunities. The degree of external expansion can thus be viewed as a proxy of 1) previous efforts to acquire new growth opportunities and 2) internal-growth opportunities available to such firms.

The sign of the coefficient is uncertain. Substantial diversification could indicate many new opportunities for internal expansion and a lower likelihood of acquisition.

On the other hand, diversification may lead firms to do more diversifying because of (1) their desire to guarantee a supply of internal expansion opportunities and (2) the short digestion period of new firms by experienced and mature acquirers, creating a need for ever more rapid external expansion.

Two related variables that are more direct measures of the effect of internal growth on merger activity are also included. The simplest form of this variable is the ratio of past internal growth in assets (growth in assets not due to acquisitions) to past total growth in assets. *Ceteris paribus*, the greater the percentage of growth that is accomplished internally, the greater the internal-growth opportunities and the less likely the firm is to engage in acquisition activity.

An alternative measure of available internal growth opportunities is a previous acquisitions dummy variable (see table 10–1). It is an indirect measure, but a better indirect measure than diversification. Such a variable captures two effects. First, it accounts indirectly for internal growth possibilities. Second, it accounts for the proclivity of managers to grow by acquisition. The expected sign of the coefficient is uncertain. Previous acquisitions may indicate the availability of new internal expansion possibilities and, hence, a negative sign would be expected. Alternatively, the variable could indicate a strong preference on the part of managers to grow through acquisitions. Thus, a positive coefficient would be predicted.

Table 10–1. Variable Names

Variable	Definition
TAC	- $ value of assets acquired, deflated by sales
ACQYES	- 0/1 dummy with value = 1 if firm made an acquisition in year of analysis
DIV[1]	- dividends/sales
INV[2]	- investment/sales
STKSHR[1]	- # of shares per stockholder
OVER[2]	- % of officers of corporation who are members of board of directors
E/S[1]	- earnings per share, adjusted for stock splits and dividends
ROREQ[1]	- rate of return on a share of common
AGE[1]	- age of firm, measured by date of incorporation
PATSAL[1]	- ratio of patents to sales
DIV2D[2]	- diversification at the two digit S.I.C. level
ACQ3YR[2]	- 0/1 dummy, with value equal to one if firm made a large acquisition in previous three years, 0 otherwise
IGR[1]	- ratio of internal growth in assets to total growth in assets
LFDS[1]	- 0/1 dummy, with value equal to one if firm was one of four leading firms in its COMPUSTAT industry in year prior to year of analysis, measured by sales
CFL[1]	- cash flow
DETEQ[2]	- debt/equity ratio
PE[1]	- price/earnings ratio
ALTCOC[1]	- alternate measure of cost of equity, measured as rate of return on shares of comparable risk

1 - appropriate test of statistical significance of coefficient is one tail t-test

2 - appropriate test of statistical significance of coefficient is two tail t-test

One statistical problem is that previous acquisitions is highly collinear with the internal-growth-ratio variable. Consequently, the significance of either (or both) variables may be obscured if both variables are included in a single equation. For this reason, the model will be estimated with and without the previous acquisitions dummy.

The leading-firm variable accounts for an important possible effect on acquisition activity. Efforts by leading firms that are potential competitors to expand into new (and sometimes related) lines of commerce through acquisition rather than *de novo* expansion invite antitrust scrutiny. There are a number of cases in which such scrutiny was begun by the antitrust authorities; such an approach has often been ratified by the courts.

The threat of such scrutiny was strongest immediately after the court decision in the *Procter & Gamble* case (1967); however, it was certainly present prior to that. (The 1964 decision in the El Paso Natural Gas case[12] invoked the potential competition line of reasoning.)

The leading-firm variable is a dummy that has a value of one if the firm was one of the four largest firms (in its COMPUSTAT industry classification) in terms of sales in the year prior to the year for which the firm was selected (see the next section, "Data and Econometric Methodology," for a discussion of the sampling procedure). A negative sign is expected. Scrutiny by antitrust authorities raises the potential cost of acquisitions; consequently, the greater the chance of antitrust problems, the lower the probability of making an acquisition, and acquisitions that do occur will be smaller.

The cost of capital variables is important in this model, because it is argued that changes in the cost of capital variables are important determinants of merger activity.

The cost of capital to a growth-maximizing manager is different from that to a profit-maximizing manager. Rather than being some measure of shareholder opportunity cost, the managerial cost of capital is some measure of managerial opportunity cost. This distinction has important implications.

Investment decisions in the neoclassical model are separate and distinct from decisions concerning finance (or, more exactly, source of finance). The optimal amount of investment is determined solely by the equality between marginal rates of return and the marginal cost of capital and, by implication, can be financed with any mix of internally and externally generated funds.

The story is different for a managerial firm. Internal capital is presumed to be cheaper than external capital. Since there is a separation of ownership and control, the cost of internal funds is not shareholder-opportunity costs; rather, it is a lower subjective figure the value of which is sensitive to preferences, pressures, and opportunities faced by managers — that is, a managerial opportunity cost. External funds are relatively more expensive to managers for several reasons. First, new stock or bond issues necessarily attract attention to a firm's investment and dividend policies. Market-imposed constraints can be tighter than shareholder constraints. Second, risks associated with borrowing may raise the possibility of firm failure and, *ceteris paribus*, reduce managerial security (although these changes may be very small). Finally, while transactions costs for using internal funds are essentially zero, they are positive and may be substantial for external funds. (Note, however, that firms do use external and internal financing.)

An important measure of the availability of internal funds is cash flow. As cash flow increases, the internal funds constraint is less severe and, *ceteris paribus*, expenditure on all uses of internal funds should increase. In particular, one would expect investment spending, be it capital expenditures or acquisitions, to increase (Grabowski and Mueller 1972, Thompson 1979).

Two measures of the cost of externally raised capital will be used. Two measures are needed since external funds can be generated in two ways: equity issues or borrowing.

One measure is (price/earnings) ratio. The P/E ratio is simplistic and is designed to serve as an approximation of the cost of issuing equity. It is a cost of capital measure in that it reflects how the market evaluates firm performance. A high P/E ratio, for example, implies that the market places a high value on the firm's earnings performance; hence, it will be more receptive to equity issued by that firm and the cost of raising equity capital will be reduced.

An alternative measure of the cost of equity capital is tried. The measure used is similar to a measure employed by Grabowksi and Mueller (1972) and is defined as the average rate of return on common stock for the fifteen firms ranked above and below the firm in question, where firms are ranked by variance of rate of return. This approximates the returns from holding stock of firms of comparable risk. The rate-of-return variable is calculated by figuring the return a shareholder would have received had he bought the stock on January 1, sold it on December 31, and collected all cash dividends paid by the firm. (This calculation fails to account for taxes and transactions costs, thus overestimating the maximum possible rate of return.) This is a direct measure of the cost of equity capital; therefore, as it rises, investment expenditures (of both types) should decline.

The second external-cost measure is firm leverage, as measured by the debt-equity ratio. One difficulty in interpreting the coefficient of the ratio is that it reflects several things. On the other hand, highly levered firms are more risky, and riskier firms pay a higher return on the debt they issue. All else being equal, investment activity in general and merger activity in particular will be reduced.

However, conglomerates are more highly levered than nonconglomerates; therefore, a high debt-equity ratio may merely indicate a predisposition towards growth by conglomeration. The variable coefficient, when interpreted this way, would have a positive sign and would merely indicate a correlation between leverage and (conglomerate) acquisition. It is not clear which effect will dominate.

Since the structural-merger equation includes two right-side endogenous variables — investment (capital expenditures) and dividends — it is useful to discuss briefly our expectations concerning these variables.

Note that the simple neoclassical model would predict insignificant coefficients for both variables (Fama 1974). It would predict, for example, that paying dividends does not limit a firm's ability to make an acquisition if that acquisition is profitable. The managerial model makes a contrary argument, suggesting that as dividend payments increase, acquisition activity will decrease.

The coefficient on investment is uncertain, depending as it does on whether capital expenditures and mergers are complementary or substitutable investments. If they are substitutes the coefficient will be negative, suggesting that mergers come at the expense of capital expenditures. A postitive coefficient implies that mergers and capital expenditures can increase simultaneously. The coefficient on this variable has important policy implications, as well, and will be discussed later.

Data and Econometric Methodology

Since the model being estimated is a simultaneous model, the ordinary least-squares-regression technique is inappropriate. However, the specification of the dependent variable means two-stage least squares is not appropriate either. Recall that the dependent variable can be expressed in two alternative ways: it can either be a truncated variable measuring the dollar value of assets acquired in a given year (zero or positive) or as a dichotomous variable with value = 1 if the firm made an acquisition in a given year and zero otherwise. Consequently, simultaneous TOBIT and PROBIT must be used. TOBIT analysis is appropriate when the dependent variable is truncated and PROBIT is used when the left side variable is expressed as a 0/1 dummy.[13] For both procedures, the conditions for identification are identical to that of a system estimated with 2SLS. It can be shown that the necessary and sufficient conditions for identification are satisfied.

Two statistical problems are encountered in this study. First, some of the variables are highly collinear. Typically, the interdependence of the right side variables results in coefficients (and t-statistics) which are lower than their true value. There is no cure for multicollinearity. One recourse is to increase the sample since large samples reduce (though they do not eliminate) the effects of multicollinearity. The difficulty, of course, is knowing when large-sample properties obtain. It is believed that the samples used in this analysis are sufficiently large for the obscuring effects of multicollinearity to be overcome.

The second problem is heteroskedasticity. The model estimated here is heteroskedastic. To remedy the problem, all nonratio, size related variables were deflated by sales (to express them in ratio form).

Current merger activity depends on past values of the independent variables. Thus, the final statistical issue is how to account for the lag between when a decision is made to acquire another firm and the time when the merger is consummated. A lag of three years was chosen because casual reviews of merger negotiations indicate that very few acquisitions take longer than three years to complete. To err by making the lag too long is viewed as less serious than making the lag too short.

Since the model is estimated on a cross-section basis, and since no estimates of the relative importance of the values of the three years preceding the year for which the firm can be made on other than an ad hoc basis, it was decided to measure the values of all exogenous variables as simple average values of the three preceding years.

The time period covered in this study is 1962–1977. This period was divided into four subperiods, each of which corresponds to a particular part of the merger cycle.

1962–1966	average merger activity
1967–1970	rapid and extensive merger activity
1971–1975	declining merger activity (to average levels)
1976–1977	rapid and extensive merger activity

The sample used for each period was drawn randomly. Each firm on the Primary Industrial File of the COMPUSTAT tape was randomly assigned an identification number. Next, a random-number table was used to choose firms for the sample for each year between 1962 and 1977. Approximately 100 numbers were drawn for each year; however, the exact number of firms is much less than 100 because (1) firms whose numbers were drawn more than once in a given year were counted only once and (2) firms for which any data were missing or incomplete were dropped from the sample. Thus, the sample only includes those firms for which a complete data set was available. The sample sizes are as follows:

1962–1966	287 firms
1967–1970	298
1971–1975	382
1976–1977	164

Results

The results of the model are generally consistent with the hypotheses outlined above, although the support is not consistently strong over all time periods.

The coefficients of the owner/manager-control variables indicate that manager control does have some effect on merger activity, although not always as hypothesized. For example, the overlap variable (see table 10-1 for abbreviations and tables 10-2–10-12 for results) is significant in two of the four periods, however, the sign is negative, contrary to our prediction. This likely indicates that one of the assumptions on which our hypothesis is based is invalid. It is probably the case that a position on the board of directors changes managerial behavior. Since a position on a board of directors is a visible one, managerial actions are more apparent to the public and subject to scrutiny. If the threat of public scrutiny represents a potential threat to managerial security, utility-maximizing managers who dominate boards of directors may act to secure their positions. This result may also indicate that managerial control is not correctly measured by the overlap variable.

The measure of the dispersion of stock ownership is either significant or almost so (at at least a 10 percent level), with the correct sign in most of the estimates. The primary exception is the 1971–1975 equation, in which number-of-shares-per-stockholder has a positive sign. This result is unexpected; indeed, it appears to be a statistical aberration.

A plot of the values of shares per stockholder in 1971–1975 shows a much greater dispersion than in other periods and has a relatively large

Table 10–2. TOBIT Equation (ACQ3YR excluded)

Var	1962-66	1967-79	1971-75	1976-77
DIV2D	.0389[b]	.0164	.0615	.0025
	(2.247)	(1.285)	(0.702)	(0.530)
AGE	.0012	.0011	.0133	-.0007
	(1.132)	(0.881)	(1.212)	(-1.16)
OVER	-.3688[b]	-.2636[c]	.4447	.0736
	(-2.24)	(-1.59)	(0.336)	(0.886)
LFDS	-.0676[c]	-.0608	-.0299	.0255
	(-1.49)	(-1.18)	(-0.15)	(1.006)
DETEQ	.0438	.0635[b]	-.1293	.0030
	(0.856)	(2.252)	(-0.29)	(0.076)
IGR	-.0182	-.0681	-.6674[b]	-.0536[b]
	(-0.63)	(-0.91)	(-1.66)	(-1.90)
PE	-.0004	.0008	-.0049	-.0017
	(-0.73)	(1.038)	(-0.77)	(-1.04)
E/S	-.0065	-.0232	.2663[b]	-.0035
	(-0.22)	(-0.71)	(1.647)	(-0.39)
PATSAL	-.0948	.2107	-4.991	-.0457
	(-0.38)	(0.927)	(-1.19)	(-0.11)
STKSHR	-.0000	-.0001[b]	.0005[a]	-.00001[c]
	(-1.15)	(-1.76)	(2.901)	(-1.34)
CFL	-.6651	.4334	-1.966	.9257[a]
	(-1.12)	(1.110)	(-0.49)	(4.181)
INV	1.7465[b]	.1833	3.6704	-.0002
	(2.149)	(0.228)	(0.682)	(-0.01)
DIV	-.8968[a]	-2.16[a]	-6.687[b]	-1.412[a]
	(-3.59)	(-3.77)	(-1.71)	(-2.36)
CONSTANT	-.0582	.0242	-3.625	-.0103
	(-0.52)	(0.161)	(-3.09)	(-0.14)
Mean Squared Error	.0080	.0225	.7143	.0020

(t-statistics in parentheses)

[a]significant at 1% level in appropriate (one or two tail) test

[b]significant at 5% level in appropriate (one or two tail) test

[c]significant at 10% level in appropriate (one or two tail) test

Table 10–3. PROBIT Equation (ACQ3YR excluded)

Var	1962-66	1967-70	1971-75	1976-77
DIV2D	.1086	.2023[a]	.0606[c]	.0833
	(1.448)	(3.914)	(1.651)	(1.196)
AGE	.0071[c]	.0008	.0047	-.0117
	(1.406)	(0.168)	(1.041)	(-1.29)
OVER	-1.266[b]	-.7294	-.0760	.6785
	(-1.94)	(-1.31)	(-0.13)	(0.548)
LFDS	-.4491[b]	-.1399[b]	.1444	-.3255
	(-2.10)	(-1.72)	(0.787)	(-0.89)
DETEQ	.5253	.1034[c]	.0013	.2422
	(1.010)	(1.815)	(0.006)	(0.629)
IGR	-.0576	-.3734	-.3708[b]	-.9858[b]
	(-0.43)	(-1.33)	(-2.16)	(-2.26)
PE	-.0023	-.0043	-.0006	-.0089
	(-1.03)	(1.146)	(-0.27)	(-0.42)
E/S	-.0149	-.1234[c]	.1567[b]	.0775
	(-0.11)	(-1.39)	(1.975)	(0.568)
PATSAL	.4043	.7530	-2.189[c]	.9548
	(0.358)	(0.871)	(-1.28)	(0.183)
STKSHR	-.0001[c]	-.0003[a]	.0001[b]	-.0002
	(-1.28)	(-2.62)	(2.014)	(-0.95)
CFL	-1.680	1.4523	-.4803	7.3938[b]
	(-0.62)	(1.020)	(-0.28)	(2.043)
INV	4.5954	-1.982	2.2479	-1.196
	(1.200)	(-0.62)	(0.538)	(-0.25)
DIV	-5.713[a]	-9.042[a]	-2.307[c]	-13.02[c]
	(-4.23)	(-4.07)	(-1.39)	(-1.49)
CONSTANT	-.0563	.4277	-1.472	-.2347
	(-0.11)	(0.736)	(-2.93)	(-0.22)
Log of Likelihood Fn.	-.114E3	-.120E3	.118E3	-.114E3

(t-statistics in parentheses)

[a]significant at 1% level in appropriate (one or two tail) test

[b]significant at 5% level in appropriate (one or two tail) test

[c]significant at 10% level in appropriate (one or two tail) test

Table 10–4. TOBIT Equation (ACQ3YR and LFDS excluded)

Var	1962-66	1967-70	1971-75	1976-77
DIV2D	.0379[a]	.0171	.0617	.0028
	(2.359)	(1.336)	(0.704)	(0.584)
AGE	.0013	.0012	.0133	-.0006
	(1.218)	(0.909)	(1.210)	(-0.97)
OVER	-.3794[a]	-.2546	.4299	.0632
	(-2.60)	(-1.53)	(0.326)	(0.743)
DETEQ	.0429	.0665[a]	-.1243	.0075
	(0.836)	(2.352)	(-0.28)	(0.185)
IGR	-.0166	-.0692	-.6685[b]	-.0528[b]
	(-0.58)	(-0.92)	(-1.66)	(-1.84)
PE	-.0004	.0008	-.0050	-.0013
	(-0.84)	(1.043)	(-0.78)	(-0.86)
E/S	-.0078	-.0373	.2656[b]	-.0015
	(-0.26)	(-1.07)	(1.644)	(-0.17)
PATSAL	-.1064	.1536	-4.989	-.0597
	(-0.42)	(0.681)	(-1.20)	(-0.15)
STKSHR	-.00001[c]	-.0001[b]	.0005[a]	-.00001
	(-1.51)	(-1.74)	(2.898)	(-1.25)
CFL	-.6891	.4091	-1.939	.9651[a]
	(-1.15)	(1.045)	(-0.49)	(4.146)
INV	1.9392[a]	.3493	3.6698	.0730
	(2.339)	(0.440)	(0.683)	(0.223)
DIV	-0.863[a]	-2.108[a]	-6.632[b]	-1.530[a]
	(-3.43)	(-3.71)	(-1.71)	(-2.54)
CONSTANT	-0.112	-0.025	-3.640	-0.047
	(-1.06)	(-0.17)	(-3.12)	(-0.698)
Mean Squared Error	.0080	.0220	.7140	.0020

(t-statistics in parentheses)

[a]significant at 1% level in appropriate (one or two tail) test

[b]significant at 5% level in appropriate (one or two tail) test

[c]significant at 10% level in appropriate (one or two tail) test

number of observations with very large values. Among these observations is a disproportionate number of acquiring firms. This is not enough to explain the shift in sign, but it is an explanation consistent with the unexpected result we obtain in this period.

The shareholder-satisfaction measures performed poorly. Rate of return on equity is never significant and earnings per share is significant only in the 1971–1975 period. This indicates either that shareholder satisfaction is unimportant or, more likely, that the suggested measures do not correctly capture the effects of shareholder satisfaction.

The life-cycle hypothesis receives modest support in the regression results. The diversification variable is significant in only one time period (1962–1966). Apparently current diversification has little relevance for determining the extent of future efforts to diversify.

The age variable performs only marginally better. It is significant only in several of the PROBIT equations (see tables 10-3, 10-5, and 10-7) and one TOBIT equation (table 10-6). This is not a complete surprise. However, the age-of-technology variable (used by Grabowski and Mueller) is not significant in any equation. This is a surprise and is a result that is difficult to explain given the theory and previous empirical results (Grabowski and Mueller 1972). These results make it difficult to support the strong formulation of the life-cycle model which suggests a direct link between maturity and acquisition activity. (Of course, better measures of maturity need to be tested before the theory is rejected outright.)

A weaker formulation of the life-cycle model is supported, however, by the internal-growth-ratio variable. In the TOBIT equations, the coefficients are significant with the correct sign at the 1 percent level in 1971–1975 and 1976–1977; in the PROBIT equation, these results also obtain for 1967–1970. These results provide a rather clear indication that a significant relationship between previous internal growth and external expansion exists. Further, the previous acquisitions variable is significant in all but one period (see tables 10-9–10-12). Note that when the previous acquisitions dummy is included in the equation, it steals the significance of the internal-growth ratio. Thus, while the direct maturity acquisition link is not supported statistically, there is a link between internal growth possibilities (measured directly and indirectly) and acquisitions.

The hypotheses concerning cash flow-cost of capital determinants receive mixed support. The cash-flow variable is significant only in 1976–1977. In this period, the coefficient is very large in each equation, suggesting a very substantial impact of changes in cash flow on acquisition activity. This result is consistent with the observed pattern of financing; that is a substantial majority of the acquisitions in that period

Table 10–5. PROBIT Equation (ACQ3YR and LFDS excluded)

Var	1962-66	1967-70	1971-75	1976-77
DIV2D	.0986	.2023[a]	.0619[c]	.0858
	(1.331)	(3.552)	(1.692)	(1.248)
AGE	.0073[c]	.0011	.0047	-.0099
	(1.469)	(0.224)	(1.057)	(-1.13)
OVER	-1.298[b]	-.7702	-.0569	.5413
	(-2.00)	(-1.28)	(-0.10)	(0.444)
DETEQ	.4952	.1085[b]	-.0200	.2856
	(1.421)	(1.861)	(-0.11)	(0.756)
IGR	-.0436	-.3772[c]	-.3621[b]	-.9714[b]
	(-0.33)	(-1.34)	(-2.12)	(-2.22)
PE	-.0024	.0043	-.0004	-.0051
	(-1.08)	(1.109)	(-0.18)	(-0.25)
E/S	-.0178	-.1324	.1622[b]	.1043
	(-0.14)	(-1.11)	(2.054)	(0.788)
PATSAL	.3187	.6462	-2.124	.6920
	(0.279)	(0.755)	(-1.24)	(1.164)
STKSHR	-.0001	-.0003[a]	.0001[a]	-.0002[c]
	(-1.22)	(-2.50)	(2.000)	(-1.30)
CFL	-1.865	1.3887	-.5802	7.3026[a]
	(-0.69)	(0.978)	(-0.34)	(2.073)
INV	5.8052	-1.569	1.2599	-.3246
	(1.546)	(-0.50)	(0.556)	(-0.07)
DIV	-5.318[a]	-8.852[a]	-2.519[c]	-.0013[c]
	(-3.98)	(-4.05)	(-1.53)	(-1.59)
CONSTANT	-.4299	.3112	-1.471	-.6834
	(-0.88)	(0.560)	(-2.84)	(-0.74)
Log of Likelihood Fn.	-.120E3	-.135E3	-.143E3	-.398E2

(t-statistics in parentheses)

[a]significant at 1% level in appropriate (one or two tail) test

[b]significant at 5% level in appropriate (one or two tail) test

[c]significant at 10% level in appropriate (one or two tail) test

Table 10–6. TOBIT Equation (ACQ3YR and LFDS excluded) ROREQ replacing E/S

Var	1967-70	1971-75	1976-77
DIV2D	.0131	.1071	.0043
	(0.951)	(1.164)	(0.909)
AGE	.0015	.0165[c]	-.0003
	(1.071)	(1.416)	(-0.54)
OVER	-.3075[b]	.5660	-.1175
	(-1.68)	(0.404)	(-1.18)
DETEQ	.1112[a]	-.0570	0.0140
	(2.217)	(-0.12)	(-0.33)
IGR	-.0565	-.5396[c]	-.0701[a]
	(-0.72)	(-1.42)	(-2.33)
PE	.0011[c]	-.0051	-.0011
	(1.383)	(-0.77)	(-0.75)
ROREQ	-.2944	1.4400	.1710
	(-0.99)	(0.363)	(0.783)
PATSAL	.1176	-5.454	.1253
	(0.467)	(-1.20)	(0.352)
STKSHR	-.00001[b]	.0005[a]	-.00001[c]
	(-1.70)	(2.446)	(-1.43)
CFL	.4603	-1.528	.8785[a]
	(1.106)	(-0.35)	(4.250)
INV	.1794	3.4296	.2421
	(0.204)	(0.578)	(0.827)
DIV	-2.266[a]	-7.488[b]	-1.515[a]
	(-3.57)	(-1.79)	(-2.58)
CONSTANT	-.0672	-3.959	-.0983
	(-0.46)	(-2.88)	(-1.44)
Mean Squared Error	.0071	.7730	.0044

(t-statistics in parentheses)

[a]significant at 1% level in appropriate (one or two tail) test

[b]significant at 5% level in appropriate (one or two tail) test

[c]significant at 10% level in appropriate (one or two tail) test

Table 10–7. PROBIT Equation (ACQ3YR and LFDS excluded) ROREQ replacing E/S

Var	1967-70	1971-75	1976-77
DIV2D	.1705[a]	.0841[a]	.1153
	(2.889)	(2.279)	(1.610)
AGE	.0029	.0061[c]	-.0059
	(0.557)	(1.326)	(-0.66)
OVER	-1.103[b]	.0353	1.4659
	(-1.69)	(0.062)	(1.159)
DETEQ	-.0387	.0267	.1047
	(-0.20)	(0.135)	(0.188)
IGR	-.3589	-.2830[c]	-1.065[a]
	(-1.25)	(-1.59)	(-2.38)
PE	.0047[b]	-.0005	-.0044
	(1.621)	(-0.20)	(-0.21)
ROREQ	1.3633	1.4958	2.3238
	(1.010)	(0.919)	(0.754)
PATSAL	.2655	-2.048	2.4104
	(0.285)	(-1.16)	(0.541)
STKSHR	-.00028[a]	.0001	-.00028
	(-2.33)	(1.428)	(1.272)
CFL	.4912	-.6746	7.9085[a]
	(0.304)	(-0.38)	(2.209)
INV	-.7590	1.2894	.8069
	(-0.22)	(0.594)	(0.168)
DIV	-9.719[a]	-2.893[b]	-15.05[c]
	(-3.98)	(-1.72)	(-1.61)
CONSTANT	.1036	-1.5489	-1.2718
	(0.1830)	(-2.819)	(-1.272)
Log of Likelihood Fn.	-.118E3	-.147E3	-.332E2

(t-statistics in parentheses)

[a]significant at 1% level in appropriate (one or two tail) test

[b]significant at 5% level in appropriate (one or two tail) test

[c]significant at 10% level in appropriate (one or two tail) test

were cash financed as opposed to earlier periods (in the 1960s) when acquisitions were generally financed with debt or a debt-equity mix.

The price/earnings ratio is not significant in any period. However, the alternative cost of equity capital measure (ALTCOC in table 10-8) is significant with the correct sign in 1967–1970. Acquisitions in this period tended to be financed with a debt/equity mix.

The debt/equity ratio variable had significant coefficients only in the 1967–1970 equation also. The coefficient is positive suggesting the positive effects of conglomeration on leverage and the general tendency to greater leverage in the late 60s dominated any cost of capital effect of the variable.

A general conclusion to be drawn from the performance of the cash flow and cost of capital variables is that their effects on merger activity are relevant only in periods of extensive merger activity. In periods of what might be termed normal merger activity, these factors provide no particular inducement to mergers. However, when merger activity speeds up, these cash flow and cost of capital factors are, indeed, important. This suggests that changes in the cost of capital and/or cash flows contribute to cyclical upswings in merger activity, although it would be too strong to suggest that these changes *cause* these cyclical upswings.

The results for the leading firm dummy are surprisingly robust (see tables 10-2, 10-3, 10-8, 10-9, and 10-10). The dummy has a significant coefficient in several of the equations estimated. This suggests that at least at some points in the past, dominance (as evidenced by status as one of the four largest firms) was sufficient to reduce both the probability of and size of acquisitions. This is consistent with our expectations; yet, it is a stronger result than might have been expected given the apparent inability of the antitrust authorities to litigate effectively against conglomerate mergers.

Finally, the endogenous right-side variables have interesting implications. First, the dividends coefficients are almost uniformly negative and significant. This implies that dividends compete with mergers for resources, as our theory would predict.

The more interesting and certainly more important result is the general lack of significance of the capital expenditures variable. In particular, the investment variable is significant only in the 1962–1966 period (and then with a positive coefficient). This is contrary to the conventional wisdom[14] which suggests that mergers use funds that would otherwise have been used for capital expansion. These results offer no hint of this; in fact, they suggest no significant relationship exists between mergers or capital expansion.

Table 10–8. PROBIT Equation (ACQ3YR excluded and ALTCOC included) 1967–70 only

Var	Equation 1	Equation 2
DIV2D	.0982 (1.496)	.0997 (1.541)
AGE	.0060 (1.095)	.0067 (1.218)
OVER	-1.604[b] (-2.27)	-1.529 (-2.18)
LFDS	-.3030[c] (-1.37)	
DETEQ	-.0910 (-0.43)	-.0432 (-0.21)
IGR	-1.162[a] (-3.77)	-1.138[a] (-3.73)
ALTCOC	-5.461[c] (-1.29)	-6.148[c] (-1.30)
E/S	1.9926 (1.128)	1.7760[c] (1.338)
PATSAL	.7035 (0.738)	.4010 (0.434)
STKSHR	-.0001[c] (-1.89)	-.0001[c] (-1.78)
CEL	.4543 (0.270)	.3781 (0.226)
INV	-.6326 (-0.17)	.0580 (0.016)
DIV	-9.132[a] (-3.63)	-8.504[a] (-3.56)
CONSTANT	.2718 (0.309)	.0813 (0.094)
Log of Likelihood Fn.	-.141E3	-.138E3

(t-statistics in parentheses)

[a]significant at 1% level in appropriate (one or two tail) test

[b]significant at 5% level in appropriate (one or two tail) test

[c]significant at 10% level in appropriate (one or two tail) test

Table 10–9. TOBIT Equation (ACQ3YR included)

Var	1962-66	1967-70	1971-75	1976-77
DIV2D	.0323[a]	.0043	.271	-.0033
	(2.047)	(0.328)	(-.300)	(-0.63)
AGE	.0008	.0013	.0147[c]	-.0003
	(0.780)	(1.053)	(1.326)	(-0.47)
OVER	-.4102[a]	-.3150[c]	.4044	.0581
	(-2.82)	(-1.91)	(0.301)	(0.693)
LFDS	-.0676[c]	-.0634	-.5643[c]	-.0155
	(-1.49)	(-1.25)	(-1.99)	(-0.61)
ACQ3YR	.2041[a]	.1959[a]	1.2325[b]	.0851[b]
	(2.740)	(2.928)	(2.370)	(2.327)
DETEQ	.0086	.0642[a]	-.0880	.0211
	(0.165)	(2.322)	(-0.20)	(0.622)
IGR	.0389	.0793	-.2169	.0072
	(0.742)	(0.865)	(-0.48)	(0.195)
PE	-.0004	.0004	-.0035	-.0018
	(-0.76)	(0.567)	(-0.54)	(-1.06)
E/S	-.0087	-.0285	.2938[b]	-.0040
	(-0.30)	(-0.87)	(1.799)	(-0.46)
PATSAL	-.0728	.2392	-3.630	-.1736
	(-0.31)	(1.079)	(-0.88)	(-0.43)
STKSHR	-.0000	-.00001[c]	.0005[a]	-.0000[c]
	(-1.26)	(-1.39)	(2.909)	(-1.40)
CFL	-.6425	.3786	-2.170	1.0144[a]
	(-1.11)	(0.979)	(-0.54)	(4.303)
INV	1.5751[b]	.4564	3.4398	-.1045
	(1.983)	(0.584)	(0.615)	(-0.31)
DIV	-.7433[a]	-1.920[a]	-6.451[b]	-1.427[a]
	(-3.14)	(-3.44)	(-1.64)	(-2.44)
CONSTANT	-.0898	-.1418	-4.013	-.0747
	(-0.79)	(-0.90)	(-3.36)	(-0.96)
Mean Squared Error	.0077	.0219	.7202	.0002

(t-statistics in parentheses)

[a]significant at 1% level in appropriate (one or two tail) test

[b]significant at 5% level in appropriate (one or two tail) test

[c]significant at 10% level in appropriate (one or two tail) test

Table 10–10. PROBIT Equation (ACQ3YR included)

Var	1962-66	1967-70	1971-75	1976-77
DIV2D	.0871	.1573[a]	.0324	.0116
	(1.127)	(2.600)	(0.824)	(0.149)
AGE	.0054	.0014	.0046	-.0078
	(1.051)	(0.274)	(1.000)	(-0.86)
OVER	-1.490[a]	-1.126[b]	-.0767	.5566
	(-2.20)	(-1.81)	(-0.13)	(0.425)
LFDS	-.4036[b]	-.1832	.0819	-.2717
	(-1.84)	(-0.92)	(0.432)	(-0.69)
ACQ3YR	1.3313[a]	.9987[a]	1.1614[a]	1.2648[b]
	(3.026)	(3.508)	(4.353)	(2.295)
DETEQ	.3785	.0978	.0693	.3579
	(1.131)	(0.804)	(0.369)	(1.102)
IGR	.3643	.3496	.0471	-.1342
	(1.138)	(0.972)	(0.232)	(-0.23)
PE	-.0020	.0025	-.0001	-.0130
	(-0.91)	(0.789)	(-0.40)	(-0.56)
E/S	-.0088	-.1024	.1575	.0480
	(-0.07)	(-1.15)	(0.197)	(0.339)
PATSAL	.4274	.9408	1.5305	-.9351
	(0.380)	(1.099)	(-0.91)	(-0.16)
STKSHR	-.00009	-.0002[b]	.0001[b]	-.0002
	(-1.00)	(-2.11)	(2.857)	(-1.26)
CFL	-1.662	1.2661	-.3539	9.0248[b]
	(-0.60)	(0.874)	(-0.21)	(2.137)
INV	3.6591	-.2998	1.0611	-2.796
	(0.955)	(-0.09)	(0.458)	(-0.52)
DIV	-4.929[a]	-8.067[a]	-1.690	-14.11[c]
	(-3.68)	(-3.67)	(-1.02)	(-1.48)
CONSTANT	-.3998	-.3650	-1.922	-.9129
	(-0.68)	(-0.59)	(-3.75)	(-0.81)
Log of Likelihood Fn.	-.112E3	-.128E3	-.133E3	-.368E2

(t-statistics in parentheses)

[a]significant at 1% level in appropriate (one or two tail) test

[b]significant at 5% level in appropriate (one or two tail) test

[c]significant at 10% level in appropriate (one or two tail) test

Table 10–11. TOBIT Equation (ACQ3YR included and LFDS excluded)

Var	1962-66	1967-70	1971-75	1976-77
DIV2D	.0314[b]	.0051	.0552	-.0034
	(1.989)	(0.389)	(0.626)	(-0.65)
AGE	.0009	.0014	.0136	-.0002
	(0.827)	(1.079)	(1.231)	(-0.32)
OVER	-.4201[a]	-.3061[b]	.2984	.0505
	(-2.88)	(-1.85)	(0.224)	(0.607)
ACQ3YR	.2138[b]	.1945[a]	.3489	.0896[b]
	(2.881)	(2.899)	(1.336)	(2.468)
DETEQ	.0065	.0674[b]	-.0834	.0247
	(0.125)	(2.429)	(-0.19)	(0.757)
IGR	.0429	.0776	0.5463[c]	.0111
	(0.813)	(0.841)	(-1.31)	(0.305)
PE	-.0004	.0004	-.0047	-.0016
	(-0.76)	(0.574)	(-0.74)	(-0.97)
E/S	-.0096	-.0328	.2720[b]	-.0030
	(-0.32)	(-1.06)	(1.675)	(-0.35)
PATSAL	-.0808	.1808	-4.551	-.1881
	(-0.34)	(0.821)	(-1.09)	(-0.46)
STKSHR	-.00001	-.0001[c]	.0005[a]	-.00001[c]
	(-1.25)	(-1.35)	(2.883)	(-1.44)
CFL	-.6571	.3515	-1.836	1.0281[a]
	(-1.13)	(0.906)	(-0.46)	(4.314)
INV	1.7027[b]	.6211	3.6245	-.0663
	(2.158)	(0.803)	(0.671)	(-0.20)
DIV	-.7132[a]	-1.850[a]	-6.314[c]	-1.509[a]
	(-3.02)	(-3.37)	(-1.62)	(-2.62)
CONSTANT	-.1301	-.1917	-3.838	-.0096
	(-1.20)	(-1.25)	(-3.24)	(-1.45)
Mean Squared Error	.0077	.0219	.7209	.0002

(t-statistics in parentheses)

[a]significant at 1% level in appropriate (one or two tail) test

[b]significant at 5% level in appropriate (one or two tail) test

[c]significant at 10% level in appropriate (one or two tail) test

Table 10–12. PROBIT Equation (ACQ3YR included and LFDS excluded)

Var	1962-66	1967-70	1971-75	1976-77
DIV2D	-.0757	.1568[a]	.0329	.0122
	(-0.99)	(2.605)	(0.839)	(0.158)
AGE	.0055	.0018	.0047	-.0061
	(1.070)	(0.362)	(1.029)	(-0.70)
OVER	-1.542	-1.097[b]	-.0658	.4269
	(-0.24)	(-1.76)	(-0.11)	(0.331)
ACQ3YR	1.3472[a]	.9791[a]	1.1707[a]	1.2694[b]
	(3.155)	(3.468)	(4.403)	(2.359)
DETEQ	.3500	.1060	.0576	.3948
	(1.248)	(0.876)	(0.310)	(1.236)
IGR	.3756	.3292	.0535	-.0967
	(1.210)	(0.920)	(0.266)	(-0.17)
PE	-.0021	.0024	.00002	-.0098
	(0.933)	(0.779)	(0.010)	(-0.42)
E/S	-.0096	-.1140	.1606[b]	.0669
	(-0.07)	(-1.19)	(2.025)	(0.483)
PATSAL	.3519	.8168	-1.486	-1.196
	(0.311)	(0.961)	(-0.88)	(-0.20)
STKSHR	-.00008	-.0002[b]	.0001[b]	-.0003
	(-0.97)	(-2.09)	(1.810)	(-1.27)
CFL	-1.847	1.1740	-.4123	9.0101[b]
	(-0.67)	(0.813)	(-0.24)	(2.161)
INV	4.7292	.1725	1.0950	-2.010
	(1.237)	(0.054)	(0.470)	(-0.38)
DIV	-4.539[a]	-7.843[a]	-1.800	-14.91[c]
	(-3.45)	(-3.63)	(-1.09)	(-1.59)
CONSTANT	-.7322	-.4983	-1.961	-1.312
	(-1.33)	(-0.83)	(-3.73)	(-1.35)
Log of Likelihood Fn.	-.114E3	-.128E3	-.134E3	-.371E2

(t-statistics in parentheses)

[a]significant at 1% level in appropriate (one or two tail) test

[b]significant at 5% level in appropriate (one or two tail) test

[c]significant at 10% level in appropriate (one or two tail) test

Conclusions and Policy Implications

The empirical results presented here do not demonstrate that the Marris-Mueller growth-maximizing/life-cycle model explains merger activity. The support for the theoretical model is simply not strong enough. However, the results are sufficiently robust to allow one to conclude that, at a minimum, growth-maximizing/life-cycle considerations form an integral part of an eclectic theory of mergers. Thus Steiner's model is made more complete. At best, one can look at previous internal growth (or previous acquisitions) to infer the relative likelihood of different firms making acquisitions and the relative size of such acquisitions. The results for the cash-flow and cost-of-capital variables seem to imply that, while cost-of-capital changes do not always affect merger activity, stock market booms, such as occurred in the late 1960s (which lower the cost of equity capital), or substantial increases in cash flows may suffice to induce cyclical upswings in merger activity or, at a minimum, sustain these increases. This suggests a role for financial factors in explaining changes in the pace of merger activity rather than in merger activity as a whole.

This study allows us to draw several policy inferences. The first implication is philosophical. There still does not exist any evidence that substantially supports a single-cause conglomerate-merger model. Unlike the merger waves of the early twentieth century, the recent conglomerate-merger wave lacks an overriding motive. We err, therefore, if we criticize conglomerate mergers because firms are using them to gain tax advantages or to play accounting games. Policy designed to limit the ability of firms to make conglomerate acquisitions must be motivated by efficiency or aggregate concentration concerns.[15] There is no obvious sinister motive underlying conglomerate-merger activity.

The second policy implication derives from the cash-flow and cost-of-capital variables. To the extent that stock market booms and cash flow increases induce, at least in part, sharp increases in stock market activity, there is no policy that the government can undertake to eliminate the generally substantial cyclical increases in merger activity that we have observed since 1960. The government does not (and cannot) control the stock market or debt markets, and confiscatory taxes on cash flows are unconscionable.

Third, there is no evidence that conglomerate mergers deprive the economy of needed (or desired) capital expenditures. The relationship between acquisitions and capital expenditures is clearly nonsubstitutable. There is no indication, based on these results, that the two expenditures compete for funds in any meaningful way. This result makes it more difficult to argue that conglomerate mergers lead to a less than desirable allocation of firm resources.

Finally, the performance of the antitrust variable suggests the possibility that the existing antitrust laws, if employed vigorously, provide a stronger legal barrier to conglomerate merger activity than is now generally believed. It is by no means a certain proposition; however, this study suggests that the threat of antitrust action against dominant firms might lead to reductions in conglomeration. Testing this proposition with vigorous antitrust action is possibly preferable to an outright ban on conglomerate activity, as has been proposed.

Appendix

Many decisions at the firm level are simultaneous. Firm managers are constantly forced to make pricing, output, and investment decisions, all of which are linked. Such simultaneity is also present in the decision as to how to distribute earnings.

A firm can either retain earnings within the firm or distribute them to the owners of the firm (the stockholders) as dividends. If earnings are retained, the firm can use the funds for research and development or for various other sorts of investments, including (though not limited to) mergers.

Micro theory tells us the basis on which firms ought to make sure decisions about how to use their retained earnings. Since, in a managerial framework, managers maximize their utility, we will assume that earnings will be distributed in a manner consistent with that end.

Recall that managerial utility is a function of growth and security.

$$U = K(G,Sec). \qquad (10A.1)$$

Earnings may be distributed as dividends, investments, and/or mergers (expenditure on acquisitions). Security is a function of dividends, investments, and mergers. Growth is a function of mergers and investments. Thus equation 10A.1 can be restated as

$$\begin{aligned} U &= K[F(I,M)),p(I,M,D)] \qquad (10A.1a) \\ &= z(M,I,D). \end{aligned}$$

In other words, utility is explicitly related to the uses and distribution of earnings.

The first order condition for a maximum is that the marginal returns from various uses of earnings (*MRR*) equal the marginal cost of finance (*MCF*), where both costs and returns are measured in utility units. That is,

$$MRR_M = MRR_I = MRR_D = MCF, \qquad (10A.2)$$

where *M, I,* and *D* are mergers, capital expenditures (investment), and dividends, respectively.

For simplicity, the marginal conditions in equation 10A.2 are written in linear form as approximations. Expressing the equations in linear form reduces the generality of the model somewhat; yet it permits us to derive structural equations that are easily estimated:

$$MRR_M = a_m + b_m I + c_m M + e_m X_m, \tag{10A.3a}$$

$$MRR_I = a_i + b_i I + c_i M + e_i X_i, \tag{10A.3b}$$

$$MRR_D = a_d + b_d I + c_d M + d_d D + e_d X_d, \tag{10A.3c}$$

$$MCF = g^*(M + I + D) + hZ, \tag{10A.3d}$$

where the X vectors contain exogenous elements peculiar to the particular type of expenditure being undertaken, while the vector Z is the vector of exogenous elements that determine the firm's marginal cost of finance.

By setting each of the marginal rate of return equations 10A.3a, 10A.3b and 10A.3c equal to the marginal cost of finance equation 10A.3d, the structural equations of the model can be derived and written as follows:

$$M = \frac{a_m}{g - c_M} + \frac{b_m - g}{g - c_m} I - \frac{g}{g - c_m} D + \frac{e_m}{g - c_m} X_M - \frac{h}{g - c_m} Z, \tag{10A.4a}$$

$$I = \frac{a_i}{g - b_I} + \frac{c_i - g}{g - b_I} M - \frac{g}{g - b_I} D + \frac{e_i}{g - b_I} X_i - \frac{h}{g - b_I} Z, \tag{10A.4b}$$

$$D = \frac{a_d}{g - d_D} + \frac{c_c - g}{g - d_D} M + \frac{b_D - g}{g - d_D} I \frac{e_D}{g - d_D} X_D - \frac{d}{g - d_D} Z. \tag{10A.4c}$$

Equations 10A.4a, 10A.4b, and 10A.4c represent the three structural equations of the model. Each equation in the system has a marginal rate-of-return component and a measure of the marginal cost of finance. The marginal cost component (the Z vector) is the same for each equation; however, the vector of exogenous variables (the X vector) is necessarily different for each equation.

Notes

1. Conglomerate mergers fall into one of three categories. Pure conglomerate mergers are mergers in which the acquired firm operates in a completely different line of business from the acquiring firm. Market-extension mergers are mergers in which the acquisition of the acquired firm extends the geographic market of the acquiring firm, while product-extension mergers enable the acquiring firm to branch out into new, but related lines of business.

2. Synergism is sometimes referred to as the 2 + 2 = 5 effect. More specifically, a synergistic effect is said to exist if the value of the merged firm exceeds the simple sum of the values of the acquiring and acquired firms.

3. Pure conglomerate mergers are mergers in which two firms with totally unrelated products (or product lines) merge. Consequently, production economies are unlikely. Marketing economies could conceivably result, although with unrelated products, they are not likely to occur.

Conglomerate mergers can also be product or market extension in nature. Production or marketing economies are possible in these cases, but only if there is substantial overlap between products or markets.

4. See, for example, Henry Manne, "Mergers and the Market for Corporate Control." *Journal of Political Economy,* 73 (April, 1965), H. Levy and M. Sarnat, Case Diversification, Portfolio Analysis, and the Uneasy Care for Conglomerate Mergers," *Journal of Finance,* 25 (September, 1970), and Dennis Mueller; "The Effects of Conglomerate Mergers," *Journal of Banking and Finance,* 1 (December, 1977).

5. If any disturbance is likely to enhance the value of a firm, managers have an incentive to make such information public. Thus, there is no reason for the asymmetry in expectations required by Gort's theory to exist.

6. Steiner (1975 p. 97). It is easy to show also that bankruptcy avoidance only makes sense from the point of view of the acquiring firm in a limited set of circumstances. Suppose the premium paid in an acquisition is .2V, where V = firm market value. The expected cost of bankruptcy equals the transactions costs arising from bankruptcy (T_B) multiplied by the probability of bankruptcy P(B). In particular, $E(C_B) = T_B \cdot P(B)$. The merger makes sense only if $E(C_B)$ is greater than or equal to P, where P = premium. If we assume $T_B = .2V$ (an estimate that is probably high), $p(B)$ must equal one for mergers to avoid bankruptcy to make economic sense. As $p(B)$ declines, the transactions costs of bankruptcy must rise for the merger to make sense. For example, with $p(B) = I$, T_B must equal $2V$.

7. The managerial utility function can be represented in the following functional form:

$$U = F(PR, NPR)$$

where PR = pecuniary returns to managers and NPR = nonpecuniary returns. It follows from Marris' model that

$$\begin{aligned} PR &= g(G,Sec), \\ NPR &= g(G,sec), \end{aligned}$$

where G = growth of the firm (measured by growth in assets) and Sec = managerial security. Thus,

$$\begin{aligned} U &= F\,[g(G,Sec),h(G,Sec)] \\ &= K(G,Sec). \end{aligned}$$

8. Mueller argues that in equilibrium the discount rate and cost of capital (to managers) will be equal. Mueller further argues that the cost of capital will be lower for the growth maximizing manager than for the profit maximizing manager. Cost of capital is some weighted average of the costs of internally and externally generated funds. The cost of internal funds is assumed relatively lower for growth maximizing managers. If the cost of externally raised funds is the same for all, the cost of capital for growth maximizing managers will be lower. Therefore, the discount rate for the growth maximizing manager will be lower.

9. A problem with this specification is that since the distribution of stock ownership is

not known, we must use a simple, unweighted average as opposed to a weighted average. As a result, there is a possibility of misrepresentating the diffusion of stock ownership. Consider the following: Suppose firm A has 1 million shares outstanding and 1,000 stockholders. The average stockholding is 1,000 shares. Suppose firm B has 1 million shares outstanding and 1,000 stockholders, but that Mr. B, the founder of the firm, owns 500,000 shares. The calculated average shareholding for firm B is also 1000 shares. Firm B appears to have stock ownership as diffuse as firm A, yet this is clearly not the case since Mr. B owns half of the shares outstanding. A weighted diffusion measure would solve this problem.

10. A disadvantage of the rate of return variable is that the data on the COMPUSTAT tape needed to calculate the variable are not complete prior to 1965; thus, the rate of return variable cannot be used for the period 1962–1966.

11. One should not set high expectations for the variable. There are many problems in interpreting patent data, as well as questions concerning the quality of the data. The variable has not worked terribly well in previous empirical analysis, particularly Grabowski and Mueller's simultaneous systems analysis of firm expenditure.

12. *Federal Trade Commission* v. *Procter and Gamble Co.*, 386 U. S. 568 (1967) and *United States* v. *El Paso Natural Gas Co.*, 376 U. S. 651, 659 (1964).

13. While it is not always the case, it can be shown that there is a single reduced form equation corresponding to each structural equation. See Robin C. Sickles and Peter Schmidt, "Simultaneous Equations Models With Truncated Dependent Variables: A Simultaneous TOBIT Model," *Journal of Economics and Business,* 31 (Fall 1978).

14. See Morris Mintz, "Playing the Takeover Game," *The Washington Post*, April 10, 1980, pp. 1, 11–12.

15. The evidence on these points is inconclusive. Substantial further research must be done in order to demonstrate the extent of efficiency or concentration problems with conglomerate mergers.

References

Amemiya, Takeshi, "Multivariate Regression and Simultaneous Equation Models When the Dependent Variables are Truncated Normal," *Econometrica*, 42 (November, 1974): 1000–1012.

Amemiya, Takeshi, "Regression Analysis When the Dependent Variable is Truncated Normal," *Econometrica*, 41 (November, 1973): 997–1016.

Beckenstein, Alan, "Merger Activity and Merger Theories: An Empirical Investigation," *Antitrust Bulletin*, 24 (Spring, 1979): 105–128.

Berle, Adolf A. and Gardiner C. Means, *The Modern Corporation and Private Property* (New York: Harcourt, Brace, and World, Inc., rev. ed. 1967).

Brittain, John A., *Corporate Dividends Policy* (Washington, D. C.: Brookings Institution, 1966).

Fama, Eugene F., "The Empirical Relationships between the Dividend and Investment Decisions of Firms," *American Economic Review* (June 1974).

Friend, Irwin and Marshall Puckett, "Dividends and Stock Prices," *American Economic Review*, 54 (September 1964): 656–692.

Gort, Michael, "An Economic Disturbance Theory of Mergers," *Quarterly Journal of Economics*, 83 (November 1969): 624–642.

Grabowski, H. G. and D. C. Mueller, "Managerial and Stockholder Welfare Models of Firm Expenditure," *Review of Economics and Statistics,* 54 (November 1972): 9–24.

Grabowski, H. G. and D. C. Mueller, "Life Cycle Effects on Corporate Returns on Retentions," *Review of Economics and Statistics*, 57 (November 1975): 400–409.

Haugen, Robert A. and Terence C. Langeteig, "An Empirical Test for Synergism in Merger," *Journal of Finance,* 30 (September 1975): 1003–1014.

Haugen, Robert A. and Jon G. Udell, "Rate of Return to Stockholders of Acquired Companies," *Journal of Financial and Quantitive Analysis,* 7 (January 1972): 1387–1398.

Herzig, Chayim L., "An Econometric Investigation of Acquisition Activity," Unpublished Ph.D. dissertation, Cornell University, 1974.

Higgins, Robert C. and L. D. Schall, "Corporate Bankruptcy and Conglomerate Merger," *Journal of Finance*, 30 (March 1975): 93–113.

Jorgenson, Dale W. and Calvin D. Seibert, "A Comparison of Alternative Theories of Corporate Investment Behavior," *American Economic Review,* 58 (September 1968): 681–712.

Kummer, Donald R. and J. R. Hoffmeister, "Valuation Consequences of Cash Tender Offers," *Journal of Finance*, 33 (May 1978), 505–516.

Larner, R. J., "Ownership and Control in the 200 Largest Nonfinancial Corporations," *American Economic Review*, 56 (September 1966): 777–787.

Levy, H. and M. Sarnat, "Diversification, Portfolio Analysis and the Uneasy Case for Conglomerate Mergers," *Journal of Finance,* 25 (September 1970): 795–802.

Lintner, John, "Distribution of Income of Corporations Among Dividends, Retained Earnings, and Taxes," *American Economic Review*, 46 (May 1956): 97–113.

———, "Expectations, Mergers and Equilibrium in Purely Competitive Securities Markets," *American Economic Review,* 61 (Spring 1971): 101–111.

———, "Optimum of Maximum Corporate Growth under Uncertainty," *The Corporate Economy,* edited by Robin Marris and Adrian Wood, eds., (Cambridge: Harvard University Press, 1971).

Manne, Henry, "Mergers and the Market for Corporate Control," *Journal of Political Economy*, *73* (April 1965), 110–120.

Marris, Robin, *The Economic Theory of 'Managerial' Capitalism.* (New York: Free Press, 1964).

Mason, Hal R. and Maurice B. Goudzqaard "Performance of Conglomerate Firms: A Portfolio Approach," *Journal of Finance*, 31 (March 1976): 39–48.

Mueller, Dennis C., "A Theory of Conglomerate Mergers," *Quarterly Journal of Economics*, 83 (November, 1969), 644–659.

———, "A Life Cycle Theory of the Firm," *Journal of Industrial Economics,* 21 (July 1972), 199–219.

———, "The Effects of Conglomerate Mergers," *Journal of Banking and Finance*, 1 (December, 1977), 315–347.

Modigliani, Franco, and M. Miller, "Cost of Capital, Corporation Finance, and the Theory of Investment," *American Economic Review,* 48 (June 1958): 261–297.

Nelson, R., *Merger Movements in American Industry, 1895–1956,* (Princeton, N. J.: Princeton University Press, 1959).

Sickles, Robin C. and Peter Schmidt, "Simultaneous Equation Models with Truncated Dependent Variables: A Simultaneous TOBIT Model," *Journal of Economics and Business*, 31 (Fall 1978): 11–21.

Standard and Poor, *Register of Corporation and Executives*, (New York, 1977).

Steiner, Peter O., *Mergers,* (Ann Arbor, Mich: University of Michigan Press, 1975).

Thompson, Donald W., "Mergers, Effects, and Competition Policy," (mimeographed) 1979.

Tobin, James., "Estimation of Relationships for Limited Dependent Variables," *Econometrica*, 26 (January 1958): 24–36.

U. S. Federal Trade Commission. *Statistical Report on Mergers and Acquisitions, 1978*. Washington, D. C.: Government Printing Office 1979.

Washington Post, "Playing the Takeover Game," April 18, 1980.

Weston, J. F. and S. Mansinghka, "Tests of the Efficiency Performance of Conglomerate Mergers," *Journal of Law and Economics*, 13 (April 1970): 919–936.

11 The Incidence of Price Changes in the U. S. Economy

Katherine Maddox McElroy
John J. Siegfried
George H. Sweeney

Both allocative and distributive effects occur whenever the price of a product is changed. If, for example, successful antitrust action against a cartel, legislative removal of an import duty or excise tax, or administrative deregulation of a product or service forces a reduction in the equilibrium price of a product to a competitive level, both a reallocation of resources and a redistribution of wealth will occur. The allocative effect, or change in the net benefit from producing and consuming the product or service, results from the increased production and consumption of units of output that cost less than the incremental value they create. The distributive effect, or transfer of benefits from producers (or government) to consumers, results from the lower expenditure paid by consumers, and, therefore, the lower revenue received by producers (or government) for the output that would have been sold at the higher price.

While economists primarily concern themselves with the allocative

This chapter previously appeared in the May 1982 issue of *The Review of Economics and Statistics* and is reprinted here with permission of the North-Holland Publishing Company. We also acknowledge the financial support of the Federal Trade Commission.

effects of price changes, policymakers, the press, and the public usually seem more interested in distributive effects.[1] Indeed, the magnitude of the distributive effect almost always outweighs the magnitude of the allocative effect.[2] Who gains and who loses from the distributive effect frequently determines policy outcomes. The gainers and losers are often described as consumers, blacks, unemployed, professionals, elderly, young, or stockholders, or by some other social or functional criterion. In this study we enumerate distributive gains and losses to consumers on the basis of family-income levels.

This study provides only a partial analysis of the relationship between income and the distributive effects that would occur in the United States if the prices of various products were changed. Specifically, the study estimates the relationship between family income and the distributive gains to consumers from a price decrease. By focusing on consumers only, we ignore the sources of consumer's gains: firm owners and other claimants on profits, or the government and the recipients of the government's revenue. The results, therefore, do not represent a complete analysis of the distributive impact of price changes.[3] By sacrificing completeness, however, we gain generality, since the distributive effect on consumers of a price change does not depend upon its cause, which may be any kind of industry-directed government action.

Two measures of the relationship between income and the price-induced distributive benefits to consumers are computed. The first measure groups consumers by products purchased and reports the weighted mean income of those consumers who purchase the products or services of an industry. This purchase may be made either directly by the consumer, or indirectly through the purchase of some other commodity or service that employs the product in question as an input. The weight applied to each consumer's income is proportional to that consumer's direct and indirect expenditure for products of the industry. The second measure groups consumers by income level and estimates the impact of a price reduction upon an average consumer of each income class.

Both measures employ input-output analysis to estimate indirect consumption of products from measures of direct consumption. Because input-output tables measure only current account transactions among industries, (that is, because input-output analysis does not measure the quantity of capital goods consumed in the production of one unit of a commodity), the measures reported should be considered to be indicative of short-run, rather than long-run, economic phenomena. The impact of price changes manifested through capital goods is ignored.

The following section describes the data and methodology. The mathematics underlying the estimates are contained in the appendix.

Data

Expenditure and income data were obtained from the 1972-1973 Consumer Expenditure Survey (CES) (U. S. Bureau of Labor Statistics) of approximately 20,000 consumer units. This survey, which was undertaken to update the consumer price index, comprises two sections which together encompass all possible consumer-expenditure categories. The diary portion contains expenditures on frequently purchased items (primarily food), which were recorded daily for two-week periods in diaries by participating consumers. The interview portion contains expenditures on less frequently purchased items (such as durables), which were collected quarterly by interviewers.[4] Monetary values of income and expenditure from both sections, having been converted to an annual basis, were combined into a single set of data standardized to 1972 dollars. The approximately 3000 product categories were translated into 1972 input-output commodity codes.

Input-output data were taken from the 365-industry level *Detailed Input Output Structure of the U. S. Economy: 1972*. The commodity-by-commodity "Total Requirements Coefficients"[5] were employed to determine the quantity of inputs required per unit of output. Transportation, wholesale, and retail margins data were obtained from the "Industry Transactions" table.[6]

Expenditure-Weighted Mean Income

The expenditure-weighted mean income for a commodity characterizes the incomes of all consumers of that commodity, including those consumers who purchase the commodity directly for final consumption and those consumers who purchase other commodities that require the commodity in question for production or distribution.[7] The weight attached to the income of each individual consumer is proportional to the sum of the dollar value of that consumer's direct purchases of the commodity, plus the dollar value of that commodity required for the production and distribution of the entire bundle of goods that he purchases.[8] Thus the expenditure weight for automobiles consists of direct expenditures on automobiles for consumption plus the indirect expenditures on automobiles, for example, the portion of insurance premiums that finances the automobiles used by insurance salesmen.

By incorporating the input requirements into the estimates for consumer products, mean income levels for the consumers of producer products such as pulp, gypsum, bearings, and surgical instruments can be evaluated and compared with those of direct consumer products such as bread, clothing, beer, toys, and cigars. These weighted mean income levels are reported in table 11-1.

Distributive Effect of a Decrease in Producer Markup

The price of any product may be expressed as the sum of two components: average cost plus a margin (or markup) over cost. In this analysis "cost" includes only the purchase cost of goods and services used as inputs in production. Therefore, the margin, or difference between price and cost, includes payments to all factors of production as well as taxes to government. Suppose that antitrust action, a tax reduction, or a negotiated wage concession causes the margin of an industry to decline. This reduction in margin implies a decrease in final price of the products of that industry, which in turn reduces average cost of commodities that use the product in question as an input. Our second measure of the relationship between income and the distributive effects of a price reduction on consumers estimates the impact of such price-and-cost changes on an average consumer at each of six income levels. It is assumed that all decreases in production costs are passed through to final prices. That is, it is assumed that a $1 decrease (increase) in average cost of a product results in a $1 decrease (increase) in price of the product.[9] With the margin of an industry expressed as a percentage of the selling price, columns 4 through 9 of table 11-1 list the percentage reduction in expenditure that an average consumer could enjoy while still maintaining an identical consumption bundle after the margin of a specific industry is reduced by ten percentage points.[10] For example, the first row of table 11-1 reveals that an average consumer of the lowest-reported income level could reduce his expenditures by .008 percent (or about one one-hundreth of one percent) and still purchase the same bundle of goods and services if the margin of the dairy industry were reduced from, say, 20 percent to 10 percent.[11] Since the estimates are linear with respect to margins, the percentage reduction in expenditure from a five-percentage-point reduction in margin would be one-half the amount reported in table 11-1, and so forth for other margin changes.

The expenditure for each product by the average consumer of an income class was defined as the average of the expenditures on that product for all consumers whose incomes were between 10 percent above or below the class income level. The lowest income level ($2,406) represents the maximum income of the poorest 5 percent of the U. S. population in

1972. The intermediate income levels ($5,612, $9,300, $12,855, and $17,760) represent the upper limits of income quintiles in 1972 (20, 40, 60, and 80 percent, respectively). The largest income ($27,836) represents the minimum income of the richest 5 percent of the population in 1972.[12]

Empirical Results

The median value of the expenditure-weighted mean income over all products is $18,109, ranging from a low of $13,258 for residential care (#7708) to a high of $29,271 for aircraft (#6001). Aircraft, jewelry and precious metals (#6401), educational services (#7704), and hotels and lodging (#7201), were purchased by people with the highest income levels. Residential care, drugs (#2901), cigarettes (#1501), primary batteries (#5802), and household refrigerators, freezers, and laundry equipment (#5402, 5403) contained the lowest average income consumers. Most producers' goods (for example, bearings (#4902), pulp (#2401), chemicals (#2701), textiles (#1603), have mean consumer-income levels near the median. Apparently the wide variety of uses for most intermediate goods diffuses the impact of price changes throughout the economy so that the burden is fairly uniform on consumers of all income levels.

In general, the income levels for purchasers of the various goods and services match a priori expectations. This supports the credibility of the data sample and the measures used to describe it. Those products that have mean consumer-income levels that are counter-intuitive become important for public policy. It is for those products that the intuition of policy makers might be misleading.

Products and services that have surprisingly high mean consumer income levels include: scales and balances (#5103), paints and allied products (#3300), brooms and brushes (#6408), floor coverings (#1701, 6409), and travel trailers and campers (#6106), each of which is in the top 13 percent of products and services ranked by income level. Poultry and eggs (#102), the U.S. Postal Service (#7801), motion pictures (#7601), and fertilizer (#2702), all have substantially above average consumer-income levels. Since both poultry and eggs, and fertilizer are primary inputs into food products, which tend to have lower-than-average-income consumers, one might have expected them to be purchased predominantly by lower income families.

Products with surprisingly low consumer-income levels include primary batteries, household refrigerators and freezers, household laundry

Table 11-1. Mean Income and Incidence of a Ten Percentage Point Change in Industry Profit Margin on Six Representative Income Levels for 349 Input-Output Industries, 1972

INPUT-OUTPUT CODE	INDUSTRY DESCRIPTION	CONSUMERS MEAN INCOME WEIGHTED BY EXPENDITURE (DOLLARS)	PERCENTAGE DECREASE IN EXPENDITURE DUE TO A TEN PERCENTAGE POINT DECREASE IN INDUSTRY PROFIT MARGIN ON SALES REVENUE FOR CONSUMERS REPRESENTING INCOME:					
			$2406	$5612	$9300	$12855	$17760	$27836
101	DAIRY FARM PRODUCTS	17199	0.008	0.008	0.007	0.007	0.006	0.006
102	POULTRY & EGGS	18429	0.013	0.010	0.009	0.009	0.009	0.010
103	MEAT ANIMALS	18233	0.067	0.071	0.060	0.063	0.063	0.067
201	COTTON	17949	0.014	0.015	0.015	0.015	0.016	0.017
202	FOOD GRAINS	18585	0.034	0.035	0.030	0.031	0.032	0.035
203	TOBACCO	13984	0.023	0.019	0.016	0.014	0.012	0.008
204	FRUITS	17115	0.004	0.003	0.003	0.003	0.003	0.003
205	VEGETABLES	17818	0.008	0.007	0.006	0.006	0.006	0.007
206	OIL BEARING CROPS	18426	0.006	0.006	0.005	0.005	0.005	0.006
207	FOREST PRODUCTS	19600	0.005	0.004	0.004	0.004	0.004	0.004
300	FORESTRY & FISHERY PRODUCTS	18519	0.012	0.012	0.012	0.013	0.014	0.015
400	AGRICULTURAL, FORESTRY & FISH SVCS	22212	0.082	0.043	0.039	0.039	0.046	0.060
500	IRON & FERROALLOY ORES MINING	18031	0.007	0.008	0.009	0.010	0.010	0.010
601	COPPER ORE MINING	18758	0.006	0.007	0.008	0.008	0.008	0.009
602	NONFERROUS METAL ORES MINING	18579	0.005	0.005	0.005	0.005	0.006	0.006
700	COAL MINING	16666	0.060	0.051	0.046	0.046	0.043	0.040
800	CRUDE PETROLEUM & NATURAL GAS	16106	0.319	0.321	0.292	0.284	0.257	0.234
900	STONE & CLAY MINING & QUARRYING	18499	0.008	0.008	0.007	0.008	0.008	0.008
1000	CHEM & FERTILIZER MINERAL MINING	18104	0.002	0.002	0.002	0.002	0.002	0.002
1201	MAINTENANCE & REPAIR, RESIDENTIAL	20465	0.595	0.576	0.537	0.584	0.792	0.761
1202	MAINTENANCE & REPAIR, NONFARM BLDGS	17831	0.199	0.181	0.170	0.169	0.165	0.166
1401	MEAT PACKING PLANTS	17543	0.067	0.064	0.058	0.058	0.058	0.060
1402	CREAMERY BUTTER	17992	0.001	0.001	0.001	0.001	0.001	0.001
1403	CHEESE, NATURAL & PROCESSED	17860	0.003	0.003	0.003	0.003	0.003	0.003
1404	CONDENSED & EVAPORATED MILK	17209	0.002	0.002	0.002	0.002	0.002	0.002
1405	ICE CREAM & FROZEN DESSERTS	18066	0.003	0.003	0.003	0.003	0.003	0.003
1406	FLUID MILK	16662	0.014	0.013	0.011	0.011	0.010	0.009
1407	CANNED & CURED SEA FOODS	17153	0.001	0.001	0.001	0.001	0.001	0.001
1408	CANNED SPECIALTIES	15196	0.003	0.003	0.002	0.002	0.002	0.001
1409	CANNED FRUITS & VEGETABLES	17050	0.006	0.006	0.005	0.005	0.004	0.005
1410	DEHYDRATED FOOD PRODUCTS	17101	0.001	0.001	0.001	0.001	0.001	0.001
1411	PICKLES, SAUCES, & SALAD DRESSINGS	18058	0.002	0.002	0.002	0.002	0.002	0.002
1412	FRESH OR FROZEN PACKAGED FISH	18275	0.003	0.003	0.003	0.003	0.003	0.003
1413	FROZEN FRUITS & VEGETABLES	17626	0.004	0.003	0.003	0.003	0.003	0.003
1414	FLOUR & OTHER GRAIN MILL PRODUCTS	17012	0.005	0.005	0.004	0.004	0.004	0.004

CODE	INDUSTRY DESCRIPTION	MEAN INCOME	PERCENTAGE DECREASE IN EXPENDITURE					
			$2406	$5612	$9300	$12855	$17760	$27836
1415	DOG, CAT, & OTHER PET FOOD	18342	0.017	0.015	0.013	0.013	0.013	0.014
1416	RICE MILLING	17157	0.001	0.001	0.000	0.000	0.000	0.000
1417	WET CORN MILLING	17812	0.003	0.003	0.002	0.003	0.003	0.003
1418	BREAD, CAKE, & RELATED PRODUCTS	17421	0.011	0.010	0.010	0.010	0.009	0.010
1419	SUGAR	17234	0.007	0.006	0.005	0.005	0.005	0.005
1420	CONFECTIONERY PRODUCTS	17713	0.003	0.003	0.003	0.003	0.003	0.003
1421	MALT LIQUORS,WINES,LIQUORS	18689	0.020	0.022	0.023	0.024	0.025	0.028
1422	BOTTLED & CANNED SOFT DRINKS	16508	0.005	0.005	0.005	0.005	0.005	0.004
1423	FLAVORING EXTRACTS & SIRUPS, N.E.C.	18057	0.003	0.003	0.003	0.003	0.003	0.003
1424	COTTONSEED OIL MILLS	17850	0.001	0.001	0.001	0.001	0.001	0.001
1425	SOYBEAN OIL MILLS	18403	0.005	0.005	0.004	0.005	0.005	0.005
1426	VEGETABLE OIL MILLS, N.E.C.	18563	0.001	0.001	0.001	0.001	0.001	0.001
1427	ANIMAL & MARINE FATS & OILS	17806	0.003	0.002	0.002	0.002	0.002	0.002
1428	ROASTED COFFEE	17403	0.005	0.004	0.003	0.003	0.003	0.003
1429	SHORTENING & COOKING OILS	17116	0.004	0.004	0.003	0.003	0.003	0.003
1430	MANUFACTURED ICE	18607	0.000	0.000	0.000	0.000	0.000	0.000
1431	MACARONI & SPAGHETTI	17993	0.000	0.000	0.000	0.000	0.000	0.000
1432	FOOD PREPARATIONS, N.E.C.	16955	0.006	0.006	0.006	0.006	0.006	0.006
1501	CIGARETTES	13984	0.150	0.124	0.105	0.094	0.078	0.052
1502	TOBACCO STEMMING & REDRYING	13984	0.040	0.034	0.029	0.025	0.021	0.014
1601	BROADWOVEN FABRIC MILLS	17848	0.138	0.153	0.152	0.157	0.162	0.172
1602	NARROW FABRIC MILLS	17561	0.006	0.006	0.007	0.007	0.007	0.007
1603	YARN MILLS & TEXTILES, N.E.C.	18278	0.062	0.066	0.063	0.064	0.069	0.072
1604	THREAD MILLS	17822	0.004	0.004	0.004	0.004	0.004	0.005
1701	FLOOR COVERINGS	20418	0.028	0.028	0.025	0.028	0.038	0.037
1702	FELT GOODS N.E.C.	18795	0.001	0.001	0.001	0.001	0.001	0.001
1703	LACE GOODS	18180	0.001	0.001	0.001	0.001	0.001	0.001
1704	PADDING & UPHOLSTERY FILLING	17520	0.001	0.001	0.001	0.001	0.001	0.001
1705	PROCESSED TEXTILES WASTE	17948	0.001	0.001	0.001	0.001	0.001	0.001
1706	COATED FABRICS, NOT RUBBERIZED	18159	0.006	0.006	0.007	0.007	0.007	0.008
1707	TIRE CORD & FABRIC	16901	0.005	0.007	0.007	0.007	0.007	0.006
1709	CORDAGE & TWINE	18397	0.001	0.001	0.001	0.001	0.001	0.001
1710	NONWOVEN FABRICS	18695	0.009	0.009	0.009	0.010	0.011	0.011
1801	WOMEN'S HOSIERY, EXCEPT SOCKS	15583	0.027	0.029	0.026	0.024	0.022	0.021
1802	KNIT OUTERWEAR MILLS	18128	0.003	0.003	0.003	0.003	0.003	0.004
1803	KNIT FABRIC MILLS	18130	0.045	0.049	0.048	0.049	0.051	0.056
1804	APPAREL MADE OF PURCHASED MATERIALS	18138	0.318	0.350	0.345	0.352	0.363	0.403
1901	CURTAINS & DRAPERIES	19508	0.009	0.014	0.011	0.013	0.017	0.015
1902	HOUSEFURNISHINGS, N.E.C.	17443	0.029	0.028	0.025	0.024	0.024	0.026
1903	FABRICATED TEXTILE PRODUCTS	18057	0.019	0.022	0.025	0.027	0.027	0.028
2001	LOGGING CAMPS & LOGGING CONTRACTORS	18504	0.019	0.020	0.021	0.022	0.024	0.024
2002	SAWMILLS & PLANNING MILLS, GENERAL	18667	0.020	0.022	0.024	0.026	0.029	0.029

CODE	INDUSTRY DESCRIPTION	MEAN INCOME	PERCENTAGE DECREASE IN EXPENDITURE $2406	$5612	$9300	$12855	$17760	$27836
2003	HARDWOOD DIMENSION & FLOORING MILLS	17837	0.003	0.004	0.004	0.005	0.005	0.005
2004	SPECIAL PRODUCT SAWMILLS, N.E.C.	19345	0.001	0.001	0.001	0.001	0.001	0.001
2005	MILLWORK	20364	0.009	0.008	0.008	0.009	0.012	0.011
2006	VENEER & PLYWOOD	19151	0.010	0.010	0.011	0.011	0.014	0.014
2007	STRUCTURAL WOOD MEMBERS, N.E.C.	18122	0.000	0.000	0.000	0.000	0.000	0.000
2008	WOOD PRESERVING	17910	0.001	0.001	0.001	0.001	0.001	0.001
2009	WOOD PALLETS & SKIDS	18443	0.008	0.009	0.010	0.010	0.011	0.012
2100	WOOD CONTAINERS	18049	0.002	0.002	0.002	0.002	0.002	0.002
2201	WOOD HOUSEHOLD FURNITURE	17569	0.039	0.048	0.053	0.057	0.061	0.063
2202	UPHOLSTERED HOUSEHOLD FURNITURE	17795	0.011	0.014	0.016	0.017	0.019	0.020
2203	METAL HOUSEHOLD FURNITURE	18327	0.002	0.002	0.003	0.003	0.003	0.003
2204	MATTRESSES & BEDSPRINGS	16301	0.006	0.006	0.006	0.007	0.007	0.008
2302	METAL OFFICE FURNITURE	17822	0.000	0.000	0.000	0.000	0.000	0.000
2303	PUBLIC BUILDING FURNITURE	17883	0.001	0.002	0.002	0.002	0.002	0.002
2304	WOOD PARTITIONS & FIXTURES	20386	0.002	0.002	0.002	0.002	0.002	0.002
2305	METAL PARTITIONS & FIXTURES	18039	0.000	0.000	0.000	0.000	0.000	0.000
2306	BLINDS, SHADES, & DRAPERY HARDWARE	19686	0.000	0.001	0.001	0.001	0.001	0.001
2307	FURNITURE & FIXTURES, N.E.C.	17424	0.000	0.000	0.000	0.000	0.000	0.000
2401	PULP MILLS	18128	0.011	0.011	0.011	0.011	0.011	0.012
2402	PAPER MILLS, EXCEPT BUILDING PAPER	18134	0.054	0.054	0.054	0.057	0.056	0.059
2403	PAPERBOARD MILLS	18116	0.018	0.018	0.018	0.018	0.018	0.019
2404	ENVELOPES	18349	0.006	0.006	0.006	0.007	0.007	0.007
2405	SANITARY PAPER PRODUCTS	17833	0.004	0.004	0.004	0.004	0.004	0.004
2406	BUILDING PAPER & BOARD MILLS	19767	0.002	0.002	0.002	0.002	0.003	0.003
2407	PAPER COATING & GLAZING	18349	0.030	0.030	0.029	0.030	0.031	0.032
2500	PAPERBOARD CONTAINERS & BOXES	18039	0.041	0.041	0.040	0.041	0.041	0.043
2601	NEWSPAPERS	16380	0.028	0.019	0.016	0.015	0.014	0.015
2602	PERIODICALS	18734	0.008	0.009	0.009	0.009	0.010	0.012
2603	BOOK PUBLISHING	18685	0.031	0.040	0.041	0.045	0.046	0.055
2604	MISCELLANEOUS PUBLISHING	18876	0.003	0.003	0.003	0.003	0.003	0.004
2605	COMMERCIAL PRINTING	18672	0.038	0.039	0.042	0.045	0.045	0.049
2606	MANIFOLD BUSINESS FORMS	18486	0.016	0.017	0.019	0.021	0.020	0.022
2607	GREETING CARD PUBLISHING	18766	0.000	0.000	0.000	0.000	0.000	0.000
2608	ENGRAVING & PLATE PRINTING	18710	0.007	0.008	0.008	0.009	0.009	0.010
2701	INDUSTRIAL CHEMICALS	17977	0.111	0.114	0.111	0.113	0.116	0.117
2702	NITROGENOUS & PHOSPHATIC FERTILIZER	18907	0.009	0.009	0.008	0.008	0.008	0.009
2703	AGRICULTURAL CHEMICALS, N.E.C.	19173	0.006	0.005	0.004	0.004	0.004	0.005
2704	GUM & WOOD CHEMICALS	18140	0.025	0.026	0.026	0.027	0.027	0.028
2801	PLASTICS MATERIALS & RESINS	18370	0.025	0.026	0.027	0.028	0.030	0.030
2802	SYNTHETIC RUBBER	17509	0.008	0.010	0.011	0.011	0.011	0.010
2803	CELLULOSIC MAN-MADE FIBERS	18014	0.008	0.009	0.009	0.009	0.009	0.010
2804	ORGANIC FIBERS, NONCELLULOSIC	17983	0.034	0.037	0.036	0.037	0.039	0.040

CODE	INDUSTRY DESCRIPTION	MEAN INCOME	PERCENTAGE DECREASE IN EXPENDITURE $2406	$5612	$9300	$12855	$17760	$27836
2901	DRUGS	13847	0.144	0.076	0.055	0.042	0.034	0.034
2902	SOAP & OTHER DETERGENTS	17893	0.015	0.014	0.013	0.013	0.013	0.013
2903	TOILET PREPARATIONS	16095	0.005	0.005	0.005	0.004	0.004	0.004
3000	PAINTS & ALLIED PRODUCTS	19849	0.045	0.045	0.044	0.047	0.059	0.058
3101	PETRO REFINING & MISC PRODUCTS	16223	0.411	0.474	0.453	0.445	0.406	0.364
3102	PAVING MIXTURES & BLOCKS	18215	0.002	0.002	0.002	0.002	0.002	0.002
3103	ASPHALT FELTS & COATINGS	20279	0.017	0.017	0.016	0.017	0.023	0.022
3201	TIRES & INNER TUBES	16862	0.045	0.065	0.066	0.067	0.064	0.058
3202	RUBBER & PLASTICS FOOTWEAR	16243	0.004	0.006	0.006	0.007	0.006	0.005
3203	RECLAIMED RUBBER	17914	0.014	0.016	0.017	0.017	0.017	0.017
3204	MISCELLANEOUS PLASTICS PRODUCTS	18093	0.059	0.061	0.060	0.062	0.064	0.064
3205	RUBBER & PLASTICS HOSE & BELTING	18109	0.005	0.005	0.005	0.005	0.005	0.005
3300	LEATHER TANNING & FINISHING	17052	0.017	0.017	0.016	0.016	0.016	0.017
3401	FOOTWEAR CUT STOCK	16704	0.002	0.002	0.002	0.002	0.002	0.002
3402	SHOES, EXCEPT RUBBER	16540	0.059	0.058	0.054	0.053	0.051	0.054
3403	LEATHER PRODUCTS	19337	0.009	0.010	0.009	0.010	0.010	0.013
3501	GLASS & PRODUCTS, EXC CONTAINERS	18314	0.020	0.021	0.024	0.024	0.025	0.027
3502	GLASS CONTAINERS	16971	0.006	0.005	0.004	0.004	0.004	0.004
3601	CEMENT, HYDRAULIC	18662	0.002	0.002	0.002	0.002	0.002	0.002
3602	BRICK & STRUCTURAL CLAY TILE	19715	0.000	0.000	0.000	0.000	0.000	0.000
3603	CERAMIC WALL & FLOOR TILE	19623	0.000	0.000	0.000	0.000	0.000	0.000
3604	CLAY REFRACTORIES	17831	0.001	0.001	0.001	0.001	0.001	0.001
3605	STRUCTURAL CLAY PRODUCTS, N.E.C.	20302	0.000	0.000	0.000	0.000	0.001	0.000
3606	VITREOUS PLUMBING FIXTURES	19746	0.001	0.001	0.001	0.001	0.001	0.001
3607	VITREOUS CHINA FOOD UTENSILS	19181	0.002	0.002	0.003	0.003	0.003	0.004
3608	PORCELAIN ELECTRICAL SUPPLIES	18051	0.000	0.000	0.000	0.000	0.000	0.000
3609	POTTERY PRODUCTS, N.E.C.	19331	0.000	0.000	0.000	0.000	0.000	0.000
3610	CONCRETE BLOCK & BRICK	19109	0.001	0.001	0.001	0.001	0.001	0.001
3611	CONCRETE PRODUCTS, N.E.C.	19105	0.003	0.003	0.003	0.003	0.003	0.003
3612	READY-MIX CONCRETE	18872	0.002	0.002	0.002	0.002	0.002	0.002
3613	LIME	18406	0.001	0.001	0.001	0.001	0.001	0.001
3614	GYPSUM PRODUCTS	20228	0.002	0.002	0.002	0.002	0.003	0.003
3615	CUT STONE & STONE PRODUCTS	19599	0.000	0.000	0.000	0.000	0.000	0.000
3616	ABRASIVE PRODUCTS	18638	0.003	0.004	0.004	0.005	0.005	0.005
3617	ASBESTOS PRODUCTS	19697	0.006	0.006	0.006	0.007	0.008	0.008
3618	GASKETS, PACKING & SEALING DEVICES	17653	0.004	0.005	0.005	0.005	0.005	0.005
3619	MINERALS, GROUND OR TREATED	19260	0.003	0.002	0.002	0.002	0.003	0.003
3620	MINERAL WOOL	18565	0.001	0.001	0.001	0.001	0.002	0.001
3621	NONCLAY REFRACTORIES	17834	0.002	0.002	0.002	0.002	0.002	0.002
3622	NONMETALLIC MINERAL PRODUCTS, N.E.C	19812	0.001	0.001	0.001	0.001	0.001	0.001
3701	BLAST FURNACES & STEEL MILLS	18005	0.101	0.119	0.134	0.140	0.140	0.143
3702	IRON & STEEL FOUNDRIES	17916	0.020	0.025	0.030	0.032	0.031	0.032

CODE	INDUSTRY DESCRIPTION	MEAN INCOME	PERCENTAGE DECREASE IN EXPENDITURE $2406	$5612	$9300	$12855	$17760	$27836
3703	IRON & STEEL FORGINGS	17899	0.007	0.008	0.010	0.011	0.010	0.011
3704	METAL HEAT TREATING	18070	0.003	0.004	0.004	0.004	0.004	0.004
3801	PRIMARY COPPER	18579	0.013	0.014	0.015	0.016	0.017	0.017
3802	PRIMARY LEAD	18610	0.003	0.004	0.004	0.004	0.004	0.004
3803	PRIMARY ZINC	18331	0.003	0.004	0.004	0.004	0.004	0.004
3804	PRIMARY ALUMINUM	18188	0.011	0.013	0.014	0.014	0.015	0.015
3805	PRIMARY NONFERROUS METALS, N.E.C.	19743	0.010	0.011	0.012	0.013	0.013	0.015
3806	SECONDARY NONFERROUS METALS	18697	0.000	0.001	0.001	0.001	0.001	0.001
3807	COPPER ROLLING & DRAWING	18493	0.011	0.013	0.014	0.014	0.015	0.015
3808	ALUMINUM ROLLING & DRAWING	18413	0.011	0.012	0.013	0.014	0.015	0.015
3809	NONFERROUS ROLLING & DRAWING, N.E.C	19442	0.004	0.004	0.005	0.005	0.005	0.006
3810	NONFERROUS WIRE & INSULATING	17925	0.009	0.011	0.011	0.011	0.012	0.011
3811	ALUMINUM CASTINGS	17405	0.009	0.012	0.013	0.013	0.013	0.013
3812	BRASS, BRONZE, & COPPER CASTINGS	19294	0.002	0.002	0.002	0.002	0.002	0.002
3813	NONFERROUS CASTINGS, N.E.C.	19230	0.002	0.003	0.003	0.003	0.003	0.003
3814	NONFERROUS FORGINGS	18067	0.001	0.001	0.001	0.001	0.001	0.001
3901	METAL CANS	17959	0.011	0.011	0.011	0.011	0.011	0.011
3902	METAL BARRELS, DRUMS, & PAILS	17604	0.004	0.004	0.004	0.004	0.004	0.004
4001	METAL SANITARY WARE	19398	0.000	0.000	0.000	0.000	0.000	0.000
4002	PLUMBING FIXTURE FITTINGS & TRIM	20182	0.004	0.004	0.004	0.004	0.005	0.005
4003	HEATING EQUIPMENT, EXCEPT ELECTRIC	20040	0.007	0.007	0.007	0.007	0.009	0.009
4004	FABRICATED STRUCTURAL METAL	17990	0.001	0.001	0.001	0.001	0.001	0.001
4005	METAL DOORS, SASH, & TRIM	20093	0.002	0.002	0.002	0.002	0.003	0.002
4006	FABRICATED PLATE WORK(BOILER SHOPS)	18573	0.002	0.002	0.002	0.002	0.002	0.002
4007	SHEET METAL WORK	20126	0.012	0.011	0.011	0.012	0.015	0.015
4008	ARCHITECTURAL METAL WORK	18862	0.000	0.000	0.000	0.000	0.000	0.000
4009	PREFABRICATED METAL BUILDINGS	18434	0.000	0.000	0.000	0.000	0.000	0.000
4101	SCREWS,BOLTS,NUTS,RIVETS,WASHERS	17954	0.014	0.016	0.019	0.019	0.019	0.020
4102	AUTOMOTIVE STAMPINGS	17847	0.042	0.052	0.063	0.065	0.062	0.066
4201	CUTLERY	18315	0.001	0.001	0.001	0.001	0.001	0.001
4202	HAND & EDGE TOOLS, N.E.C.	18184	0.005	0.006	0.005	0.006	0.006	0.006
4203	HARDWARE, N.E.C.	17913	0.013	0.016	0.019	0.020	0.020	0.021
4204	PLATING & POLISHING	18079	0.007	0.008	0.009	0.009	0.010	0.010
4205	MISC FABRICATED WIRE PRODUCTS	18100	0.010	0.011	0.012	0.013	0.013	0.013
4207	STEEL SPRINGS, EXCEPT WIRE	17828	0.003	0.003	0.004	0.005	0.004	0.005
4208	PIPE, VALVES, & PIPE FITTINGS	17590	0.005	0.005	0.005	0.005	0.005	0.005
4210	METAL FOIL & LEAF	17062	0.002	0.002	0.001	0.001	0.001	0.001
4211	FABRICATED METAL PRODUCTS, N.E.C.	18299	0.010	0.011	0.011	0.011	0.012	0.012
4301	STEAM ENGINES & TURBINES	16444	0.002	0.001	0.001	0.001	0.001	0.001
4302	INTERNAL COMBUSTION ENGINES, N.E.C.	17947	0.011	0.012	0.015	0.015	0.016	0.018
4400	FARM MACHINERY & EQUIPMENT	16704	0.007	0.013	0.013	0.016	0.014	0.013
4501	CONSTRUCTION MACHINERY & EQUIPMENT	17560	0.004	0.003	0.003	0.003	0.003	0.003

CODE	INDUSTRY DESCRIPTION	MEAN INCOME	PERCENTAGE DECREASE IN EXPENDITURE $2406	$5612	$9300	$12855	$17760	$27836
4502	MINING MACHINERY, EXCEPT OIL FIELD	17361	0.001	0.001	0.001	0.001	0.001	0.001
4503	OIL FIELD MACHINERY	16280	0.002	0.002	0.002	0.002	0.002	0.002
4601	ELEVATORS & MOVING STAIRWAYS	20223	0.004	0.004	0.004	0.004	0.006	0.005
4602	CONVEYORS & CONVEYING EQUIPMENT	19102	0.001	0.001	0.001	0.001	0.002	0.002
4603	HOISTS, CRANES, & MONORAILS	20128	0.003	0.003	0.003	0.003	0.004	0.004
4604	INDUSTRIAL TRUCKS & TRACTORS	18239	0.000	0.000	0.000	0.000	0.000	0.000
4701	MACHINE TOOLS, METAL CUTTING TYPES	17918	0.000	0.001	0.001	0.001	0.001	0.001
4702	MACHINE TOOLS, METAL FORMING TYPES	18191	0.000	0.000	0.001	0.001	0.001	0.001
4703	SPECIAL DIES, TOOLS & ACCESSORIES	17976	0.008	0.009	0.010	0.011	0.011	0.011
4704	POWER DRIVEN HAND TOOLS	16466	0.004	0.005	0.005	0.008	0.008	0.006
4801	FOOD PRODUCTS MACHINERY	18129	0.000	0.000	0.000	0.000	0.000	0.000
4802	TEXTILE MACHINERY	17865	0.002	0.002	0.002	0.003	0.003	0.003
4803	WOODWORKING MACHINERY	18232	0.000	0.000	0.000	0.000	0.000	0.000
4804	PAPER INDUSTRIES MACHINERY	18168	0.001	0.001	0.001	0.001	0.001	0.001
4805	PRINTING TRADES MACHINERY	18507	0.001	0.001	0.001	0.001	0.001	0.001
4806	SPECIAL INDUSTRY MACHINERY, N.E.C.	17827	0.003	0.003	0.003	0.003	0.003	0.003
4901	PUMPS & COMPRESSORS	17668	0.005	0.005	0.005	0.005	0.005	0.005
4902	BALL & ROLLER BEARINGS	18034	0.006	0.006	0.007	0.008	0.007	0.008
4903	BLOWERS & FANS	18357	0.001	0.002	0.002	0.002	0.002	0.002
4904	INDUSTRIAL PATTERNS	18001	0.001	0.001	0.001	0.001	0.001	0.001
4905	POWER TRANSMISSION EQUIPMENT	17821	0.005	0.005	0.007	0.007	0.007	0.007
4906	INDUSTRIAL FURNACES & OVENS	18163	0.000	0.000	0.000	0.000	0.000	0.000
4907	GENERAL INDUSTRIAL MACHINERY,N.E.C.	18695	0.003	0.003	0.003	0.003	0.003	0.003
5000	CARBURETORS, PISTONS, RINGS, VALVES	17948	0.018	0.021	0.023	0.024	0.024	0.025
5101	ELECTRONIC COMPUTING EQUIPMENT	18494	0.003	0.003	0.003	0.003	0.003	0.004
5102	TYPEWRITERS	19353	0.001	0.002	0.001	0.002	0.002	0.003
5103	SCALES & BALANCES	19525	0.000	0.000	0.000	0.000	0.000	0.000
5104	OFFICE MACHINES, N.E.C.	17793	0.001	0.001	0.001	0.001	0.001	0.001
5201	AUTOMATIC MERCHANDISING MACHINES	18067	0.000	0.001	0.001	0.001	0.001	0.001
5202	COMMERCIAL LAUNDRY EQUIPMENT	16980	0.000	0.000	0.000	0.000	0.000	0.000
5203	REFRIGERATION & HEATING EQUIPMENT	18294	0.038	0.048	0.050	0.050	0.053	0.053
5204	MEASURING & DISPENSING PUMPS	18824	0.000	0.000	0.000	0.000	0.000	0.000
5205	SERVICE INDUSTRY MACHINES, N.E.C.	19102	0.001	0.001	0.001	0.001	0.001	0.001
5301	INSTRUMENTS TO MEASURE ELECTRICITY	17926	0.000	0.000	0.000	0.000	0.000	0.000
5302	TRANSFORMERS	18472	0.002	0.002	0.002	0.002	0.002	0.003
5303	SWITCHGEAR & SWITCHBOARD APPARATUS	19021	0.004	0.004	0.003	0.004	0.004	0.004
5304	MOTORS & GENERATORS	17572	0.012	0.014	0.014	0.014	0.015	0.014
5305	INDUSTRIAL CONTROLS	18154	0.003	0.004	0.004	0.004	0.004	0.004
5306	WELDING APPARATUS, ELECTRIC	18295	0.001	0.001	0.001	0.002	0.001	0.002
5307	CARBON & GRAPHITE PRODUCTS	17982	0.002	0.002	0.002	0.002	0.002	0.002
5308	ELECTRICAL INDUST APPARATUS, N.E.C.	18540	0.001	0.001	0.001	0.001	0.001	0.001
5401	HOUSEHOLD COOKING EQUIPMENT	16136	0.010	0.014	0.009	0.013	0.011	0.010

CODE	INDUSTRY DESCRIPTION	MEAN INCOME	PERCENTAGE DECREASE IN EXPENDITURE					
			$2406	$5612	$9300	$12855	$17760	$27836
5402	HOUSEHOLD REFRIGERATORS & FREEZERS	14997	0.018	0.023	0.023	0.021	0.021	0.015
5403	HOUSEHOLD LAUNDRY EQUIPMENT	14765	0.012	0.022	0.022	0.022	0.020	0.012
5404	ELECTRIC HOUSEWARES & FANS	17210	0.015	0.017	0.015	0.017	0.017	0.015
5405	HOUSEHOLD VACUUM CLEANERS	15710	0.005	0.007	0.008	0.008	0.008	0.006
5406	SEWING MACHINES	16963	0.002	0.005	0.006	0.008	0.006	0.007
5407	HOUSEHOLD APPLIANCES, N.E.C.	20524	0.014	0.014	0.014	0.017	0.022	0.020
5501	ELECTRIC LAMPS	18096	0.005	0.004	0.004	0.004	0.004	0.005
5502	LIGHTING FIXTURES & EQUIPMENT	19944	0.010	0.011	0.012	0.013	0.014	0.016
5503	WIRING DEVICES	18287	0.008	0.008	0.007	0.008	0.008	0.008
5601	RADIO & TV RECEIVING SETS	15752	0.078	0.089	0.087	0.080	0.067	0.068
5602	PHONOGRAPH RECORDS & TAPES	16983	0.006	0.012	0.013	0.012	0.011	0.011
5603	TELEPHONE & TELEGRAPH APPARATUS	16353	0.012	0.010	0.009	0.008	0.008	0.007
5604	RADIO & TV COMMUNICATION EQUIPMENT	18065	0.002	0.001	0.001	0.001	0.001	0.001
5701	ELECTRON TUBES	15960	0.013	0.015	0.015	0.014	0.012	0.012
5702	SEMICONDUCTORS & RELATED DEVICES	17748	0.008	0.009	0.009	0.009	0.008	0.009
5703	ELECTRONIC COMPONENTS, N.E.C.	16717	0.019	0.021	0.021	0.020	0.018	0.020
5801	STORAGE BATTERIES	18085	0.002	0.003	0.003	0.003	0.003	0.003
5802	PRIMARY BATTERIES, DRY & WET	14178	0.008	0.010	0.008	0.008	0.007	0.005
5803	X-RAY APPARATUS & TUBES	16806	0.000	0.000	0.000	0.000	0.000	0.000
5804	ENGINE ELECTRICAL EQUIPMENT	17895	0.009	0.011	0.014	0.014	0.014	0.015
5805	ELECTRICAL EQUIPMENT, N.E.C.	18815	0.002	0.002	0.002	0.002	0.002	0.002
5901	TRUCK & BUS BODIES	17833	0.001	0.001	0.001	0.001	0.001	0.001
5902	TRUCK TRAILERS	18099	0.000	0.000	0.000	0.000	0.000	0.000
5903	MOTOR VEHICLES	17867	0.404	0.535	0.687	0.722	0.679	0.716
6001	AIRCRAFT	29271	0.001	0.001	0.001	0.001	0.001	0.001
6002	AIRCRAFT & MISSILE ENGINES & PARTS	19744	0.002	0.002	0.002	0.002	0.002	0.003
6004	AIRCRAFT & MISSILE EQUIP, N.E.C.	20262	0.002	0.002	0.002	0.002	0.002	0.003
6101	SHIP BUILDING & REPAIRING	17592	0.001	0.002	0.001	0.002	0.002	0.001
6102	BOAT BUILDING & REPAIRING	18188	0.000	0.002	0.007	0.009	0.020	0.026
6103	RAILROAD EQUIPMENT	17919	0.002	0.002	0.002	0.002	0.002	0.002
6105	MOTORCYCLES, BICYCLES, & PARTS	17700	0.016	0.020	0.037	0.035	0.037	0.037
6106	TRAVEL TRAILERS & CAMPERS	20503	0.000	0.002	0.011	0.016	0.026	0.013
6107	TRANSPORTATION EQUIPMENT, N.E.C.	18577	0.002	0.002	0.008	0.005	0.005	0.011
6201	ENGINEERING, SCIENTIFIC INSTRUMENTS	18663	0.000	0.000	0.000	0.000	0.000	0.000
6202	MECHANICAL MEASURING DEVICES	17705	0.002	0.002	0.002	0.002	0.002	0.002
6203	AUTOMATIC TEMPERATURE CONTROLS	19117	0.006	0.006	0.006	0.006	0.007	0.007
6204	SURGICAL & MEDICAL INSTRUMENTS	16364	0.001	0.001	0.001	0.001	0.001	0.001
6205	SURGICAL APPLIANCES & SUPPLIES	15190	0.019	0.007	0.006	0.005	0.004	0.004
6206	DENTAL EQUIPMENT & SUPPLIES	16689	0.001	0.001	0.001	0.001	0.001	0.001
6207	WATCHES, CLOCKS, & PARTS	19292	0.013	0.014	0.013	0.015	0.015	0.022
6301	OPTICAL INSTRUMENTS & LENSES	18995	0.000	0.000	0.000	0.000	0.000	0.000
6302	OPHTHALMIC GOODS	15145	0.003	0.004	0.003	0.003	0.002	0.002

CODE	INDUSTRY DESCRIPTION	MEAN INCOME	PERCENTAGE DECREASE IN EXPENDITURE $2406	$5612	$9300	$12855	$17760	$27836
6303	PHOTOGRAPHIC EQUIPMENT & SUPPLIES	18909	0.030	0.034	0.038	0.041	0.042	0.046
6401	JEWELRY & PRECIOUS METALS	24970	0.012	0.014	0.020	0.026	0.025	0.039
6402	MUSICAL INSTRUMENTS	19360	0.005	0.005	0.009	0.010	0.013	0.021
6403	GAMES, TOYS, & CHILDREN'S VEHICLES	15811	0.004	0.006	0.009	0.009	0.007	0.006
6404	SPORTING & ATHLETIC GOODS, N.E.C.	19870	0.006	0.010	0.014	0.019	0.021	0.021
6405	PENS & MECHANICAL PENCILS	18616	0.005	0.005	0.005	0.005	0.005	0.006
6406	ARTIFICIAL TREES & FLOWERS	19474	0.001	0.001	0.001	0.001	0.001	0.001
6407	BUTTONS	18103	0.007	0.008	0.008	0.008	0.008	0.009
6408	BROOMS & BRUSHES	20074	0.003	0.003	0.003	0.003	0.004	0.004
6409	HARD SURFACE FLOOR COVERINGS	20437	0.003	0.003	0.003	0.003	0.004	0.004
6410	BURIAL CASKETS & VAULTS	16761	0.002	0.003	0.003	0.003	0.003	0.003
6411	SIGNS & ADVERTISING DISPLAYS	18327	0.001	0.001	0.002	0.002	0.002	0.002
6412	MANUFACTURING INDUSTRIES, N.E.C.	25475	0.012	0.013	0.015	0.015	0.013	0.018
6501	RAILROADS & RELATED SERVICES	17851	0.064	0.069	0.071	0.073	0.073	0.074
6502	LOCAL,INTERCITY HWY PASSENGER TRANS	18671	0.042	0.031	0.027	0.025	0.026	0.035
6503	MOTOR FREIGHT TRANS & WAREHOUSING	17790	0.161	0.165	0.158	0.162	0.162	0.162
6504	WATER TRANSPORTATION	17354	0.030	0.034	0.032	0.033	0.033	0.029
6505	AIR TRANSPORTATION	19790	0.108	0.098	0.104	0.104	0.107	0.161
6506	PIPE LINES, EXCEPT NATURAL GAS	16215	0.022	0.025	0.024	0.024	0.022	0.019
6507	TRANSPORTATION SERVICES	18881	0.005	0.005	0.006	0.006	0.006	0.007
6600	COMMUNICATIONS, EXCEPT RADIO & TV	16298	0.553	0.457	0.405	0.384	0.346	0.336
6700	RADIO & TV BROADCASTING	18127	0.000	0.000	0.000	0.000	0.000	0.000
6801	ELECTRIC SERVICES (UTILITIES)	16282	0.555	0.456	0.395	0.389	0.354	0.329
6802	GAS PROD & DIST (UTILITIES)	15395	0.565	0.404	0.302	0.277	0.240	0.229
6803	WATER SUPPLY & SANITARY SERVICES	16654	0.177	0.134	0.114	0.113	0.115	0.110
6901	WHOLESALE TRADE	17032	0.680	0.724	0.709	0.708	0.680	0.650
6902	RETAIL TRADE	17435	0.969	1.058	1.047	1.065	1.052	1.061
7001	BANKING	18380	0.310	0.372	0.523	0.676	0.635	0.662
7002	CREDIT AGENCIES	18455	0.063	0.076	0.111	0.146	0.137	0.144
7003	SECURITY & COMMODITY BROKERS	18286	0.049	0.053	0.063	0.073	0.070	0.075
7004	INSURANCE CARRIERS	18322	1.015	1.086	1.177	1.269	1.280	1.459
7005	INSURANCE AGENTS & BROKERS	18325	0.375	0.401	0.435	0.468	0.472	0.538
7102	HOUSING	19514	3.109	3.143	3.260	2.931	2.938	2.427
7201	HOTELS & LODGING PLACES	22947	0.026	0.028	0.032	0.037	0.051	0.076
7202	PERSONAL & REPAIR SERVICES	16760	0.112	0.156	0.144	0.150	0.135	0.136
7203	BEAUTY & BARBER SHOPS	16357	0.042	0.051	0.044	0.044	0.039	0.037
7301	MISCELLANEOUS BUSINESS SERVICES	20470	0.391	0.313	0.313	0.350	0.346	0.411
7302	ADVERTISING	18040	0.205	0.207	0.208	0.212	0.208	0.211
7303	MISCELLANEOUS PROFESSIONAL SERVICES	18378	0.128	0.130	0.126	0.130	0.131	0.134
7400	EATING & DRINKING PLACES	18990	0.181	0.195	0.204	0.217	0.227	0.265
7500	AUTOMOBILE REPAIR & SERVICES	17521	0.242	0.282	0.292	0.276	0.269	0.301
7601	MOTION PICTURES	18740	0.012	0.012	0.012	0.012	0.013	0.014

CODE	INDUSTRY DESCRIPTION	MEAN INCOME	PERCENTAGE DECREASE IN EXPENDITURE					
			$2406	$5612	$9300	$12855	$17760	$27836
7602	AMUSEMENT & RECREATION SERVICES	20075	0.091	0.151	0.116	0.126	0.141	0.175
7701	DOCTORS & DENTISTS	16662	0.252	0.268	0.253	0.225	0.227	0.213
7702	HOSPITALS	17217	0.126	0.091	0.067	0.049	0.032	0.027
7703	OTHER MEDICAL & HEALTH SERVICES	16716	0.062	0.059	0.047	0.042	0.041	0.035
7704	EDUCATIONAL SERVICES	25569	0.035	0.065	0.073	0.095	0.142	0.239
7705	NONPROFIT ORGANIZATIONS	22528	0.386	0.293	0.279	0.296	0.307	0.407
7706	JOB TRAINING & RELATED SERVICES	18729	0.001	0.001	0.001	0.001	0.001	0.001
7707	CHILD DAY CARE SERVICES	17124	0.000	0.001	0.002	0.002	0.001	0.001
7708	RESIDENTIAL CARE	13258	0.008	0.001	0.003	0.004	0.003	0.003
7801	U.S. POSTAL SERVICE	18570	0.062	0.061	0.064	0.069	0.068	0.074

Detailed descriptions of the industries and their component S.I.C. codes are available from the authors on request.

Input-output industries 1101, 1102, 1103, 1104, 1105, 2301, 7101, 7709, 7802, 7803, 7901, and 7902 are excluded because there were no direct or indirect purchases by private consumers of the products or services of these industries. The industries include buildings and structures, which were all assigned to 7102, products and services purchased exclusively by government, products and services that are exclusively capital goods, and wood office furniture, which could not be distinguished from wood household furniture in the Consumer Expenditure Survey and was therefore classified into 2201.

equipment, household vacuuum cleaners (#5405), ophthalmic goods (#6302), natural gas distribution (#6802), and games, toys and children's vehicles (#6403).

While the income level of consumers of security and commodity services (#7003) is about a hundred dollars above the median, it is lower than commonly expected. The reason, of course, is that business firms consume substantial amounts of brokerage services, and the eventual burden of these costs, depending on the degree of competition, falls on their customers. Since businesses of all types use these services, it is not surprising that the overall impact of price changes in brokerage services seems to hit middle- and lower-income consumers with substantial force.

The extent to which price changes are regressive or progressive can be evaluated from the trend in columns 4 through 9 for individual products or services. For example, row 1 of table 11-1 indicates that consumers at the first quintile in the 1972 income distribution would enjoy an 0.008 of 1 percent decrease in their expenditures if the average margin on sales of dairy farm products (#101) were to decline ten percentage points. Consumers at the second and third quintiles would enjoy an expenditure decline of 0.007 of one percent, while consumers at the fourth quintile (80 percent through the income distribution) would gain only a 0.006 percent reduction in their expenditures. Therefore, a price reduction in dairy-farm products is progressive; a price rise in those products, regressive.

The size of the percentage decrease in expenditure resulting from a ten-percentage-point reduction in margins indicates the importance of the product in consumers' budgets. For example, crude petroleum and natural gas (#800) has an effect on the lowest income class ($2,406 in 1972) that is four times greater than dairy-farm products, while the effect of electric services (utilities, #6801) is seven times as great as dairy-farm products.

The numbers in table 11-1 can be used to assess the incidence of various governmental policies on consumers of different income levels. To illustrate one use of these numbers, we compute (admittedly arbitrarily) a one-dimensional index of incidence, *I*, which is the ratio of the effect of a change in prices on consumers at the ninety-fifth percentile of the income distribution (wealthier) to the effect of a change in prices on consumers at the twentieth percentile of the income distribution (poorer) (that is, column 9 divided by column 5). We believe these consumers represent the common interpretation of what is meant by the terms "high income family" and "low income family." Their mid-1981 income levels (the latest available inflated by the GNP deflator), were $11,484 and $59,268 respectively.

The index *I* indicates the progressiveness or regressiveness of price decreases. A lower index (less than unity) implies progressiveness of price decreases, since the advantage of the lower price accruing to wealthier consumers is relatively less than the advantage to poorer consumers. The following table summarizes the interpretation of *I:*

Value of I	*Price Increase*	*Price Decrease*
$I < 1$	Regressive	Progressive
$I = 1$	Neutral	Neutral
$I > 1$	Progressive	Regressive

If the current big cases in antitrust were successful in reducing prices, then it appears that their results would be generally progressive. The proportionate income-enhancing effect on high-income consumers' budgets would be only 81 percent of the effect on poor families' budgets if the price of cereals (#1414) were to decline ($I = 0.81$). For petroleum refining (#3101) $I = 0.77$, and for telephone services and equipment (#6600, 5603) $I = 0.74$. On the other hand, if the myriad of antitrust actions against IBM were eventually to reduce price in electronic computing equipment (#5101), we would expect higher income consumers to have their expenditures reduced more than proportionately vis-à-vis poor families ($I = 1.21$). The size of the impact of a price reduction in these industries varies considerably. The increase in consumers' welfare from a ten-percentage-point reduction in margin of petroleum refining or telephone service would be approximately 100 times as large as that of a ten-percentage-point reduction in the margin of cereals or computers.[13]

The Federal Trade Commission has for years seemed to target antitrust violations in the food-processing industry. Price reductions in that area appear slightly progressive, since the index for all food-processing industries combined is 0.90.

The impact of the government on prices is even more direct in the regulated industries. The degree of progressivity of price reductions in these industries varies. Price reductions in hospitals (#7702), natural-gas production and distribution, electric utilities, and telephone and telegraph services, would all be progressive ($I = 0.30, 0.57, 0.72$, and 0.74, respectively), while those in the U. S. Postal Service, insurance (#7004, 7005), and banking (#7001), would be regressive ($I = 1.20, 1.34$, and 1.78, respectively).

Some of these industries command a large share of a consumer's budget. A ten-percentage-point reduction in margins of the natural gas, electric, or communications utilities would yield increases in consumer well-being of 0.23 to 0.57 percent. A similar reduction in the margins of insurance carriers would confer benefit to consumers of about 1.2 percent. A ten-percent reduction in the margin of the U. S. Postal Service would yield consumer benefits of only 0.06 to 0.07 percent of their total expenditures.

In the case of recent deregulation, the major benefits of price reductions appear to have accrued to higher income families. For air transport (#6505) I is 1.64, and for stock-and-commodity brokerage services I is 1.41. For crude petroleum and natural-gas deregulation (expected to raise the price of gasoline and natural gas) the burden would fall more heavily on lower income families (I = .73). Thus its incidence is consistent with airline and brokerage deregulation (because price changes in the opposite direction). On the other hand, motor-freight (#6503) deregulation (expected to reduce rates) would have almost the same impact on high-income and low-income families (I = 0.98). The impact of changes in margins of the petroleum industry is comparable to those of the energy utilities (abnout 0.28 for crude petroleum and natural gas, and about 0.40 for petroleum refining). The impacts of changes in margins of the transportation industries are somewhat smaller (about 0.16, 0.11, 0.07, and 0.03 for the truck, airline, railroad (#6501), and water (#6504) transportation industries, respectively).

The data can even be used to assess the incidence of certain regulations emanating from the regulatory agencies that protect the environment and safety. In these cases, induced price increases serve to reduce effective spending power, thereby reversing the interpretation of the index. For example, controls on asbestos (#3617) that raise the price of asbestos and products that use it as an input appear to have a progressive incidence (I = 1.30), the costs of a price increase falling more heavily on the wealthy. The stringent environmental controls on pulp mills appear to have had a slightly progressive impact on consumers of all income levels (I = 1.10).

The data in table 11-1 can also be used to evaluate the incidence of policy areas beyond direct regulation and antitrust. For example, the incidence of excise taxes on specific products can be assessed. Many local governments impose a tax on hotels, which appears to be a progressive tax (I = 2.73). The federal tax on air transportation also appears to be very progressive (I = 1.64). But for other major products subject to excise taxes, the tax seems regressive, as the values of I for telephone services, gasoline, and cigarettes are 0.74, 0.73, and 0.42, respectively.

An induced price reduction caused by elimination of protection from import competition in shoes (#3402) would be only slightly progressive (I = 0.92), while price reductions due to greater competition from foreign steel producers would be regressive (I = 1.19). Were the automobile industry (#5903) to be successful in increasing protection from foreign competition, the incidence of the resulting rise in prices would be progressive (I = 1.34).

The impact of certain agricultural policies that raise prices appears to be neutral (food grains, #202, I = 0.99) or regressive (milk, #1406, I = 0.74). Subsidies to educational institutions that facilitate across-the-board reductions in tuition appear to be highly regressive (I = 3.69).

The data could be used to assess the impact of changes in the prices of any factor payments. For example, a wage settlement negotiated by the United Auto Workers that increases wages in the motor-vehicle (#5903) industry would be progressive (I = 1.34), whereas an increase in wages to migrant farm workers, which raises the gross margin of the vegetable sector (#205), would be neutral (I = 1.0).

Conclusions

This chapter presents two indicators of the income distribution consequences that would result from changes in prices in specific industries. The information provides a basis for evaluating the often controversial income-redistribution effects of policies, and the range of these measures across industries suggests the potential to accommodate diverse equity goals.

The weighted mean income of the consumers of products varies from \$13,000 to \$29,000. The percentage impact on the welfare of a rich consumer relative to that of a poor consumer ranges from 0.3 to 10.3. A ten-percentage-point reduction in the margin of an industry would yield increases in consumer welfare ranging from less than one ten-thousandth of one percent to over 3 percent.

Income distribution consequences are certainly important aspects of public policy. The quantification of these consequences permits the debate to shift from the issue of what the effects of a policy might be to the question of whether those effects are desirable.

Appendix

Calculation of the Expenditure Weighted Mean Income of Consumers by Commodity

Let C_j^i = Dollars of direct personal consumption expenditure by the ith consumer for products of the jth industry (measured in producers prices),

X_j^i = Dollars of products of the jth industry required for final consumption and for production of consumption bundle of the ith consumer,

Y^i = income of ith consumer,

A_{jk} = i, kth element of the total requirements matrix (in monetary units), where A_{jk} represents the amount of output required both directly and indirectly from industry i to produce a dollar of deliveries to final demand by industry j,

s = total number of consumers in the sample,

n = total number of commodities.

Table 11-1 reports the weighted mean income level of all consumers who directly or indirectly purchase the jth commodity:

$$\bar{Y}_j = \sum_{i=1}^{s} X_j^i Y^i \Big/ \sum_{i=1}^{s} X_j^i. \tag{11A.1}$$

Assuming that production is accurately characterized by a fixed coefficients input-output model, the input vector X^i required to produce the final consumption vector C^i may be calculated as follows:

$$X_j^i = \sum_{k=1}^{n} A_{jk} C_k^i. \tag{11A.2}$$

The mean income level, weighted by direct and indirect purchases may be derived by substituting equation (11A.2) into equation (11A.1):

$$\bar{Y}_j = \sum_{i=1}^{s} \sum_{k=1}^{n} A_{jk} C_k^i Y^i \Big/ \sum_{i=1}^{s} \sum_{k=1}^{n} A_{jk} C_k^i. \tag{11A.3}$$

Calculation of this mean income level is facilitated by reversing the orders of summation:

$$\bar{Y}_j = \sum_{k=1}^{n} A_{jk} \sum_{i=1}^{s} C_k^i Y^i \Big/ \sum_{k=1}^{n} A_{jk} \sum_{i=1}^{s} C_k^i. \tag{11A.4}$$

Calculation of the Distributive Effect of a Change in Producer Markup

Assume the economy is composed of n separate industries. Within each industry, every firm produces the same homogeneous product, subject to the same fixed coefficients and constant returns-to-scale technology. Furthermore, every firm within an industry charges the same price for its product by setting price equal to average cost, plus a mark-up, or margin, that is independent of cost.[14]

Let $\tilde{a}$ represent the $n \times n$ "direct requirements" matrix, the i,jth element of which indicates the number of (physical) units of the ith good directly required to produce one (physical) unit of the jth good. Let P represent the $n \times 1$ vector of prices of the n goods. And finally, let M designate the $n \times 1$ margin vector, the ith element of which represents the margin above average cost charged by firms in the ith industry.

The assumption about pricing behavior of each firm implies that

$$P' = P\tilde{a} + M'. \qquad (11A.5)$$

Equation (11A.5) may be solved for the vector of equilibrium price levels:

$$P' = M'(I - \tilde{a})^{-1}. \qquad (11A.6)$$

Let $\tilde{A}$ represent $(I - \tilde{a})^{-1}$, or the "total requirements matrix." The effect upon final prices of a change in the margin of one industry may be derived by differentiating equation (11A.6):

$$\frac{\partial P'}{\partial M'} = (I - \tilde{a})^{-1} = \tilde{A}. \qquad (11A.7)$$

The input-output tables published by the U.S. Department of Commerce measure input requirements in monetary units (the number of dollars' worth of an input required to produce one dollar's worth of an output). The relationship between physical units and monetary units may be derived as follows. Let $\bar{P}$ denote an $n \times n$ diagonal matrix, the ith diagonal element of which equals the price of product i. Let a denote the coefficients matrix measured in monetary units. It must be true that $a = \bar{P}\tilde{a}\bar{P}^{-1}$. Let A denote $(I - a)^{-1}$. Then

$$A = (I - \bar{P}\tilde{a}\bar{P}^{-1})^{-1} = \bar{P}(I - \tilde{a})^{-1}\bar{P}^{-1} = \bar{P}\tilde{A}\bar{P}^{-1}. \qquad (11A.8)$$

Equations (11A.7) and (11A.8) may be employed to calculate the change in expenditure required to purchase a given bundle of goods when prices change. Let $\tilde{C}$ represent the $n \times 1$ consumption vector of a consumer, the ith element of which represents the quantity (in physical units) of good i

that he purchases. Let C represent the consumer's expenditure vector or consumption vector, measured in monetary units:

$$C = P\tilde{C}. \tag{11A.9}$$

An increase in the margin of the ith industry will affect prices in numerous industries. The effect of these changes upon the money required to purchase the commodity bundle $\tilde{C}$ equals

$$\frac{\partial C}{\partial M_i} = \frac{\partial \bar{P}}{\partial M_i} \tilde{C},$$

where subscripts denote elements of a vector or matrix. Equation (11A.7) implies

$$\frac{\partial C}{\partial M_i} = \begin{bmatrix} \tilde{A}_{i1} \tilde{C}_1 \\ \tilde{A}_{i2} \tilde{C}_2 \\ \cdot \\ \cdot \\ \cdot \\ \tilde{A}_{in} \tilde{C}_n \end{bmatrix} \cdot \tag{11A.10}$$

Premultiplying the right-hand side of equation (11A.10) by the unit matrix $\bar{P}^{-1}\bar{P}$ and postmultiplying both sides of the equation by the scalar P_i implies

$$\frac{\partial C}{\partial M_i} P_i = \begin{bmatrix} P_i \tilde{A}_{i1} \frac{1}{P_1} P_1 \tilde{C}_1 \\ P_i \tilde{A}_{i2} \frac{1}{P_2} P_2 \tilde{C}_2 \\ \cdot \\ \cdot \\ \cdot \\ P_i \tilde{A}_{in} \frac{1}{P_n} P_n \tilde{C}_n \end{bmatrix}, \tag{11A.11}$$

or, equivalently,

$$\frac{\partial C}{\partial M_i} \frac{1}{1/P_i} = \begin{bmatrix} A_{I1} C_1 \\ A_{i2} C_2 \\ \cdot \\ \cdot \\ \cdot \\ A_{in} C_n \end{bmatrix} \cdot \tag{11A.12}$$

The left-hand side of equation (11A.12) represents the vector of derivatives of expenditure with respect to the margin of the *i*th industry, when margin is expressed as a fraction of the base year price (i.e., as a fraction of the price of the *i*th good in the year of the input-output table).

Finally, the total dollar effect upon expenditures of the consumer can be derived by summing the elements of the vector on the right-hand side of equation (11A.12).

Notes

1. The recent debate over the "windfall profits" accruing to the oil industry from decontrol provides a good example of the popular concern about distributive effects of government policies. See also Comanor and Smiley (1975) and Scherer (1980).

2. If an individual firm believes that the elasticity of its demand, with respect to a firm-initiated price decrease, exceeds the elasticity of its demand with respect to an industry-wide price decrease, and if that firm chooses price to maximize profit, then the magnitude of the distributive effect of an industry-wide price decrease must exceed the magnitude of the allocative effect. Let k represent the ratio of the elasticity of firm demand with respect to a firm-initiated price decrease divided by the elasticity of firm demand with respect to an industry-wide price decrease. If the firm's perceived-demand curve is smooth at the profit-maximizing price, then an industry-wide price decrease will result in a transfer of benefits from the firm to its customers, which is (approximately) k times as large as the resulting increase in surplus of that producer and its customers. If the perceived demand curve is kinked at the profit-maximizing price, then the transfer of benefits of a price decrease will exceed k times the increase in surplus. A similar relationship holds in the case of an industry-wide price increase if the firm's demand curve is smooth. If the firm's perceived demand curve is kinked, however, the distributive effect of a price increase need not necessarily outweigh the allocative effect.

3. See Siegfried, Sweeney, and Maddox (1980) for a discussion of the conceptual and empirical difficulties of estimating the relationship between income and the losers of the distributional effect of a price decrease.

4. See Carlson (1974) for an overview of the Consumer Expenditure Survey.

5. Bureau of Economic Analysis IED 79-004 or Table B.

6. Bureau of Economic Analysis IED 79-003 or Table A.

7. This measure reflects only the private consumption of commodities. That is, purchases of commodities by government agencies are not included in the measure. The task of determining the beneficiaries of the services provided by government purchases is beyond the scope of this investigation.

8. The input-output table measures output in producer prices, which approximately equal the per-unit revenues received by the producer after paying transportation costs and retail and wholesale commissions. The CES consumer data measures purchases in consumer prices, which include transportation, wholesale, and retail margins in consumer-based price units. Purchases from the transportation and wholesale and retail industries were increased accordingly to include the margins which were subtracted from purchases from all other industries.

9. Possible effects upon final price of a change in the average cost of a profit-maximizing

firm and of a firm that maximizes revenue subject to a (binding) minimum-profit constraint are enumerated in Sweeney and Siegfried (1979). The magnitude of the effect of a change in cost upon the price of a profit-maximizing firm in a large part depends upon the curvature of the demand function facing the firm. For a firm-maximizing revenue subject to a binding minimum-profit constraint, a change in average cost will lead to a greater change in price. Thus the assumption that a $1 change in a firm's marginal cost will lead to a $1 change in that firm's price is extremely difficult to justify on strictly theoretical grounds. This assumption must be made on pragmatic grounds and the hope that such an elemental pricing assumption gives reasonable approximations to reality.

10. This measure also represents an indicator of the welfare gain to the average consumer from the price decrease. Under the assumption that a consumer maximizes utility subject to a budget constraint, the derivative of the maximum utility with respect to the price of any commodity is proportional to the quantity of that commodity purchased by the consumer. That is, the first order approximation of the dollar value of the welfare gain to a consumer due to a price decrease is equal to the number of dollars that can be taken away from the consumer while still allowing him to purchase his original consumption bundle.

11. The effects of a 10-percent change in margin may be expressed as percentages of gross income rather than as percentages of expenditures by multiplying the numbers in table 11-1 by the following factors:

Income level	*To convert to percentage of income, multiply by*
$ 2,406	.90
5,612	.72
9,300	.68
12,855	.62
17,760	.60
27,836	.52

12. The income levels for the fifth, twentieth, fortieth, sixtieth, eightieth, and ninety-fifth percentiles for mid-1981, using the latest available data (1978) inflated by the GNP deflator, to 1980 and inflated by 12 percent from 1980 to 1981, are $4,713, $11,484, $19,404, $27,192, $37,752, and $59,268, respectively. If consumption patterns are relatively invariant to relative position in the distribution of incomes, these figures can be substituted for those in table 11-1 to update the table.

13. The reason for these large differences is obvious: consumers spend (both directly and indirectly) a much greater share of their budgets on petroleum products and telephone services than on cereals or computers. But the magnitudes of these differences are striking.

14. A similar analysis is presented in Klass (1970).

References

Carlson, Michael D., "The 1972–73 Consumer Expenditure Survey," *Monthly Labor Review* (Dec. 1974): pp. 16–23.

Comanor, William S. and Robert H. Smiley, "Monopoly and the Distribution of Wealth," *Quarterly Journal of Economics* 89 (May 1975): 177–194.

Klass, Michael, *Inter-Industry Relations and the Impact of Monopoly,* Ph.D. Thesis, University of Wisconsin-Madison, 1970.

Scherer, F. M., *Industrial Market Structure and Economic Performance,* 2nd ed. (Chicago: Rand McNally, 1980): 471–473.

Siegfried, John J., George H. Sweeney, and Katherine E. Maddox, "The Incidence of Monopoly Profits in Consumer Goods Industries," in J. Siegfried (ed.), *The Economics of Firm Size, Market Structure, and Social Performance* (Washington, D. C.: U. S. Government Printing Office, 1980).

Smiley, Robert, "Firm Size, Market Power and the Distribution of Income and Wealth," in J. Siegfried.

Sweeney, George H. and John J. Siegfried, "The Effects of Price Changes of Intermediate Goods Upon Expenditures for Final Goods," unpublished manuscript, Vanderbilt University, 1979.

United States Department of Commerce, Bureau of Economic Analysis, *1972 Detailed Input-Output Structure of the U. S. Economy.*

List of Contributors

David B. Audretsch, Assistant Professor of Economics, Middlebury College.

Ralph M. Bradburd, Assistant Professor of Economics, Williams College.

Catherine M. Garber, Student, University of California, Santa Cruz.

Alfred E. Kahn, Robert Julius Thorne Professor of Economics, Cornell University.

Edwin Mansfield, Professor of Economics, University of Pennsylvania.

Katherine Maddox McElroy, Economist, TCS Management Corporation.

Peter J. Meyer, Assistant Professor of Economics, University of California, Santa Cruz.

Willard F. Mueller, William F. Vilas Resident Professor of Economics, University of Wisconsin-Madison.

A. Mead Over, Jr., Associate Professor of Economics, Boston University.

Barbara A. Pino, Student, University of California, Santa Cruz.

Steven Schwartz, Assistant Professor of Economics, Miami University.

William G. Shepherd, Professor of Economics, University of Michigan.

John J. Siegfried, Professor of Economics and Business Administration, Vanderbilt University.

Robert E. Smith, Professor of Economics, University of Oregon.

George H. Sweeney, Assistant Professor of Economics and Business Administration, Vanderbilt University.

Oliver E. Williamson, Charles and William L. Day Professor of Economics and Social Science, University of Pennsylvania.